The Invisible Job

About the Author

Paula Fyans has experienced first-hand what it is like managing the Invisible Job from the perspective of a working mother with an international career (in pharma and university) and as a stay-at-home mum. When she gave up her job to restore balance to family life, she learned about life as a full-time parent. She discovered that the grass is no greener, instead it just presents a very different set of challenges.

The Invisible Job features insights from many interviews she has conducted with women about their personal experiences of the challenges of managing parental and home responsibilities, either full-time or on top of a career. Drawing on her scientific background, it also examines extensive demographic, economic and gender-based global research into how responsibility for parenting and running a home is shared by couples and the way an imbalance in this role impacts women.

Paula has lived and worked in the UK, Ireland, Australia, Germany, France, Malawi and South Africa. She now lives in Dublin where she is (most days!) very happily married with two children. In addition to gender equality, she is also a passionate advocate for climate justice.

Follow Paula on Instagram and Twitter @InvisibleJob or find more information at www.theinvisiblejob.com.

The Invisible Job

How Sharing Home and Parental Responsibilities Leads to Happier Lives

PAULA FYANS

ORPEN PRESS

Published by
Orpen Press
Upper Floor, Unit B3
Hume Centre
Hume Avenue
Park West Industrial Estate
Dublin 12

email: info@orpenpress.com
www.orpenpress.com

Paperback ISBN 978-1-78605-128-8
ePub ISBN 978-1-78605-129-5

Printed in Dublin by SPRINTprint Ltd

To my mother, who excelled at the Invisible Job, and my father, who allowed me to grow up without ever contemplating whether there might be anything that a girl could not do as well as any boy

Acknowledgements

As the saying goes, it takes a village to raise a child. This book is no different. I owe huge thanks to all of the following for making it a reality.

My dear friend Dr Jenny Tooze, whose brilliant work on shortening the first draft was pivotal to the book being published.

Dr Marie Murray, for her belief in the book from the start.

Dr Seán Ruth, for his guidance and support.

My editors at Orpen Press, Eileen O'Brien and Kerstin Mierke, whose painstaking work improved the text immeasurably.

Niamh O'Regan, Aoife Ruth, Síomha Ní Aonghusa, Emma Skelly and Eleana Skelly for their valuable help with research.

Anne Fyans, for assisting with proofreading.

Saverio Campione, for his lovely artwork.

Claire Kilroy, for her encouragement and advice.

Imelda May, for graciously giving me 'her blessings with bells on' to quote her beautiful song.

Jason Hazely and Joel Morris, for allowing me to include some lines from their razor-sharp book, *The Mum — How It Works*

Sue Collins and Sinéad Culbert, better known as Dirt Birds, who understand better than anyone what being a mother involves.

Avril Stanley and Zan Comerford for all their technical advice.

Ann Corcoran for her guidance on communications.

Krzysztof Wlodarsksi of KW Solutions, for creating the website www.theinvisiblejob.com

Most importantly, I wish to thank all the women who shared their personal stories of the Invisible Job with me over the last few years, as these formed the vital pieces that revealed what this jigsaw puzzle really looked like. As promised, no names have been included!

I also wish to thank all the women who took part in creating the videos on @ invisiblejob that illustrate the transformation that occurs to women's lives between our early twenties and late thirties.

And thank you to my wonderful husband and my children, for their understanding and kindness while trying to make it to the finish line.

Foreword

Would you apply for a job in which the more perfectly you executed it the less visible your efforts would be? Would you undertake it without remuneration or recognition? Would you accept it impinging on every other aspect of your life: your career prospects, your financial status, your social outlets, your sense of identity and your personal time? Such is the topic of this book, *The Invisible Job: How Sharing Home and Parental Responsibilities Leads to Happier Lives*. It is a book in which the author, Paula Fyans, gives the reader a detailed description of the demands of family life; the workload it entails; the gendered division of labour that arises in the execution of that workload; and the negotiation of roles, rights and responsibilities that is required to balance work fairly between couples, especially if children arrive.

One of the main tenets in the book is that men are given the opportunity to 'opt in' to their share of household responsibility. They 'help', they offer support, they undertake specific tasks, they give time, they abandon activities in the service of *helping* their wives, which by definition means that household tasks are *not* their primary remit but gifts bestowed rather than work shared. The experience of this for many women is that they are the drudges who cry out for help when they are unable to cope rather than there being an agreed fair division of work undertaken as a couple. Men, who have grown up with a separate-gender ideology that defines tasks as either male or female, can feel resentment that their contributions are not appreciated, leading to a situation where both men and women feel hard done by in the relationship, which can suffer as a result.

What is remarkable about *The Invisible Job* is the manner in which it identifies, enumerates, analyses and articulates the issues that many couples struggle with in family life today. The topic will resonate with anyone who has ever argued about household tasks or couples who have found themselves overwhelmed by the sheer volume and diversity of the demands of raising children while both parents work full time. For as the author points out, it is with the arrival of children that 'the mountain of things' that absolutely must be done grows exponentially and parents of young children usually find themselves 'sleep-deprived, stressed and exhausted', putting an inevitable strain on otherwise harmonious relationships.

Of course, Covid-19 added another dimension to the distribution of work and home tasks and to situations of gender inequality as the burden of caring increased for women. The fact that the majority of essential teaching and caring roles are occupied by women meant that they were disproportionately impacted in the workplace and disproportionately burdened by additional caring roles at home. The timing of this book is therefore opportune because work and home life are bi-directional and this book calls upon us to understand work–home dynamics in new and creative ways, not just in a time of pandemic, but by carrying the lessons of working from home during Covid-19 into future work–home practices in a beneficial way.

The book is set out in a clear, comprehensive, incremental style. It explains how the disparity in workload between men and women essentially arises when women have unfair responsibility for domestic and childcare issues in addition to working full-time. This is the time when 'women's work is never done', when women find themselves engaged in the Invisible Job – one for which they never officially signed up and would be unlikely to do so if they had advance access to a formal job spec of what it entails. For, as Paula describes, with impressive detail, it is not the individual tasks that parenting entails that are onerous, it is 'the cumulative burden of having too many jobs to do and the "mental load" associated with managing them all.' It is finding yourself emptying the washing machine at midnight. It is the time urgency of tasks. It is routine and repetitive housework; health and hygiene; headlice and threadworms; teeth brushing and toenail cutting; fitting shoes and buying, sorting, mending and organising clothes, toys, games, books and art supplies; children's social life, birthday parties and parental participation in school activities. It is knowing how to manage WhatsApp etiquette. It is choosing crèche and school, interviewing au pairs and the relative merits, demerits, affordability or otherwise of acquiring paid home help. The Invisible Job requires the holder to be a project manager, short-order chef, events organiser, medical consultant, teacher, nurse, financial manager, taxi driver, diplomat, psychologist and peacekeeper.

While Paula does not regard The Invisible Job as a parenting book, nor is it intended to be, yet in narrative and practicality it is an invaluable guide to meticulous parenting, sensitive childcare and the minutiae of family life. Paula knows what life is like when you are a new mother. She has lived through the annihilating impact of sleep deprivation, has felt the despair of making a list of 'must do' actions that evaporate because the day is devoted to the immediacy of baby care. She recognises the alarm women often feel when they find their identity altered from organised, time-managed working life to the chaos of new motherhood and the dismay of self-neglect. She prioritises listening to a child's woes in an exceptionally moving account of the significance of being available for this task. All in all, one would search far to find a more useful book about parenting and childcare.

But apart from the educational value that reading her personal accounts of the challenges that motherhood brings, the humour with which they are told, the richness of the illustrative links to which the reader is directed, and the lively images Paula conjures up in her writing, the book also provides important documentation and analysis of the negative gender-defined roles foisted on women and the extent of unpaid care which women have no alternative but to provide. In presenting this information the book combines extensive global research with insights from Paula's own lived experiences and her interviews with women from the UK and Ireland on their personal experiences of the Invisible Job. She provides statistical data to support the reality that women are still disadvantaged in the workplace by the career interruption that motherhood entails and that women do more than 76.2% of all unpaid caring work. She notes pay disparities and diminishing opportunities as the gap widens between men and women who began their careers as equals. She is concerned that women today are led to believe 'that gender imbalance is largely a thing of the past; that we live in an era where women are free to achieve their potential on an equal footing with men'. The reality, she says, is that we are still miles away from gender equality because of the time spent on the Invisible Job: the unpaid caring and household responsibilities that most women subsume.

The book distinguishes itself by the abundant flow of ideas, the clarity with which they are written, the wry humour that often emerges in her domestic accounts, and the vivid descriptions the author provides of life as lived. Paula writes in a disarmingly honest way, yet in each example there lies additional perspectives on the topic. Section by section the book advances her description of the lived reality of gender-determined conscriptions that neither men nor women may wish to have but that have not yet been dismantled. Dominant discourses take time to be diluted. Reading The Invisible Job, it becomes disappointingly clear that 'the doctrine of separate spheres' (which denies the extent to which gender differences in society are culturally defined) still implicitly, if not explicitly, pertain.

In identifying the Invisible Job Paula is not denigrating men's motivations but simply addressing gendered inequalities of power and privilege. The book exposes the hidden societal structures that define men and women, thereby consigning each of them to pre-determined gender-defined roles that do a disservice to both and that can threaten relationships in family life. If women are caught in a bind, so too are men in a culture where the dominant discourse does not encourage men, for example, to avail of paternity leave, to abandon their power or to recognise their privilege. Society could also give more recognition to the nurturing role men play in their children's lives and how central fathers are to their children's happiness, self-esteem, safety and psychological development.

The manner in which men and women organise their lives, what influences their choice of career, how they negotiate work and home arrangements, the rationale for their decisions about this, societal expectations and that of employers, family and friends – all are addressed in this extraordinarily comprehensive book. The author also emphasises that no one size fits all, that there is no rigid prescription about how people should lead their lives, how couples should divvy up household tasks, how they should undertake the Invisible Job together, or whether or not the parent who voluntarily opts for full-time parenting should do otherwise. The choice is between couples to decide together what works for them in their own relationships. But what the author calls for in her Afterword is for employers and governments to recognise the enormous economic and societal contribution made by the Invisible Job and to support it as 'a worthwhile investment towards building a better world for everyone'.

Dr Marie Murray
Clinical Psychologist, Systemic Psychotherapist and Author
Health Publications and Commissioning Editor, Orpen Press
@drmariemurray

Contents

Preface

The number of responsibilities and tasks associated with any household is huge. Often, but not always, most of these are managed by women, even where both partners are in paid employment. When children arrive, women often continue to perform this role alongside childcare and, once maternity leave is over, alongside paid employment. The better they do this job, the more invisible it becomes. This frequently leads to exhaustion and resentment and in the long term can have many other negative consequences for women's wellbeing and their ability to achieve their goals. The process through which women acquire this Invisible Job is based on beliefs so ingrained in our conditioning that many women don't even realise it is happening. A sleep-deprived young mother is simply too busy trying to survive and do her best for her baby amidst the bewildering sea of messages that battle to define her new role in the world.

Becoming a parent is possibly both the best and the hardest thing any person will ever do (the latter is especially true when you don't have adequate support). It is therefore important that both partners have a clear idea beforehand of exactly what it will entail.

A QUICK NOTE ABOUT HOW THIS BOOK IS STRUCTURED

Part I outlines a Job Description for this *Invisible Job* so that there is some clarity for all parties as to what is involved. If you are a mother, you will already be familiar with most of the elements it entails. Therefore you may wish to skip through much of the detail in this part for now. However if you have not yet reached this stage in your life, understanding what lies ahead of you will be hugely useful. There are myriad ways to tackle it and it is for couples to determine how they plan to tackle the job between them. It requires honest discussion and making important joint decisions about your family, career and financial priorities.

Part II looks at how the Invisible Job tends to be shared between men and women in reality. It also reviews the consequences for women when they end up bearing most of this burden – the impact on their physical and mental health, their career and financial prospects, their personal goals and, importantly, how it affects their relationship with their partner. It includes the perspective of a mother with a full-time paid job and that of a 'stay-at-home' mother.

Part III explores the reasons for this gender imbalance in relationships when it comes to responsibility for the Invisible Job. It discusses how we can prevent it happening in our own relationships, as well as how to put an end to it in society overall.

Introduction

When I was pregnant with my first child, a wonderful woman I worked with at the time, Dr Jane Anderson, took me aside and gave me a piece of advice. If I had realised then the importance of what she was telling me, I would have had it tattooed on the back of my hand. Sadly, it wasn't until a decade later that I finally realised just how critical her three words were.

What she shared with me was a wise insight into the inequity between the roles women and men often take on in a relationship, especially when they become parents. 'Men opt in', she said.

Seeing the puzzled look on my face, she went on to explain ...'OK, let's say I ask my husband to do something: he will, absolutely. For instance, if I say "Clive, I have an appointment at the hairdresser's at 10 a.m. next Saturday, can you look after the kids?" He'll say, "Of course, darling! Let me just put that in my diary ... did you say 10 o'clock? That should be absolutely no problem. Don't you worry, I've got it covered".'

In other words, he opts in.

A few moments later he will add, with a slightly worried look on his face,

'Er, darling, can I just check: what time will you be back?'

(In other words, 'Just how long will I be committed to this responsibility that I've temporarily agreed to take on?')

Jane went on, 'On the other hand, if Arsenal is playing at home and Clive is planning to spend all day Sunday at the stadium with his season ticket pals, it wouldn't even cross his mind to check if I would be free to mind the children at all, never mind for how long!'

What Jane had identified, and was revealing to me in this brief conversation, is the default situation in many male–female relationships: when it comes to children or the management of household activities, unless a man is specifically asked to do something (at which point he opts in), he will not spontaneously assume this responsibility. The default presumption is that it rests with his wife/partner.

At the time, the implications of this little revelation were not clear to me at all. Looking back now, I'm not entirely sure why. I guess I was like many other professional women in their late twenties and early thirties; that is, just busy with my career and generally enjoying life. My husband and I lived in a flat in central London and had a good social life, both as a couple and individually. We went out with friends, saw a lot of theatre, did a fair bit of sport and enjoyed travelling. Although I never managed to get to everything on my mental to-do list each week and felt I still had a list of so-called 'big rock' life goals to achieve, overall, things were going well. I felt confident that we would be able to cope with whatever curveballs becoming parents might throw at us. We were both independently minded and financially self-sufficient. While I felt lucky to be married to a wonderful and very capable individual, I had never felt dependent on anyone (including him) for help. We functioned synergistically, as a team. So, interesting as Jane Anderson's 'opting in' theory was, I didn't envisage it having any major implications for me. My husband and I were about to have a baby; no doubt it would be a steep learning curve but I felt we would manage just fine.

I now realise that I simply had no clue what was about to happen to my life and understood very little about the role I was about to take on.

Before I go any further, I just need to make two important disclaimers:

1. The relationship dynamics described in this book are in the context of male–female heterosexual couples. There are two reasons for this: firstly, the research referenced in various places in the book is based on heterosexual couples; secondly the individual relationships mentioned by the people I have interviewed are male–female. I simply don't know enough about the relationship dynamics in same-sex couples with children to represent them properly in this book. However, the responsibilities involved in the Invisible Job apply equally to all couples.

2. While this book describes many parenting and relationship challenges associated with being a mother, I realise that there are women who would give anything to be a mother but have been denied this opportunity, which can be a source of huge grief and feelings of loss. Equally, not every woman wants to be a mother and there are many happily childfree couples in the world. Therefore, many relevant points regarding the male–female distribution of household and life administration tasks will apply equally to couples without children.

BORING HOUSEHOLD JOBS

In every household, whether you live by yourself or with a partner or family, there are certain household tasks that simply have to be done. Annoyingly, many of them need to be repeated with surprising frequency – even several times a day. Some might need to be done weekly, others (thankfully) only monthly or annually. Different people approach these tasks with varying degrees of enthusiasm, while some are blissfully ignorant of the necessity to do many of them at all!

A scene from the film *Notting Hill* comes to mind, in which Hugh Grant's character William Thacker asks why his housemate Spike is wearing Thacker's wetsuit and diving mask while munching his breakfast cereal in the kitchen. Spike replies it's because he has no clean clothes.

Thacker then casually points out, 'There never will be, you know, unless you actually *clean* your clothes'.

Spike acknowledges in his Welsh accent, with sad resignation, 'Right … Vicious circle!' (1)

Before you and your partner start living together, there probably isn't an issue about who is responsible for doing what. You will each have your own standards and expectations about what things you feel need to be done, and when – such as how often bedsheets need to be changed, whether it's critical to have fresh milk in the fridge and whether you need house insurance. It's nobody's business but yours. You can watch Netflix for the whole weekend while eating takeaway if you wish (… provided someone has remembered to renew the Netflix subscription).

When you move in together, a new dynamic comes into play. Initially, the exciting and romantic side of setting up home together will predominate, but eventually the 'grown-up' part of your brain will highlight to one (or both) of you that there are basic household activities that you need to manage between you if this living together thing is going to work. According to many couples I have asked, it appears that formal discussion around this rarely takes place. Instead, a pattern usually just evolves whereby each person naturally gravitates to tasks that they either:

a. notice need to be done, and/or
b. don't mind doing.

One person admitted to me that she and her partner have a system for sharing responsibilities where certain tasks are labelled as 'pink jobs' or 'blue jobs'. (No comment on how any feminist would feel about that terminology!) Their blue jobs largely included what might have been traditionally male activities in my parents' generation – for instance, bringing out the rubbish bins, mowing the lawn and getting the car serviced. Pink jobs tended to be either nurturing/home-making activities – like cooking and buying groceries – or organisational/planning roles like booking holidays and arranging house insurance. Interestingly, blue jobs tended to be more visual or urgent – in other words, if someone doesn't mow the lawn or bring out the rubbish for months, it serves as its own visual reminder that it needs to be done. At the same time, although urgent (in other words, time-sensitive), the consequences of not doing a blue job might not be truly significant: an overflowing rubbish bin in the back yard for a week is annoying and might smell ... but that's about it.

Conversely, pink jobs are often less visual and therefore don't appear to be urgent but in fact may be more important – (i.e. the consequences of not doing them are greater). For instance, if you let your car/house insurance lapse or don't remember to book your holiday in good time, while there may be no visual trigger nudging you to do it, you have no financial comeback if your house is burgled or end up paying twice as much for your holiday.

A friend of mine is a successful television producer and enjoys her job. However, she is even more enthusiastic about her side-line job as landlord of a one-bedroom flat, which she bought as a rental investment. Having rented out a flat myself, I couldn't understand her enthusiasm for being a landlord. In my experience, managing a property involved nothing but hassle – arranging plumbers and electricians to fix shower mixers or heating systems that are playing up, along with hours spent cleaning ovens and emptying drawers of random items left behind every time a tenant moves out. Intrigued, I asked my friend why her experience of owning a flat was so positive. She revealed to me her secret (and highly effective!) strategy for ensuring her tenants always took really good care of her flat:

'I always choose new couples moving in together for the first time. The women want to show their partner that moving in together was a great step forward in their relationship. They really want to make it work and therefore subconsciously start *nesting*, i.e. making the flat into a home. So they keep the place immaculate!'

Wow. An eye-opening insight. As I thought more and more about it, I realised that it is certainly true that in many relationships, women take on a much greater share of the joint household responsibilities than their partner. But why?

- Is it linked to a desire to ensure the relationship thrives (as my friend's tenant-selection strategy proposes)?
- Or do women believe they are simply better at managing household responsibilities than their male partners? Might they even enjoy it?
- Could it be that men and women have different aspirations regarding what needs to be done in a household (or how well such tasks need to be done)?
- Or are we are simply following scripted messages from society that teaches us that the responsibility for maintaining a successful relationship and perfect home lies with women, and where this doesn't happen, it's on them?

We'll come back to this question later.

Let's say you and your long-term partner live together without children. You are both capable people with busy lives and careers, but between you, you manage to stay on top of your life and household responsibilities. Chances are that, like the couples I have asked, you probably never formally sat down to discuss what this entails and who (in theory) is responsible for doing what. Instead, it sort of just happened. If you are a woman, you may strongly suspect that you do quite a lot more than he does but don't dwell on it too much. Perhaps you get a bit fed up sometimes – there may be days when you wonder if your partner is even aware of the existence of a mop in the flat. But he is essentially a good guy, so even if you are doing more than your fair share of household management, it's not worth making a big deal of. Life may feel too busy at times but we just need to crack on with it. Before you have children, the consequence of an imbalance between you and your partner when it comes to sharing household tasks is often no more than this.

CHILDREN: THE GAME CHANGER

Figure 1.1: Juggling responsibilities, age 25, Saverio Campione

Before you have children, you only have *you* to look after. Even so, it may never feel as if you are truly on top of everything in your life. Mostly, this reflects the endless choices we have and the challenge of balancing everything on our 'would-like-to-do' list with what we can realistically pack in. There are internal and external pressures to be on top of every aspect of our lives and the reality is that we never feel we are. Overall, though, we are doing OK.

Once you have children however, life gets much more complicated. Time feels as if it has warped and is accelerating mercilessly. The mountain of things you absolutely *must* do grows exponentially, while the available time to manage this mountain has been sucked into a black hole. Parents of young children are usually sleep-deprived, stressed and exhausted. It can be hard to remember what 'free time' even means.

When you find yourself in this situation, if there is a significant disparity in workload between you and your partner in managing children and household responsibilities it can, for the first time, put significant strain on an otherwise harmonious relationship.

Among my friends and family, I do not know of a single relationship that has not endured major arguments and unhappiness caused by one person in the relationship feeling exhausted, unfulfilled and overwhelmed because they are shouldering an unmanageable workload – usually on top of paid employment – that they feel their partner is not sharing equally. If a relationship is rocky before children come along, their arrival will really test its durability. However, even 'match-made-in-heaven' couples with no worries or strains were now facing serious challenges to their relationship, fuelled by resentment over an issue that took both too long to appreciate.

Perhaps surprisingly, it doesn't happen overnight. From the moment your child is born, it is like letting go at the top of the world's highest waterslide and not being able to catch your breath for months; you are simply propelled along by the rapids in a semi-conscious state brought about by wonder (OMG that tiny, beautiful person is mine!), anxiety (I hope I am going to be a good parent) and crucially, lack of sleep. You are flying by the seat of your pants for a long time, ever-hopeful that the gradient will flatten out around the next bend. But it doesn't. Not for a very long time. And because we don't realise that we now *live* on this waterslide, for far too long we fail to grasp the differences between this new reality and our former, much more manageable life.

This is why it is important for both people in the relationship to be open and realistic about the Invisible Job that they will have to manage once they start a family: so that they can come up with a realistic plan for how to go about it. In other words, they need to have 'the Talk'. And not when they bring their new baby home from the hospital. It needs to happen well before that – ideally at the point when the idea of even having a baby is still just that: an idea. Or better still, even earlier: at the point when you decide to make a long-term commitment to each other. Why? As we'll see later, wrapped up in your expectations of how you are going to manage being parents are layers of beliefs and values that neither of you may realise you hold and it is very easy to presume that our partner shares our vision of what life as a family will look like. The sooner you have the Talk, the less time you will spend tumbling down the waterslide on your own.

Now I *get* that the mere idea of floating this topic for discussion will probably make you cringe and might feel a little OTT – 'Surely it's something we will just figure out as we go along!' But as we will see later, in most relationships, the Talk (in whatever form it takes) ends up happening sooner or later. And the later you leave it, the greater the risk of causing unnecessary struggle in your relationship. So it's important to get on with talking openly and honestly to ensure you and your partner don't have fundamentally different aspirations or unrealistic expectations of your future roles from the outset.

Until you find yourself in the thick of it – i.e. as a new parent doing your best to keep your head above water in unfamiliar territory – it's hard to grasp what a huge undertaking becoming a parent is going to be. We underestimate the mountain of tasks involved and how hard it will be to manage them all. Therefore, we don't tend to worry too deeply beforehand about what exactly they will entail – or who is going to do them. The purpose of Part I of this book is to try to map out exactly what is involved by listing these tasks in the form of a job description. That way, couples can work out between them the best way to handle it. This is not rocket science; it is being forewarned. When you do not have a realistic sense beforehand about what is coming down the track and have not agreed in advance how you will manage it, it is likely that much of the responsibility will fall to the mother, putting her under enormous pressure and ultimately damaging your relationship.

Balance can be restored eventually but by then much damage has often occurred, both to the mother and to the relationship. Much better to mitigate this by ensuring that as you and your partner enter this new and exciting phase of your life, you

- are fully aware of what the Invisible Job will entail;
- engage in an honest discussion about what you envisage your roles will be;
- agree a plan for how you aim to handle it *together*.

PART I

THE INVISIBLE JOB DESCRIPTION

1

A Job Easily Misunderstood

Before getting into what the Invisible Job Description entails, I must make one important point:

No single element of the Invisible Job is in itself overly onerous or even unpleasant.

This is important to explain because one partner is sometimes confused as to why, for example, the other finds it stressful to cook a midweek meal, yet seems to enjoy cooking at the weekend while listening to the radio, with a glass of wine in their hand. The thing is, doing any one element of the Invisible Job at a time can be perfectly delightful. When my children were about eleven and nine years old, I took a career break. Shortly after I gave up my job, I remember spending an uninterrupted hour in the kitchen one morning washing dirty pots while listening to a podcast. Strange as it may sound, it was sheer bliss!

Doing any individual element of the Invisible Job is no problem whatsoever. I am perfectly happy to clean a toilet or scrub an oven – provided I'm not doing it at 9 p.m. while simultaneously trying to put children to bed, knowing I need to get back to an urgent work email after that!

The issue is the cumulative burden of having too many jobs to do and the 'mental load' associated with managing them all – i.e. the constant thinking ahead, scheduling/rescheduling and prioritising. It's when you find yourself emptying the washing machine at midnight, or arriving home after a tough day at work and needing to cook dinner in fifteen minutes because the children are already hungry and one of them needs to tell you all about a bad day at school that you start to appreciate the full weight of the Invisible Job, a commitment you never knowingly signed up for, and feel that it is all becoming too much. To the uninitiated, the Invisible Job can appear deceptively manageable. Like many jobs though, the better you do it, the easier it looks to a casual observer.

If you were going to hire someone to manage everything that the Invisible Job entails on behalf of your family, however, you would need to articulate clearly what was expected of them so they had a realistic sense of what it entailed. The best approach might be to write an actual job description, much like what you would get from an employer when taking on a new role. In corporate organisations clear job descriptions are often required to be ASMART, an acronym that stands for:

- **A**ligned with the goals of the organisation
- **S**pecific – what exactly needs to be done
- **M**easurable – outcomes that can be objectively measured
- **A**chievable
- **R**ealistic
- **T**ime-bound – by when it needs to be done

Try to keep these criteria in mind when completing your Invisible Job Description, as this will help ensure you have a shared, clear understanding of what it entails and that you are focusing your efforts on the things that matter most.

ALIGNED WITH THE GOALS OF THE ORGANISATION

In this case, the 'organisation' is your family (i.e. you and your partner (+/-children). It is entirely up to you what your goals are, and they will evolve over time. At a certain stage in your relationship, your focus might be on your careers, trying to buy a place of your own or start a family, while later it may shift to spending as much time as possible with your children and building a nurturing base from which they can learn and develop happily. Obviously, the goals and aspirations of every couple/family will be unique and depend on many factors. Because of this, the relative importance of the elements in the Invisible Job Description will vary between (and even within) couples. Discussing and agreeing what your current life priorities are is an important first step in determining what your Invisible Job Description will involve.

SPECIFIC

To avoid misunderstandings or arguments about whether a job has been carried out as envisaged, it's important to agree on the expected outcome. Unless this is specified clearly, misunderstandings will inevitably occur. It's important to remember that nobody is a mind reader! Instead of presuming that it is obvious to your partner what 'doing the bins' means, it is clearer to specify what this means – e.g. 'empty contents of all internal bins once a week to the outside wheelie bin and put a new liner in each bin'. Being specific makes it much easier to determine objectively whether something has been completed as envisaged and avoids unnecessary arguments. It is also one of the main reasons that women's efforts to establish fair sharing of responsibilities tend to fail and they simply revert to doing it themselves. But there's no point getting annoyed with someone about not cleaning the kitchen properly if you haven't been specific about what exactly needs to be done. There's no need to go over board but you must provide enough guidance on what needs to be done (and how) so that the person responsible for a given element has full autonomy to do it, without the need for further assistance or reminding.

MEASURABLE

This is a very important factor where the Invisible Job is concerned. As a recent report by the Economic and Social Research Institute identified, 'unpaid labour is not routinely measured or made visible; as a result, it is often undervalued' (2).

Therefore, an essential way to stop this work from being invisible – and therefore unvalued – is to measure it. This also facilitates more equitable sharing. Estimate roughly how much time each element is likely to take. Granted, this is not always an exact science: estimating how long it takes to bring your children to a swimming class every Tuesday is straightforward, but how can you predict the volume of related administration and WhatsApp correspondence? It's also important to consider how frequently a particular element will need to be done, as it significantly impacts the actual workload involved – e.g. while the car might only need to be insured once a year, the kitchen table may need to be cleared several times a day.

TIME-BOUND

This is an important criterion because time is the main limitation for couples when it comes to doing the Invisible Job. When children are hungry, they need dinner now; when a baby has a wet nappy, it needs to be changed now; when you discover nits in your child's hair, it needs to be treated this evening. Therefore, the challenge is trying to do everything within the limited time available by prioritising, multitasking and working at speed to accommodate all demands. Elements that are highly time-bound afford very low flexibility around when they need to be done, meaning they tend to cause the most conflict when trying to manage the Invisible Job on top of paid work and all your other commitments.

It is useful for couples to list all the elements in their Invisible Job Description for three reasons:

a. To ensure that both people have a clear overall picture of all the things being done between you for the benefit of your household/family.
b. To assess whether there is anything important missing – i.e. not currently being done – that you both feel should be.
c. More importantly, to identify if there is anything in the job description that is not critical and can be eliminated to make the other things you are trying to manage more **R**ealistic and possibly even **A**chievable!

ACHIEVABLE AND REALISTIC

Note that it may not always be possible to apply these two ASMART criteria to the Invisible Job Description, especially elements linked to parenting. Since trying to stay on top of everything often feels impossible (especially without adequate support), few parents may feel that managing everything they think they should be doing is either **A**chievable or **R**ealistic. In fact, it's quite likely that, on reading the job description, nobody in their right mind would apply for this job at all! And as many parents will testify, there are certainly days when we are all tempted to hand in our resignation.

DRAFTING YOUR INVISIBLE JOB DESCRIPTION

Where do you begin, when it comes to putting down on paper the millions of things that need to happen every day/week/month/year for family life to function?

Those not yet in the thick of things don't know what it entails and those who are in the thick of things barely have time to breathe, never mind draft a detailed list of all the things swimming around inside their heads. Although your Invisible Job Description will be personal to you and your current circumstances, many of the elements are common to most couples. And the child-related elements will be common to most parents.

To save time, I have drafted a template Invisible Job Description, which you can download at www.theinvisiblejob.com. Use it as a starting point which you can edit to create your own Invisible Job Description by adding/deleting elements so it reflects your personal situation as a couple right now. You can then discuss together how to divide these responsibilities fairly between you.

You'll notice that beside each element in the job description are some columns, indicating:

- **Frequency** (how often that job element needs to be done)
  * Daily/several times a day
  * Weekly
  * Monthly or less often

- **Flexibility** (how much freedom you have around when to do it)
  * Low
  * Medium
  * High

- **Responsibility** (who is responsible for ensuring this job element gets done). Note this person can either do the job themselves or outsource it to someone else (e.g. if you are responsible for gardening, you could either do the gardening yourself or hire a gardener to do it). Either way, you are responsible for ensuring it gets done and for managing all associated administration and liaison (i.e. finding, hiring, overseeing and paying). There are therefore two columns:
  * Person responsible (which must be one of you)
  * Outsource (Yes/No)

If you don't have children, many of the elements in the job description template won't apply to you. However, if becoming parents is something you are considering soon (or even in the distant future), before you do, it is important to talk through these elements beforehand, so you both appreciate the huge amount of time these additional responsibilities will take up. That way, you can come up with a realistic plan for how you will manage it between you.

Choose a neutral moment to tell your partner that you'd like to have a chat about balancing your time and priorities as a couple. Identify when would be a good time for both of you to have a quiet night in with a bottle of wine or (even better), to go out for a bite to eat somewhere local, and put it in your diaries.

Print two copies of the draft Invisible Job Description and have them to hand when you have your scheduled date/chat. With hopefully a glass of something nice in hand (and no children to attend to!), begin by giving a bit of background: i.e. that life is busy for both of you, as there are lots of things you are each trying to achieve and many activities and social things you also love to do. On top of this, there are many things that may not feature on the fun list but just have to happen somehow – because sadly, we don't have magic elves to do them for us. The trick is trying to balance it all. Therefore the reason for having this chat is so that you and your partner:

1. Have a clear understanding of what the Invisible Job entails (i.e. all the things that must happen routinely for life in your home to run smoothly, efficiently and happily)

2. Direct your (finite!) energy towards the elements you both feel matter most (leaving as much time as possible for all the other things you want to do in life)
3. Agree how best to manage these responsibilities fairly, i.e. in a way that respects your right to free time equally. (Note that this applies regardless of whether you both work full-time, part-time or do not currently have a paid job)

Explain that you have already drafted a list of these responsibilities to get the ball rolling and that you'd like to go through it together. Give a copy of the draft job description to your partner.

1. The first thing you need to decide together is whether there are any elements currently in the draft job description that you agree are not important or not applicable to your life right now and therefore do not need to be done at all. Delete them.
2. Next, go through each of the remaining elements and agree on two things: roughly how frequently each needs to be done (tick which category best fits). The frequency in the template may or may not reflect your life, so just edit it to whatever you feel does.
   * Daily/several times a day
   * Once a week or more
   * Once a month or more
   * Once or twice a year
   * Less frequently
3. Next, consider how much flexibility there is around when each element must be done. This is important because it is a lack of freedom to choose when to do something (i.e. opt in when it suits) that really impacts our autonomy and ability to balance conflicting responsibilities.
   * Low – i.e. must be done now, whether it suits you or not – an example might be preparing dinner for hungry children.
   * Medium – i.e. it might not need to be done in the next hour but must be done by tonight – an example might be putting out the wheelie bin for collection.
   * High – i.e. something associated with a high degree of choice around when to do it – e.g. booking an annual holiday.
4. Now put a star next to any elements with both high frequency and low flexibility around when it must be done, as these constitute the 'heavy lifters' of parenting and home responsibilities that can really wear us down. For this reason, it's particularly important that when you get to Step 6 (Dividing up responsibilities in the Invisible Job), you each volunteer for your fair share of starred elements.
5. Identify if there are any elements it would make sense to outsource (if you can afford it) – for instance, hiring a cleaner to do some of the weekly housework tasks. Note that even if you decide to outsource an element, overall responsibility for this element will still need to be assigned to one of you as someone

has to find, hire, manage and pay this person. Similarly, even if you decide to outsource a service, such as having your car valeted at the garage instead of hoovering and washing it yourself, someone still needs to arrange to take the car to the garage. Note that outsourcing an element doesn't necessarily mean hiring a professional. For instance, you could check if a grandparent would be willing to bring your children to an after-school activity on a certain day.

6. Now for the most important part: Go through each of the elements and select the ones that you both agree are essential. Then discuss which of you will take responsibility for each of these elements from now on. Write this person's name next to each element in the 'Responsibility' column. Ideally, where possible, you would each choose elements you either have some aptitude for or don't mind doing. Pay particular attention to the starred elements (i.e. the ones with high frequency and low flexibility). As we will discuss later, the key factor that determines whether couples feel they are both doing their fair share of the Invisible Job is how these heavy lifter elements are shared, not whether all elements are shared 50:50. Unsurprisingly, there may be no great rush to volunteer for too many of these elements, but it is important that you each accept your fair share of responsibility!

7. Having assigned responsibility for all the essential elements, go back through the remaining ones and see which additional elements you each feel you have the capacity to take on. Don't forget that even elements you have decided you will outsource still need to be assigned to one or other of you as the person accountable for that element.

8. Having gone through every element, if there are any that remain unclaimed – i.e. neither you nor your partner is willing to accept responsibility for doing them right now – you must delete them. This doesn't mean they are not important. It just means that for the foreseeable future at least, you both accept that they won't get done. If you realistically can't fit in any more right now, attempting to do so will only lead to frustration and friction. Perhaps you will have sufficient capacity between you to take them on in a few months, or a few years.

WHAT CONSTITUTES A 'FAIR SHARE' OF THE INVISIBLE JOB?

A fair share does not necessarily mean doing 50% of the elements in the job description because, as we have already identified, some elements need to be done once a year, while others need to be done several times a day. Similarly, some might take fifteen minutes to do, while others may take hours. While these are important factors in determining what constitutes a fair division of responsibilities, it is more important to take a step back and look at the Invisible Job in the context of your overall free time. If you both work similar hours per week in a paid job, it would be reasonable to expect that the time you each commit to the Invisible Job is also equal. Note that it doesn't matter whether one person earns more than the other; regardless of whether one of you earns £300/hour and the other £10/hour, you are equally important and your free time is equally valuable. Therefore, having decided together what the key responsibilities for your home/family are, you should be equally responsible for managing them.

Obviously where one person spends significantly more hours per week in a paid job (forming part of your joint household income), it would make sense for the other person to spend more time on the Invisible Job. However, both paid and unpaid work that contribute to your joint welfare should be recognised equally. If you are each doing your fair share, you should end up with a similar amount of free time each week to spend on non-work activities (whether paid or unpaid) and similar flexibility to manage this time.

Warning for new mothers

This bit is important: New mothers should not allocate themselves responsibility for too many elements!

When you wake up in the Brave New World of being a new mother, it can be hard to figure out what your role is. Before you had this little person to look after, you were capable of doing a million things. Your instinct might be to continue trying to do all these, plus one more (looking after your new baby). It took me far too long to realise that when you have just had a baby, you need to focus on attending to the baby, getting adequate sleep and the small number of activities which absolutely must be done that day.

This may sound like the lowest bar set for personal goals ever – especially if you are used to being a highly productive person, but life is very different once you have a baby. While I knew there would be some late nights/early mornings and a lot of baby clobber to buy, before having children my vision of what my new life would be like was wildly inaccurate. (I will admit that leisurely strolls to coffee shops to meet up with other mums from the NCT group featured strongly!)

The reality was more like being spun around in a churning wave all day with only brief gasps of air (or coffee) keeping me alive. In the beginning, the idea of staying at home on maternity leave while my husband went out to work in the morning felt a bit like playing hooky from school, or being given an unexpected afternoon off at work, and I planned to put my time to good use. I was used to being an active, efficient and productive person with multiple projects and to-do lists always on the go. For the first few months I ploughed on trying to be this person, oblivious to how misguided I was.

Some of the things on my to-do list were the perennial household chores, which for some reason (perhaps because I was no longer contributing equally to our relationship financially) I felt were now my responsibility.

Lots of the things on the list were baby-related – such as hospital, physiother-apist, immunisation or breastfeeding appointments, along with official things like registering her birth and applying for a passport.

There were also many things that I felt I should be doing to be a good mother; things that had been mentioned by well-meaning people or in baby books that I dutifully tried to read during the only moments in the day I was not running around, i.e. while breastfeeding. Things like:

- **Mum from my hospital antenatal group:** 'Have you learned how to do baby massage? It's so good for sore tummies!'
- **Work colleague:** 'Have you got her name down for a good crèche? And have you told HR what date you are coming back?'
- **Leaflet in the post:** 'Have you applied for the free child savings account new parents are entitled to?'
- **Mum from my NCT group:** 'Is she (my six-week-old daughter) doing baby yoga yet?'
- **Nurse at my GP surgery:** 'Are you doing your pelvic floor exercises four times a day?'
- **Family:** 'When's the christening?!'

Each morning I would scribble a to-do list for the day, not realising how unre-alistic it was. As time wore on, I became increasingly frustrated at my continuing inability to get through what (on paper) should have been a straightforward day. What I failed to grasp was that it would only constitute a straightforward day for someone who had slept the night before and did not have a baby to look after! It took me a very long time to realise that looking after my baby was the one and only thing I absolutely had to do.

The impact of sleep deprivation is real. Nobody can function without adequate sleep, as the neurologist Professor Matthew Walker explains in his brilliant book, *Why We Sleep*. According to Prof. Walker, we need between seven and nine hours of sleep every night and the long-term consequences of failing to give our bodies this rest are sobering. (We'll come back to this later.)

The consequences of sleep deprivation are obvious to me now. Yet during my maternity leave (when the amount of sleep I got each night was at best four hours), I did not understand the impact this was having on my brain. When you are up several times every night, you lose the ability to do simple things the following day, like plan or do mental arithmetic. A simple decision about whether it makes more sense to wake your baby now and feed her before going to the doctor or to transfer her to the pram asleep and feed her when you get there feels like a Mensa-level conundrum.

Your short-term memory also deserts you completely, especially when it comes to repeated activities.

'What time did you last feed her?' the nurse at the breastfeeding clinic asks with an expectant smile ... and I have no idea. I rack my brain, knowing this is a simple question that I should of course know the answer to, but nope ... total blank.

You are also likely to frequently misplace things and leave the house without essential items like your wallet, keys or phone. I ended up sticking Post-it notes with checklists by the front door.

Sleep deprivation, coupled with the immediate nature of a new baby's demands, leaves you in a fog of chaos with multiple half-finished activities: the phone rings when I am on my way to put a nappy in the bin with baby on hip. It's the doctor's surgery and I put the nappy down on the hall table to answer the phone, then run into the lounge looking for a pen to note the details. I can't find a pen but do find half a piece of toast I didn't finish an hour ago because baby woke up crying from her nap. I find a pen in the kitchen and see the half-loaded washing machine, abandoned when I realised we were out of detergent. Many hours later my husband will come home and wonder why there is a dirty nappy on the hall table.

The good news is that, while most of us are used to getting our daily quota of sleep in one (nightly) block, we can also function well on two solid blocks of four hours of sleep. Therefore, if we manage to get a four-hour block during the night, we will feel reasonably rested – and sane! – as long as we prioritise grabbing the other four hours whenever possible during the following day. If I could go back in time, the main thing I would tell thirty-year-old me is 'Sleep! Whenever you can!'

WHAT DOES THE INVISIBLE JOB ENTAIL?

Deciding what the Invisible Job entails in your relationship/household is completely up to you. The list in the Invisible Job Description template is not exhaustive and is mainly intended as a guide to help you figure out what yours entails.

The process of examining it may highlight for the first time the disproportionate responsibility one partner has been shouldering, perhaps for quite some time! Discussing it offers an opportunity to make conscious changes to the Invisible Job so that life becomes more manageable and more fulfilling for both of you. What matters is that your Invisible Job Description represents the goals and responsibilities that you and your partner both believe are most important and can realistically be managed between you.

You both need to understand exactly what it involves and appreciate its vital contribution to the welfare of your family.

Being responsible for a given element means taking responsibility for every aspect of it, from researching and planning through to execution – and all the communication in between. Without relying on help or reminders from your partner. For instance, taking responsibility for your child's Saturday football doesn't just mean driving them to training and back each week. It encompasses everything from finding a suitable football club to figuring out whether the training time would fit with their existing schedule, managing the logistics of getting them to training and matches, taking care of enrolment and club fees, managing all the communications about training and matches, and scheduling all football commitments in your diary each week. It also includes ensuring your child owns the right size football boots, socks, shin pads and gumshield, and that they have it all in their bag when leaving the house, ensuring that the jersey and socks go in the laundry basket when you get home so they are clean in time for the next match. It also means helping your child through the ups and downs of learning new skills and possibly even having to volunteer for the club coaching or fundraising committee. Cheering on the sideline on a Saturday is just the tip of the iceberg, the glory part.

Therefore, when one of you takes responsibility for a given element, they need to own it. It is only when someone agrees to be fully accountable for an element that their partner gets to cross it off their mental list. And as we will see later, it is the overall mental load of being accountable for too many things that is the biggest burden of the Invisible Job. Therefore the rest of Part I delves a little deeper into what each element really involves and possible ways of handling it. Once someone fully understands what is required, they should be ready to run with it solo.

2

I'm Hungry!

PREPARING LUNCH AND DINNER FOR THE FAMILY

Frequency: Once or twice a day
Flexibility around timing: Low

Although my husband managed to feed himself perfectly well before he met me, for some reason when we moved in together cooking became my responsibility. I'm not sure how this happened but I distinctly remember that he was in semi-denial about the need to cook at all. Because he regularly had lunch out with colleagues, he claimed he 'didn't really eat in the evening' but the double portions I made rarely made it as far as the fridge because he would always 'just finish off' whatever was left over, leaving me to cook from scratch again the next day.

My husband claims that the range of meals he can cook is very limited and says, 'You're a much better cook than me'. However, what this pseudo-compliment really means is, 'It therefore makes much more sense that you cook (... and I don't)'. In fact, flattering someone about their capabilities is a classic technique used in work environments to persuade an already busy (but capable) person to take on additional projects.

Anyway, somehow I became the default cook. When Jamie Oliver brought out an app, it inspired a sudden keen interest in cooking in my husband. Not only did the app download the ingredients as a shopping list to his phone, it also video-guided him through the cooking process. Despite copious (and genuine!) praise for various wonderful culinary outputs, sadly, this gadget-inspired interest was short-lived.

Many women with whom I discussed the topic of who does the cooking in their home highlighted an interesting pattern when it comes to men's involvement: while their partners usually showed little appetite to contribute in any way to the never-ending job of preparing midweek lunches and dinners for the family, they happily took over when it came to more prestigious culinary undertakings. One woman described how her husband was more than happy to cook a roast for Sunday lunch and invite extended family, while another recounted how her husband loved masterminding a barbeque in the garden for friends. To my surprise, one woman I know told me her husband insisted on managing the entire menu when hosting a dinner party for friends. However, none of these men exhibited the slightest interest in cooking midweek meals for hungry children or preparing school lunches. Perhaps this is because cooking for friends or special occasions is a visible role that gets copious recognition, in addition to being something we can do at a time when we are not normally under conflicting pressure from work. On the other hand, cooking midweek dinner for your partner and children tends to attract much less recognition and must usually be done at the end of a busy day in a limited time.

IS COOKING A NECESSARY ELEMENT OF THE INVISIBLE JOB DESCRIPTION? COULD IT BE OUTSOURCED OR EVEN DELETED?

Napoleon was not wrong when he said, 'An army marches on its stomach'. The only thing worse than a hungry child when dinner isn't ready is a hungry and tired child. Few of my friends are of the view that serving healthy food twice/three times a day is an easy or joyful experience. My children sometimes ask me questions like, 'Mommy, if you could have superpowers or magical items, what would they be?' They are usually disappointed with my unimaginative answers because they don't include being able to morph into different animals or conjure up magical vehicles with gravity-defying powers. Instead, I often reply that I would love to have a magical dumbwaiter hatch in the kitchen that instantly popped out whatever dish my stomach was dreaming about. When you are the person who cooks 99% of the time, there is something wonderful about someone else cooking for you. It is no coincidence that my husband, who is a fan of home-cooked food, defaults to eating out when he is in charge of the children on a Saturday or Sunday.

When it comes to cooking, like many jobs, there are three basic factors to juggle when deciding how best to manage it: quality, time, and cost.

Quality

When I was a child, we rarely ate processed food. My mother, who was an excellent cook, prepared all our meals from scratch, so we grew up on a healthy diet of home cooking. Potatoes were a mandatory component of all meals (my English husband is still coming to terms with the Irish obsession with potatoes). As my mother had given up her job to stay home and look after children, in theory she had time to cook (although in practice I now realise she couldn't have had much time between managing four children, doing all the housework and supporting my father's business). However, the main reason we rarely ate processed food was because back then, it was just too expensive. In 1980s Ireland, processed food was also very exotic – I still remember pleading for Uncle Ben's boil-in-bag rice, having seen the TV advert, along with another exotic-sounding food called 'pasta'.

Time

However, home cooking requires of a lot of time. Not just the actual cooking, but planning ahead to ensure you have all the right ingredients and then cleaning up afterwards! If we had unlimited time to devote to cooking, we could probably all prepare tasty meals using quality ingredients without spending a fortune. The reality for most working parents, though, is that time is a very scarce commodity. Even sitting down to eat together might not be possible for many couples, owing to the daily whirlwind of commuting, drop-off/pick-up from childcare, getting home at different times and attending to children's needs. For many years, my husband and I both worked full-time in demanding jobs involving frequent overseas travel. Both of us being home on a weeknight was rare enough; sitting down to a home-cooked meal together was usually wishful thinking. Although our children ate proper meals, the *plat du jour* for exhausted parents was sometimes late-night muesli.

Cost

Money is a constraint for almost everyone. We think before we buy things and (consciously or subconsciously) budget to make sure money goes as far as possible. While the cost of food might be small in comparison to say, the mortgage, it accounts for a considerable portion of most people's weekly outgoings.

There may be some very lucky individuals for whom money is no object whatsoever. If this applies to you, just scratch the whole 'Cooking' thing off your Job Description and hire a private chef to cook for you – and, of course, do the washing up! For most people, this is more one to keep in mind for when they win the lottery.

A balancing act

If both you and your partner work, time for cooking during the week may be scarce. Therefore, you may need to compromise as follows:

a. Even if the quality is less than ideal, sometimes the only practical option might be microwave meals or takeaway food.
b. If eating healthily is important (i.e. you're not willing to compromise on quality), you could try mastering a few simple but healthy dishes from recipe books that promise meals in fifteen minutes. Alternatively, you might decide to dedicate time at the weekend to cooking healthy food. (Every so often I would spend Saturday making lasagne, casseroles and stews to stock the freezer for days when I'd have no time to cook.)
c. Or you might accept the increased cost of buying freshly prepared meals that you can stick straight in the oven when you get home from work. While these will get a big thumbs up from most adults, finding healthy meals that your children will also eat can be challenging.

Cooking can feel like a never-ending job and is definitely one of the heavy lifters in the Invisible Job. No sooner has my son finished his breakfast cereal on a Saturday morning than he is already asking, 'What's for lunch?' When we come home after a busy afternoon, often the first thing he'll say is, 'Mom, what's for dinner?!' Curious about his understanding of the logistics involved, I asked him once how he thought it was possible that Mom could have been out with him all afternoon while somehow simultaneously preparing dinner at home ... but he just looked at me blankly.

While cooking is time-consuming, it can be quite a pleasant activity. Chopping, frying, stirring, tasting, adjusting – it's all good, especially if you are not doing it under pressure (which is normally the case when it comes to midweek meals). The real killer about cooking is the thinking and planning it requires.

I remember starting to make stew one evening and moaning to my husband that I was sick of always being the one who has to cook. Seemingly surprised, he looked at the semi-peeled vegetables and other ingredients on the chopping board and said, 'I'll do it then. Just show me exactly what I need to do'.

'No!' I shouted back.

He looked confused.

Last-minute offers like this to stand in and 'cook dinner', while well-intentioned, are not to be confused with being responsible for the job in question. Much of the work has been done by this stage so the 'cooking' is only a minor part of the overall task. Preparing food requires planning, and someone has had to give consider-able thought in advance to what the family will eat for the week (working around various after-school and work commitments) and purchase whatever ingredients need to be bought, while being mindful of what needs to be used up.

Planning what meals to cook for the week is eminently sensible in theory but requires time. My retired mother-in-law likes leafing through recipe books 'just for fun'. When working full-time, the only time I ever managed to open a recipe book was if we were having friends over for dinner at the weekend, as I searched frantically for something tasty to prepare in under two hours.

When allocating responsibilities in the Invisible Job Description, consider carefully the total time involved in preparing meals, as this is easy to underestimate (especially if you are not the one doing it!) It also varies according to the age of your children. To share the load, you might consider splitting the job of preparing family meals into two parts, with one of you managing this Monday to Friday while the other is in charge at weekends (which usually involves cooking lunch and dinner).

Job element	Time needed (excluding shopping and clearing up)	Frequency	Flexibility around timing
Preparing family meals	Anything from 30 mins to 2 hrs	Daily Mon–Fri and twice daily on weekends	Low
Preparing baby food	Approx. 30 mins to 1 hour	Daily (but only for about 6–9 months)	Low–medium
Preparing children's lunches	10–20 mins	5 days a week during school term	Low–medium

BABY FOOD

When your baby is about five or six months old, she will probably be ready to move from a diet of milk, milk (and more milk) to real food. Exciting times for all! After sampling bland baby rice, she will be ready to start exploring a world of new tastes – fruits, vegetables, cereals, pasta, rice, fish, meat, spices and all the amazing ways we humans combine these to create delicious sensations in our mouths. Initially, though, baby may be a table for one special order, as she isn't able to just eat whatever you're having because she doesn't have any/enough teeth and her dining schedule won't match the rest of the family's. In addition, there are some foods that babies simply can't eat (like honey) or can only tolerate in tiny quantities (like salt). So bespoke menu it is!

Luckily, there is ample guidance available regarding what a baby can/should eat and how to gradually introduce all these exciting foods to her palate. Annabel Karmel is a guru of baby food recipes, with intriguing delicacies for the young and dentally challenged (like pear and cinnamon purée or mashed banana with avocado), progressing gradually to mushed-up versions of adult meals. Any baby lucky enough to enjoy such five-star dining will have a whale of a time navigating this learning curve, but being a baby chef takes time! Not only are you preparing a separate menu, but there is a ton of steaming, mashing and blending involved – not to mention washing up!

One way of trying to minimise the work involved in home-made baby food is to make large batches that you can freeze in ice-cube trays. Additional preparation time upfront, but you can then unfreeze a broccoli and carrot, lamb and potato or beetroot and apple baby meal whenever you need it.

On the plus side, it's also the cheapest option. A less time-intensive, but more expensive solution would be to buy jars or packages from one of the many baby food ranges now widely available. Once baby is old enough to sit upright in a highchair, many parents take an approach called baby-led weaning, which basically entails giving your baby food in manageable sized pieces they can pick up and feed themselves (e.g. cooked carrot batons, half a boiled egg or a tiny serving of whatever the family is having for dinner). While this may eliminate the need for purées, it means factoring in all baby requirements when preparing family meals (e.g. low sugar, low salt, no nuts or honey) and preparing suitable baby alternatives whenever you all just fancy a takeaway.

CHILDREN'S SCHOOL LUNCHES

Even if one person is responsible for cooking the main meals, the other person might take on the more straightforward job of preparing school lunches. When I say straightforward, I'm referring only to the level of culinary talent involved. After all, everyone knows how to make a sandwich, right?

What makes this job less than straightforward, however, is the unpredictable nature of your clientele! It can be very challenging to reach an agreement with children about what constitutes an acceptable lunch. When my son was in kindergarten, there was nothing he would agree to eat for lunch. For months, I presumed he enjoyed the ham sandwiches he took with him in his little lunchbox every morning because it always came home empty. It was only when the mother of another little boy said her son was delighted with the sandwiches that my son brought him every day that I realised he never ate them at all. When I asked him why, he looked puzzled, as he thought the answer was obvious: although he really liked bread, ham and butter, he did not like ham sandwiches. Or any sandwiches. Oh. Neither was he prepared to try any fruit, yoghurt or cheese. Note that if you ever manage to hit on an acceptable lunch for all your children simultaneously, don't be lulled into a false sense of security, because children regularly change their minds. Check out a sketch called 'When making the school lunches sends you over the edge' by Dirt Birds (Irish comedians Sue Collins and Sineád Culbert) on YouTube.

CLEARING UP AFTER MEALS

Although linked to preparing meals, this element deserves a separate mention. Not only because it is very time-consuming and may need to be done several times a day, but also because when someone has just spent significant time and effort preparing a meal for the family, they might not be in the mood to then clear the table, load the dishwasher, wipe kitchen counters and scrub pots. In fact, it might be an ideal opportunity for someone else to say, 'I've got this covered, you sit down.' Clearing up also needs to happen after simple meals that may not involve cooking, such as breakfast and/or impromptu snacks as, unfortunately, the shoe-making elves don't do cereal bowls and milk spills.

IDENTIFY AND FULFIL ALL GROCERY SHOPPING NEEDS

Frequency: Daily to weekly
Flexibility around timing: Medium

Everyone knows about grocery shopping. When we first moved out of home, we all figured out quickly that if nobody went out to get milk and bread, well ... you didn't have any milk or bread. The principle remains the same but the scope of the job grows a bit when you have a family because you are buying for more people and have less time. You also need to manage the near-impossible permutations of things your children will and won't eat.

Food shopping is an activity that can be handled in a variety of ways.

My children were born in London and while working full-time with two young children, I was deeply in love with an online grocery shopping service there called Ocado. The platform was wonderfully straightforward, enabling you to put an order together in under fifteen minutes, and deliveries arrived punctually in your chosen 30-minute time slot. What truly made it amazing though was that the website was linked to real-time stock availability.

When we moved from London to Dublin, Ocado was possibly the thing I missed most. Critically, to someone struggling to juggle full-time work, international commuting and the Invisible Job, Irish supermarkets at the time could not compare to Ocado in terms of reliability – i.e. delivering the things you had ordered when you needed them!

I got so fed up dashing out to the local shop for missing items I needed to make dinner that I eventually I gave up on online grocery shopping and switched to going to the supermarket and local butcher once a week. My well-meaning husband couldn't understand why I insisted on shopping in person instead of ordering online, while constantly saying I had too much to do. Looking up expect-antly from his laptop, poised to submit an online order, he would say 'Just quickly tell me all the food we need for the week'.

But this was not something I could answer at 11 p.m. off the top of my head! At least not until I had gone through the fridge to see what needed to be used up soon, then worked out the family's comings and goings for the week and based on this information, formed a mental plan of what meals we should cook. And don't forget that online deliveries also have to be put away! On days I was working from home, the delivery van always managed to arrive in the middle of a conference call. I would scramble downstairs on mute and mime directions to the driver to drop everything on the kitchen floor, before running back upstairs to my desk, returning to put the chilled food in the fridge whenever I had a minute between meetings.

Job element	Time needed		Flexibility around timing
	Amount	Frequency	
Grocery shopping in person, not including time to compile shopping list or unpack shopping	45–60 mins (plus travel time to/from shop)	Once a week should cover most things	Medium
Grocery shopping online	20–30 mins	As above	High
Unpacking/sorting groceries and throwing out anything out of date in the fridge/cupboard	20 mins	As above	Low

3

Housework

LAUNDRY

There is nothing special to note about laundry, except that it is repeatedly mentioned in studies as one of the jobs that most people find boring and repetitive and which therefore weighs heavily in couple's estimates of whether household responsibilities are being shared fairly between them. (A number of people I spoke to specifically listed 'hanging socks' as their ultimate nemesis when it comes to the Invisible Job.) While the washing machine needs to be fed at least twice a week, if you have babies/small children this may need to happen daily as there is an awful lot of laundry to do!

GENERAL HOUSEWORK

Although people's views will differ on how clean a home should be, nobody wants to live in a pigsty. Therefore, cleaning is unfortunately something that has to happen on a regular basis. When couples disagree about what 'clean' means, it can become a bone of contention. One person may appear completely oblivious to a level of dirt/untidiness that the other finds intolerable. Some may deem people who clean the inside of cupboards as 'tidy freaks'. Others may hold people who don't seem to know what a toilet brush is for in very low regard. Couples will never score exactly the same on the tidy vs messy scale and therefore expectations of what 'cleaning the house' entails will differ. There may be some jobs that one partner considers necessary to do every week but which the other partner had no idea needed doing – ever! Each couple will be different. And that's fine. All that matters is that you agree between you what jobs need to be done, and how often.

Housework is such a tedious subject that rather than spend too much time on it, I suggest you look at the Invisible Job Description template in the Appendix for a breakdown of the more obvious elements to consider. The key thing to be mindful of when dividing up responsibility for housework is frequency. Jobs that only need to be done once a month are not only likely to take up less time overall than something that needs to be done three or four times each day, but in addition, generally feel more satisfying to complete, knowing you won't have to do them again in a few hours.

The workload involved with housework will vary according to the age of your children. If you have a baby starting on solid food or a toddler learning to feed herself, your kitchen floor is likely to be freshly covered in porridge, vegetables and half-chewed pieces of cheese on a daily basis, earning you frequent flyer miles with a dustpan or mop.

The frequency of some jobs is also linked. For instance, if you hardly ever cook, there will be little pot washing to do and the stove top and oven won't be permanently covered in spills. Because jobs are linked, it's important not to fall into the trap whereby the person who takes on responsibility for one job (e.g. cooking) automatically acquires a related job (e.g. cleaning up afterwards).

The thoroughness with which the job is done will also influence how long it takes. Herein lies another common misunderstanding that can lead to arguments: If one partner considers that the shopping has been put away when they have just crammed everything into the nearest cupboard, they are failing to understand what the full job entails and the efforts of the other partner to do it more thoroughly are likely to be undervalued. For instance, when putting away groceries from the supermarket, although it takes a bit longer, I will put the tins of tomatoes from today's shopping behind the ones already in the cupboard, as they have a longer expiry date. This involves shuffling things around in the cupboard, during which I might come across some tins of food which are out of date (bin) or in the wrong place (relocate). The same thing applies in the fridge. Although my goal was simply to put away some cheese and a carton of milk, sometimes I may end up taking out all the jars on the top shelf in order to wipe the jam off the bottom and scrub the (remarkably sticky) shelf with hot water and detergent. All too often, one job can lead to another – that is, if you are predisposed to noticing the other job.

My nemesis, in terms of one job leading to another, is trying to clear the kitchen table. In theory, the kitchen table is for eating meals, and indeed we do use it for that. But it is also the default place where everything else in our house seems to end up, meaning whenever you want to sit down and eat, you first need to remove the mountain of things that have taken up temporary residence. Recognising that it is not always practical to do so immediately and that space in the kitchen is frequently needed by children for matters of great importance (like colouring or homework), we eventually decided to just buy a bigger table. Our current kitchen table can therefore (in theory) seat ten people. Perfect for when extended family come over for Sunday lunch, but it also means that during the week, it's always possible to find space for four plates, even if that means pushing a pile of things down to the end of the table. The downside of having a bigger table is that the pile down the end of the table can grow quietly for days or weeks until you realise that an urgent intervention is needed to fit even a mug of coffee!

STRATEGIES FOR MANAGING HOUSEWORK

Sadly, there is no way to get out of doing housework completely. Like most jobs, it can be tackled in different ways, depending on how much time and money we are prepared to invest and how much we are bothered by the quality of the outcome.

It's easiest to start with the last one, which comes down to deciding what needs to be done, how well and how often. One simple way to minimise the amount of housework that needs to be done is to set a low target for quality. If both partners are happy for bed sheets to be changed every second week, for example, rather than every week, that reduces the time spent on this by 50%. Equally, you may decide you don't need your clothes ironed. And if you feel cleaning windows is an obsession applicable only to older generations, scrub that off the list too. However, this approach will only go so far. For instance, none of us can survive too long without clean clothes and dishes

This brings us to the other variables: time and money. Let's be honest, nobody really likes doing housework. Therefore, those who can afford it usually opt to outsource as much housework as possible, for instance by hiring a cleaner for a few hours each week or sending the ironing to the local laundrette. Before I had children, it had never occurred to me to hire a cleaner. While no more a fan of housework than anyone else, I just accepted it as a part of life admin that we all have to attend to.

However, two months after becoming a parent, I finally understood why people who are lucky enough to be able to afford a cleaner would not think twice about hiring one. Despite being constantly sleep-deprived, instead of catching 40 winks myself whenever my baby was having a nap, I would run around the flat desperately trying to do as much housework as possible before she woke up. Finally, the penny dropped that this was both insane and unsustainable. So I hired an amazing woman who came to the flat for three hours each week. She accomplished more in those three hours than I ever could (even without a baby!), but more importantly, any snippets of time while my baby slept could instead be spent napping myself, or catching up on the millions of other things I was constantly behind on.

There are several elements of general housework that can be effectively managed by accepting the additional cost of outsourcing it to someone else to help with it, leaving you with a better-quality living environment and more time to spend on other things. But don't think that a weekly clean will remove cleaning from your task list entirely!

4

The Health and Hygiene Needs of Your Children

When I was 25, I would never even have considered this element, but older, wiser me now appreciates what it entails. Like many other parenting responsibilities that form part of the Invisible Job, it is very important for your children's welfare and someone needs to be responsible for it. However, it is not really an element you are specifically conscious of; it is simply one more current in the ocean of child-related activities you are swimming (or drowning!) in.

Looking after your baby/child and keeping her safe and well is part and parcel of what you signed up for as a parent; your most important priority. And even if you had not fully got your head around this before, once your baby is born, something hormonal thing kicks in that instinctively makes you want to do this to the best of your ability.

PREVENTIVE HEALTH

Life as a new mother can be pretty chaotic. Succeeding in being only half an hour late to meet a friend for coffee with baby in tow feels like an achievement worthy of an award for strategic planning. However, as your baby's health is your top priority, you make sure to schedule all necessary health appointments with the GP, hospital and elsewhere, and that you (and baby!) turn up for them on time. These include:

- GP baby assessments
- Postnatal and physiotherapy assessments
- Hearing and other tests
- Immunisations

Some of these visits are painless and straightforward (e.g. sitting next to your baby and smiling while the doctor sees if he reacts to a series of bleeps and noises).

Others can be traumatic – such as big needles in the upper thigh to immunise against diseases like diphtheria, tetanus, whooping cough and meningitis. Be aware that health visits take up considerably more time than just the scheduled appointment, as you aim to achieve the happiest possible outcome by structuring the day through a fine balancing act of naps, feeds and paracetamol. I'll never forget one particularly painful injection visit that defied all my efforts at pain management; baby and I spent the whole afternoon afterwards snuggled up together on the couch, crying inconsolably.

There are very important health issues you need to keep an eye on as your child grows up, for instance whether their eyesight and hearing seem to be OK. Chances are, your child will not have any issues with either but if he does, it may not be obvious.

After a routine eye test in my son's class at school, I received a phone call from the health service saying they were making a follow-up appointment for him with a specialist. When I enquired why, they provided no further details; I was simply advised there might be a twelve-month wait. I thought no more about it at the time. When the appointment finally came around, my son and I attended a clinic where an ophthalmologist informed us that one of his eyes had a focusing deficiency. Because his other eye was perfect, the ophthalmologist explained, my son compensated for the weak eye by relying on the stronger eye (and had probably been doing so since birth). He added that this would normally be picked up in early childhood, before the age of four. When this inability to focus is detected in younger children, it can easily be corrected with the help of glasses to support the weak eye, encouraging the brain to use it. The infant brain is very underdeveloped at birth, a state described as plastic. But during childhood, it develops neural pathways to transfer visual information from the optic nerve of the eye to the brain – enabling the eye to see. At a certain age, however, the brain stops trying to build or maintain any neural network for the weak eye, as it appears to be inefficient. Instead, it relies almost entirely on the stronger eye. Once this occurs, the weak eye never learns to see properly.

I asked the ophthalmologist what age this 'switch off' process happens and was horrified by the answer. In his experience, he said, the age limit for restoring vision in a weak eye was around eight years old. My son was already eight and a half! Perhaps to make me feel better, the ophthalmologist added there was some chance it might still work if the child was slightly older than eight.

He sent us off with a prescription for glasses with plain glass on one side (for the good eye) and a prescription lens for the weak eye to encourage it to focus properly. He advised that my son should wear the glasses all the time if possible and come back in three months. By then, he would know whether it was helping or whether it was too late to correct the problem.

Now, imagine this had happened to a rational adult, instead of an eight-year-old boy. The rational adult patient would probably diligently wear his glasses all day every day in the hope of being able to restore his eyesight.

But that's not how an eight-year-old boy sees it when you explain to him that one of his eyes is not working properly and that he will need to wear glasses for a while to see if we can fix it.

'What?! You must be joking! There is no way I am going to wear glasses. You can't make me! Everyone will laugh at me.'

I tried to get him to understand how much was at stake and reassured him that glasses are no big deal whatsoever; lots of people wear glasses.

'That's fine for you to say. You're not the one who has to wear the glasses! Absolutely no way! And nothing you can try to bribe me with will make me do it, either!' (Clearly he was already familiar with my tactics).

I tried to bribe him anyway, with every possible tool I could think of. He then disclosed that he already knew there was something wrong with that eye and explained that was why he didn't really use it for reading. (What?!) Instead, he told me, he squinted to make it easier to see with the other eye. When I asked him why he had never told me about this before, he just shrugged and said, 'I dunno. Never thought about it'.

So I went home with a prescription, a heavy heart and an eight-year-old adamant that he didn't care whether that eye ever worked.

I tried every approach I could to try to persuade him to give it a go. Eventually, we hit on a solution: if he agreed to wear glasses during the day, he would be allowed to use his iPad for half an hour every day after school.

Over the next three months, with coaxing and reassurance every day to make sure that he did wear the glasses at school, eventually he accepted the idea. Conscious that his brain had never practised hand–eye coordination with this eye, I also played badminton or catch with him in the back garden after school while wearing the glasses.

We carried on diligently every day in the hope it wouldn't be too late after all. The appointment finally came around. After testing both eyes, the optometrist announced with surprise that the weak eye was responding extremely well and told us to carry on with whatever we were doing and twelve months later, we were told that the neural pathways had progressed so well that the vision in the weak eye was now almost indistinguishable from the good eye. I almost cried with relief. The only caveat (which my son was not too happy with!) is that in order to ensure that all this development does not regress, he should wear the glasses in school for another three years!

Enormous time and effort had to be put into remedying this important issue but it was essential to prioritise. If my son had to wear glasses for life when it could have been prevented, I would have beaten myself up about it forever. And there are many such issues on the task list and mental load of a parent who is the default carer!

EMERGENCY HEALTH

Frequency: Variable
Flexibility around timing: Low

When your baby/child is sick, as a parent you feel almost as upset as they do and will do absolutely anything to try to make them well, or at least feel better. Thankfully, most incidents are not serious and will resolve themselves with the help of paracetamol, ibuprofen, the odd plaster and importantly, lots of cuddles.

Ensuring you are stocked up on essential medical supplies – both for children and adults – is a really good idea. This includes painkillers, plasters, sun cream, antiseptic cream, liquid worm medication and oral rehydration sachets.

Ailments like blocked noses, chest infections, high temperatures, earaches, sore throats, vomiting and diarrhoea are common, but you learn how to manage them. Things like chickenpox or colic can be more challenging. Watching your child wriggle in frustration with chickenpox is tough but you do your best to soothe the itching by applying various creams/powders. But the most important thing is simply being there to hold and reassure them, perhaps distracting them by reading favourite stories or watching cartoons together. Whatever you were meant to be doing – work, a tax return or sleeping – goes to the back of the queue, as it should.

When your child is sick, this may mean one parent can't go to work that day – or must come home early when the childminder, kindergarten or school calls saying they are unwell. It is important to discuss which of you will be responsible for looking after children when they are unwell – is it something you plan to share or will it mainly be one person's responsibility? This may depend on several factors, including whose job permits them to leave at short notice should the need arise.

If one parent is attending to a sick child, it will mean that other things they are meant to be doing are piling up. It is important that both parents understand this fully. Ideally, the other parent would swoop in and keep all the other plates spinning so the parent taking care of the sick child gets a chance to rest, eat and catch up.

HYGIENE

Bath/shower time

Frequency: Daily to weekly
Flexibility around timing: Medium

Giving your baby a bath at home is one of many lovely, exciting activities for new parents. It feels so special, you may even be loath to let anyone else do it. Like Tom Sawyer painting the fence, you jealously guard this opportunity to cradle your baby while gently washing her in water at a temperature you have diligently checked with a thermometer. You watch with delight her reaction to being immersed in water and experience what it feels like to float, splash, kick and listen to the sound of water. You carefully pick her up in a fluffy towel and revel in the lovely smell of newborn baby while you gently dry her. You might even attempt the soothing baby massage you learned, delighted when she seems to like it.

But all this takes time. When Baby No. 2 comes along, this idyllic, indulgent scene can become a battlefield as you juggle the demands of both children. The task becomes more functional and it can be quite a relief when both children are out of the bath and out of danger! Twenty to thirty minutes from beginning to end may be optimistic.

Hair – washing and drying; haircuts

Frequency: Washing, weekly; Haircuts, every few months
Flexibility around timing: Medium

You wouldn't think of washing/drying/cutting children's hair as a job but like everything else, someone needs to take responsibility for getting it done! Children need their hair washed about once a week and need it cut every few months.

With a baby or toddler, you might attempt cutting their hair yourself but before long you will find yourself in need of a professional. Since she was little, my daughter loved the ceremony associated with going to the hairdresser, sitting importantly in a big chair with a cloak around her shoulders. However, my son refused to let anyone near his hair, resulting in many abortive trips to the hairdresser. Despite every conceivable bribe, distraction and threat, invariably he victoriously led the way back out the door with hair intact.

It doesn't take a huge amount of time to get a child's hair cut – perhaps thirty minutes plus the time to get to the hairdresser and back – but you also need to find a day/time when it is possible to make it there with children in tow while juggling work commitments, school, after-school activities, traffic and getting home in time to eat. When you're working full-time, evening appointments may be too late to accommodate dinner and bedtime, so the only option is to go on a Saturday (if you can find a time that doesn't clash with activities or birthday parties!) One of you will need to need to find the time! Unless this task is delegated, the default carer will likely take on this responsibility while the other partner, having not opted in, continues with their chosen weekend schedule.

Teeth – brushing, dentist appointments

Frequency: Twice daily
Flexibility around timing: Low

Twice a day, every day, children need to brush their teeth, at least from the time their first little tooth appears. In fact, most dentists would advocate starting this routine even earlier, from whenever teething begins.

Toothbrushing is a routine you need to establish as soon as possible so that it becomes a natural activity children do every day at breakfast time and before going to bed. Obviously, babies and very small children can't do it themselves so you must do it for them, but as they get bigger, you will want to encourage them to take responsibility for doing it themselves and teach them how to do it properly – so you don't have to do it!

Children aged two or under need toothpaste with very low fluoride levels, from three onwards they need a medium level of fluoride and eventually they move on to using adult toothpaste. Toothbrushes also need to be replaced whenever they are worn or lost. Therefore, somebody needs to notice what toothpaste/toothbrushes your children need and stock up accordingly. Depending on the child's age you may either need to supervise or do the actual toothbrushing. This can sometimes be reasonably straightforward, but often involves a long game of 'Catch me if you can!' followed by 'How to prise a tightly-shut mischievous mouth open'.

Someone will need to book and attend dental appointments and the same considerations apply to these as for hair appointments. Advance notes to teachers may be needed if the appointment is during school hours. And there are often surprises, regardless of how good a job you think you are doing! On one occasion, we left the dentist with tooth charts, floss, plaque disclosing tablets and recommendations for child-friendly mouthwashes. It was the beginning of a relentless campaign to progress from a red traffic light (the worst score from the dentist to describe the health of your child's teeth and gums) to orange and eventually a hard-won green. However, when a child is adamant that every one of the mouthwashes you have bought to date is 'horrible' and won't open his mouth wide enough to enable you to brush (never mind floss!) his teeth properly, the twice daily toothbrushing struggle can be soul-destroying. What should in theory take only two or three minutes would regularly consume half an hour or more. Not a big deal when you are not under pressure but no fun on nights when you have at least an hour of work to complete afterwards.

Cutting nails

Frequency: Every few weeks
Flexibility around timing: Medium

I'm pretty sure children's fingernails and toenails grow at twice the rate of adult nails. Well, possibly not! But it honestly feels like it. Just a few days after clipping, somehow they appear to have already grown half a centimetre. We would be out to dinner at someone's house or at a restaurant when I'd suddenly spot that my daughter's fingernails were long enough to pass for a small grappling hook and my son had amassed half a centimetre of black gunk under his. Mortified, I'd scuttle off with two children in search of the nearest sink, trying to scrape off as much black gunk as possible without the benefit of a nailbrush and wondering whether some parents carry emergency nail clippers.

Keeping children's nails short feels as interminable a job as painting the Golden Gate Bridge. Furthermore, whereas cutting your own nails is fast, with children it is anything but. You need to factor in negotiations about why we need to cut them at all (generally they will disagree entirely and clench both hands firmly shut), where we are going to cut them (while the bathroom was perfectly acceptable last time, this time they insist we do it in the bedroom), then do your best to prepare the area with a sheet of paper so you don't end up having to sweep/vacuum the entire floor afterwards, then referee the eternal debate over whose nails will be cut first.

I have two children, which equates to 40 fingernails and toenails that need cutting, on average every second week from the time they were born up until maybe age twelve (I'm optimistic that they'll be doing it themselves after that). By my calculations, per child that means cutting ten fingernails and ten toenails 26 times a year for twelve years, which is 6,240 nails. Multiply this by the number of children you have and you will appreciate why cutting nails should really be included in those pie charts revealing a breakdown of how you spent your life.

OTHER CHILD MEDICAL/HYGIENE DELIGHTS

Headlice

Frequency: Variable
Flexibility around timing: Low

Unless you are a primary school teacher or parent, as an adult you could be forgiven for thinking that headlice had been eradicated years ago. But oh no, those little guys are very much alive and kicking and have quite a stage presence. And boy do they eat your time! If ever there was an unexpected and thankless task requiring immediate intervention, this is it.

It feels like headlice have been around forever. Apparently, the incidence of headlice in Britain has remained reasonably stable over the last 30 years, with about 8% of schoolchildren affected at any one time. Studies have found that as many people without lice itch as those with lice, which means you can't even rely on children scratching their heads as an indicator of anything being amiss (3).

Although nit treatments are no longer the fire hazard they were 30 years ago and are available in an array of easy-to-use shampoos and sprays claiming '100% efficacy', unfortunately the wily headlice have upped their game since then and are now almost invincible. A study published in the *British Medical Journal* (4) showed that when using any of the main headlice treatments you can buy at a pharmacy, even if you follow the instructions carefully, you have only a 13% chance of having a lice-free child two to four days later! Or put another way, an 87% failure rate.

To have any hope of eliminating headlice, parents embark instead on a gruelling regime of diligent nit combing called 'bug busting', which involves painstakingly combing your child's hair, slicked with conditioner, using a nit comb. You must remove and flush down the sink every delightful nit you find, as well as try to pull off all the eggs – tiny black dots that stubbornly cling to individual hairs. If you are the parent of a girl with thick, long hair, this takes forever! And although you may be the one with a pain in your back/neck/arm as you strain to examine every inch of her head while positioned under an ultra-strong lamp, your daughter (whose only job is to sit still), will feel *she* has drawn the short straw! You may feel mildly victorious at the end of this delightful evening but before cracking open the bubbly, be warned: this will have to be repeated every few days for a fortnight. You will also need to check (and treat if necessary) everyone in the house to avoid a nit siege continuing for weeks.

Remember the ASMART criteria? Well, eliminating headlice is one task where what needs to be done is highly **S**pecific. Equally, success can be easily **M**easured – are your children nit-free or not? Being nit-free may also seem like a **R**ealistic goal. However, given how arduous the process is and how useless the chemical treatments are today, it's debatable whether success is actually **A**chievable. It's certainly not easy.

Threadworms

Frequency: Variable
Flexibility around timing: Low

If you are an adult living in the Western world without children, you might not have encountered threadworms of late, although you will almost certainly have experienced them at some point in your life.

Threadworms (also known as pinworms) are tiny white cylindrical worms, about 1mm in diameter and 1cm long, that infect the large intestine of humans, particularly children under the age of ten. In fact, it is estimated that the prevalence of threadworms in children this age is as high as 40%.

Sometimes threadworms don't cause any symptoms, in which case it is possible that neither you (nor your child) would be aware of an infection at all, unless you happened to spot them (either still or wriggling) in your child's stools. (What a pleasant image.) However, they can cause very uncomfortable itchiness in children in and around the anus and/or vulva. This occurs especially at night, when worms migrate to the anus to lay eggs and in the process leave behind a mucus that irritates the skin. The itchiness can be so severe that it significantly disturbs the child's sleep or can make it impossible for them to fall asleep at all.

The good news is that, unlike nits, threadworm infections can be successfully eradicated with medicine and some due diligence. The bad news is that there is quite a bit of work involved.

The treatment consists of taking a single spoonful of a liquid anti-worm medicine, repeated after a fortnight to kill any worms that may have hatched in the previous fourteen days. Everyone in the family needs to be treated at the same time, whether they have symptoms or not!

You also need to ensure that reinfection does not happen by doing your best to get rid of any worm eggs present throughout the fourteen-day period (this is where the work comes in):

a. *In clothes*: all pyjamas, nighties and underwear currently or recently worn by any member of the household must go in the wash.
b. *In beds*: sheets, duvet and pillow covers from everyone's beds must also go in the wash and fresh ones must be put on all beds. Same goes for teddy bears.
c. *On bottoms*: each of your children will need a shower or bath every day, ensuring their bottoms and genitals get a good wash with a flannel and hot soapy water.
d. *Under fingernails*: one of the most common ways threadworms are spread to others is through people scratching the (itchy) anus area, inadvertently picking up eggs under the fingernails and then transferring these eggs to worksurfaces, food or other people's hands. If ingested, they create a new worm infestation. The best way to limit reinfection is therefore to keep everyone's fingernails short and ensure hands are washed frequently, especially before meals.
e. *On contaminated surfaces*: those same fingers have no doubt been in contact with many surfaces that should be wiped down (kitchen and bathroom surfaces, door handles). Regular hoovering is also advised.

If you do all these things, within two weeks your home and everyone in it should be happily threadworm-free ... that is, until the next time you notice your five-year-old scratching their bottom.

SUMMARY OF CHILDREN'S HEALTH AND HYGIENE RESPONSIBILITIES

Job element	Daily (or more)	Weekly	Monthly (or less)
Bath/shower		X	
Washing/drying hair		X	
Haircuts			X
Brushing/flossing teeth	X		
Visits to the dentist			X
Emergency health issues			X
Cutting fingernails/toenails			X
Other medical delights	X	X	X

For whoever takes on these responsibilities, it is important to appreciate the time they take up because often, they can fall to one partner (usually Mommy, who is at a loss to understand where her time has gone) while the other partner appears strangely oblivious to the need to attend to them at all or the time taken by the other partner to do so!

BIRTH CONTROL

For obvious reasons, women have a strong vested interest in ensuring that birth control is one job that never falls through the cracks, NO MATTER WHAT. Yet it is a responsibility that some men fail to acknowledge, much less actively consider assuming responsibility for. When a woman is on the pill, receives contraceptive depot injections or has had an intrauterine device (IUD) inserted, this may be very convenient for her partner but how many men actively consider what this entails?

If their partner is on the pill, do men realise the time involved in getting a prescription from the GP every six months, going to the pharmacy to pick up the tablets and then remembering to take them religiously at the same time every day (ensuring not to forget to bring them whenever you are away from home for a night)? And while oral contraceptives and the GP visit are at least free of charge to women in the UK, this is not the case in all countries. Women who choose depot injections have to attend their doctor or a women's health clinic every twelve weeks to receive the injection. And while an IUD provides effective contraception for up to ten years, it involves a delightful visit to a women's health clinic or your GP where you lie on your back with your knees splayed while it is inserted. Sometimes IUDs can cause discomfort or become dislodged, requiring a return visit to reinsert it.

And like all medication, hormonal contraceptives are not without side effects. They commonly cause weight gain, bloating, acne, mood changes and changes in menstrual cycle. However, of much greater concern is the fact that oral contraceptives significantly increase the risk of a stroke caused by a blood clot in the brain, an event which can result in death or other serious consequences. A meta-analysis (i.e. a review of all the relevant published data) published in 2015 found that in women aged 15–50 years, taking oral contraceptives increased the risk of a stroke seven-fold, compared to women who are not taking oral contraceptives (5). While the absolute risk of having a stroke while taking oral contraceptives is relatively low – estimated at about three to five cases per million of the population each year – this still accounts for 0.5–1% of all strokes. And since strokes are relatively rare in younger people, this risk merits consideration. In women with additional risk factors, for instance women who smoke, the risk is even higher.

But there are many options when it comes to birth control, some of which make this an element of the Invisible Job that men are just as well-placed as women to take responsibility for. For instance, ensuring you always have sufficient stocks of condoms. And if you have reached a point in your life where you are both sure you don't want any more children, men opting for a vasectomy is a highly effective option that avoids the risk posed to women by contraceptive medication. While it involves minor surgery (which in many countries needs to be paid for privately) and a few days of local discomfort, with the help of some painkillers for a few days it's an effective means of deleting 'birth control' from the *Invisible Job* permanently.

5

Childcare

LONG-TERM CHILDCARE NEEDS

For most women, going back to work after maternity leave was always the plan. It might not have been a fully formed plan; bits of the picture were probably a little fuzzy around the edges, such as, 'How many months maternity leave should I take?' or, 'How exactly will we look after baby once I go back to work?' While these questions were certainly noted as Important Things to Figure Out, for most women they fell down the priority list as they navigated their way through being pregnant and the mental lead-up to D-day (birth). At work, there were probably project deadlines they were hoping to meet before finishing up, and handover lists to prepare for the maternity leave replacement. During their free time, they were busy going to antenatal classes, reading books about babies and buying or acquiring a vast list of items that would apparently be needed, such as a buggy, a baby car seat, a Moses basket and a breast pump (viewed with a mixture of amusement and suspicion). The issue of figuring out how life would function with a baby once both parents went back to work would just have to wait. Optimistically (and naïvely) one hoped that it would all just become clear along the way.

However, this big question doesn't really solve itself. While a woman is at home on maternity leave trying to cope with the demands of a small baby, lurking in the back of her mind, like a patient but insistent monster, is the little voice that says

'You've gotta come up with a plan pretty damn soon because you told work you were coming back on 1 October and it's already August!'

Regardless of which parent chooses (or is obliged) to stay home for the available period of paid parental leave, if both parents plan to return to work after that, someone needs to come up with a satisfactory childcare option in time to make this transition back to work feasible. And by 'in time', I mean way ahead of when they plan to return to work, as it can take a long time to investigate the available options and set this up. In fact, researching and managing childcare is a time-consuming element of the Invisible Job Description, easily overlooked by anyone who has never had to tackle it. So, what are the options?

Crèche

A crèche typically caters for children aged between three months and five years and provides care from 8 a.m. or 9 a.m. to 6 p.m., with some half-day options. A kindergarten (also called playschool or preschool) is similar but is usually understood to be a place of creative learning and play for children who are a year or two younger than school age. Hours may be more limited. When trying to decide if a crèche would be your preferred option for looking after your baby, you will need to consider all the aspects of the childcare they offer, e.g.

- Who exactly will be looking after your baby? (Who has possibly not been out of your sight for more than a few hours since she was born and whose personality, needs and wants you feel nobody else truly understands). The mere thought of leaving her with anyone can be traumatic at this stage and even more so if you are chronically sleep-deprived and therefore highly emotional.)
- Are the staff well trained and dedicated to caring for children?
- Will your baby have the same familiar face looking after her each day or could this change on a random basis?
- What is the ratio of crèche staff to babies/children?
- Are babies mixed in with older children or are they kept separate?
- Does the crèche prepare meals for children/babies or do you need to provide it? If they do provide food, is it healthy?

There are also logistical considerations:

- Would it make more sense to choose a crèche near home or near work? Which would make more sense for ease of drop-off/pick-up by you or your partner?
- How long would it take to get there from your home/work, bearing in mind the likely traffic in the mornings and evenings?
- What hours do they cover each day?
- Is there any space to park nearby for drop-off and pick-up?

- If you envisage arriving with a pushchair (possibly with another child in it), will that work or is the crèche located on the second floor of a building with no lift?

You will probably also want to know:

- How much outdoor time do the babies/children get each day?
- What kind of activities do they do? (e.g. music, dancing or messy play)
- How much will it cost per week, including any extra costs that may apply, e.g. charges for nappies, registration or other fees?
- And crucially, once you have found one that seems to meet all your requirements and you like the feel of, have they got any spaces available for the times you need, starting from the date you go back to work, or perhaps even earlier? Or if this crèche is full, how long is the waiting list?

Kindergarten/Playschool/Preschool

Some people use the words crèche and kindergarten interchangeably but traditionally, they are not the same thing. While a crèche will look after both young children and babies, kindergarten is usually for children who are a year or two younger than school age. At kindergarten, children engage in lots of messy artwork, stories and games and it is a great place for learning to socialise with other children as well as developing skills like manual dexterity, listening, singing, sitting still and the general notion of following a routine.

Some kindergartens are better than others, some are more expensive than others, some are in very convenient locations, some may be attached to a specific primary school, meaning children in the kindergarten are guaranteed a place in the primary school (often parents will put their kids into such a kindergarten just for this reason). It should therefore come as no surprise that once you have discovered the 'Goldilocks' kindergarten (the one that is *just right*), it will probably already have a waiting list for the year your child will be ready to start there. Damn those über-organised other Moms!

Childminder

An alternative to a crèche is to leave your baby/child in the care of a person who looks after several children in their own home.

Leaving your child with a childminder is not quite the same as putting them in a crèche. While it varies from country to country, the legislation governing crèches tends to be more stringent compared to childminders. Although there are generally government guidelines for registered childminders, not all childminders might be registered, often having started out perhaps just looking after a neighbour's child informally. The ratios governing how many children a childminder can look after tend to be more relaxed than those mandated for crèches, as are the rules around staff having a formal qualification in childcare. A kindergarten will usually be set up in a building that has been either purpose-built or modified to look after children, while a childminder will usually be looking after them in her own home. Some parents will find the idea of their child spending the day in a 'home-from-home' environment more appealing, while others would feel more comfortable with the structure and oversight of a kindergarten. Much may come down to the rapport you have with the childminder or the caregiver at the kindergarten: does this person make you feel confident that your child will be looked after lovingly and stimulated to develop?

When it comes to finding out what your crèche/childminding options are, doing the research is not complicated but takes time. Options must be identified, visits scheduled (always tricky as crèches do not schedule appointments around the feeding and sleeping patterns of your baby) and important decisions need to be made. This task tends to land on the parent who is on parental leave to look after the baby – usually the mother! For someone (usually in a sleep-deprived state) who is already busy looking after a baby all day, this can be very challenging. In addition, it often sets a precedent, whereby the mother takes on the onerous responsibility for organising/managing childcare from that point onwards.

Nanny

For many mothers, the thought of leaving a young baby in a crèche all day, when he has rarely been separated from her for more than a few hours up to now, can be traumatic. When you go back to work, whether it is to keep up the one-to-one attention your baby has been used to, or to accommodate the needs of parents with irregular work schedules, getting a nanny can seem like the ideal solution. Having a 'live-in' nanny enables you to manage even on days when you need to be at an early-morning client meeting or be on call overnight at the hospital. A 'live-out' nanny is slightly less flexible but has the advantage that you do not have to share your house with someone, giving you both more privacy. A nanny provides the freedom to tailor-make each day to suit the circumstances – for instance getting out to the park to make the most of good weather or choosing to take it easy at home on days when baby is not well. A nanny can also make full use of whatever child-friendly facilities are in the area, such as taking your baby/toddler to the swimming pool or attending story time at the children's library. A nanny can also prepare healthy food that even the fussiest eater will like. But perhaps one of the nicest things about having a nanny is the continuity of care from the same person, something that is not guaranteed at a crèche. All sounds great, right? The main drawback, however, is that relative to other childcare options, having a nanny is expensive and therefore not always a feasible option, especially when you have only one child. If you have two or more, the cost per child relative to other childcare options becomes comparable to (or even cheaper than) putting them in a crèche. And for many working parents, having a good nanny during the period before children start school can be the Holy Grail.

Finding a good nanny requires time and effort. You could go through a nanny agency, who will help define your requirements as well as provide you with a stream of potential candidates who they will have pre-screened to some extent. Obviously, there will be fees attached. Alternatively, you can draft a summary advert yourself of what you are looking for and publish it online or just put up a few 'nanny wanted' signs on noticeboards in your local area. Finding a nanny recommended by someone you know is ideal; perhaps a friend or acquaintance who employed the nanny up to now but whose children are at an age where they no longer need that type of care. Before you speak to potential candidates, you'll need to draft a clear job description of what the nanny will be expected to do, along with any required or desired qualifications or experience. Whether you are recruiting someone yourself or using the services of a nanny agency, you'll still need to sift through the applications you receive, shortlist a few and arrange to interview them. Once you've found someone you feel would be good, you'll need an employment contract, which both you and the nanny sign and which clarifies their duties, hours, payment and rights. Someone also needs to take on the responsibility of managing their contract and payment, covering their absences and of recruiting a new nanny should they leave. Without a doubt, having a nanny considerably lightens the load when managing life and work with young children. But be warned: it also means that all your eggs are in one basket, so the stakes are higher should anything go wrong.

Au pair

At first glance, getting an au pair sounds like an exciting multicultural solution to childcare needs. An au pair is a young person, usually in their late teens or early twenties (but can in theory be any age) who lives in your home as a member of the family. They help you look after children and babysit, as well as possibly doing some light housework, while in return you offer them a room in your home and treat them a bit like a niece/nephew. That means providing all their food/drink, broadband, along with perhaps a mobile phone, paid travel and access to local amenities like a gym. You also invite them to participate in all family activities, whether it's going to the zoo, going out for a meal or possibly even coming on holidays with you. You also pay them a modest weekly allowance, but au pairs don't do it for the money. Instead it's usually about the chance to experience life in another country in a safe environment while learning a foreign language.

Having an au pair can be brilliant but it depends completely on the individual. We've had about a dozen au pairs over the years and each experience has been different. The first was a bit of a disaster, but we didn't know any better at the time.

She would sit in front of the TV in the middle of the kitchen with France 24 blaring loudly while my husband and I tried to dress and feed our two- and almost four-year-old before rushing out to work. France 24 would still be blaring when we got home.

I remember finding a raw chicken breast she had left draped over a half-eaten yoghurt in the fridge. That's when I realised that what I had previously assumed were universally understood rules of basic food hygiene may not yet feature in the life of a nineteen-year-old who has never lived away from home. In fact, accepting such inexperience is a big part of what you need to consider before inviting someone to live with you as an au pair. You cannot expect too much from someone who has not yet lived independently, and you must also be cognisant that they may not be able to cope with this first flight from the nest, let alone be capable of helping your family.

When a nineteen-year-old says they say they 'know how to cook', this may just mean they know how to boil rice. So if you are hoping they will be able to prepare food for your children as part of their responsibilities, you'll probably need to regularly set aside time to teach them how to.

Over time, I got better at understanding how to help our au pairs integrate into this new role and adjust to their surroundings. So each time we got a new au pair, I would set aside two full days for 'au pair boot camp':

- Getting familiar with the locality: this involved providing a map of the local area (with a big X on our house) and taking them around, showing what there was to do – e.g. signing them up at the library so they could take out free books and DVDs, joining the gym and checking out the timetable for classes. I would also get them a travel card and explain how to get around on nearby tubes, buses or trams.
- Communications: sorting out a SIM card for their phone and setting them up on the home wi-fi.
- Doing trial runs of the route from home to kindergarten/school – in London this was a walk or short bus trip, in Dublin it meant cycling or scooting. I'd teach them how to lock the bikes, then show them the children's classrooms, along with the places the children were most likely to forget their coats every day.
- In the house: going through things like how to open the fiddly front door, set/unset the alarm, work the microwave and washing machine and figure out which cupboards contained what. I would find out what they did/didn't like to eat, explain where to leave any clothes that needed ironing, where we store coats and shoes and how to turn the heating on for an extra blast anytime they felt cold.
- I would then go through their responsibilities with them in detail – all of which had been clearly communicated beforehand.

- Most of our au pairs also wanted to do English classes in the mornings, so I would help them research the available options and enrol in whatever class suited them best.

I also learned that it was really important to schedule time in the diary each week to sit down with our au pair and just ask how it was all going; find out if there was anything they were struggling with or wanted information on, or anything they were keen to do/see during their stay. We'd also discuss how their au pair responsibilities were going and any difficulties they were having. When we didn't have anything specific to discuss, we'd often use the time to do some 1:1 English conversation practice or go through any difficulties with their English classes. This is akin to a management role that would most definitely feature in any office job description but which is not acknowledged in the Invisible Job.

Having a successful au pair experience requires investing quite a lot of time, not only while they are with you, but also in finding the right person in the first instance. Finding someone suitable – who, in turn, thinks your family might be suitable for them – involves a lot of homework. You need to put together a concise summary of what you are looking for (i.e. woman/man/either), specifying whether there is any minimum/maximum age, minimum language capability, if there is a minimum/maximum period you need the au pair to stay, whether they need any specific skills – e.g. being able to ride a bike or read music. In turn, you need to paint a clear and honest picture of your family and the role the au pair will play in it. You post this summary on an au pair website and then spend days wading through the hundreds of replies you receive, saying no thanks to those you don't think are remotely suitable (picture Robin Williams as the applicant on the phone in *Mrs Doubtfire* saying, 'I am job!') and finding out more about the ones you feel have potential. Once you've narrowed it down to a handful, you arrange to video chat so you can both decide whether six to twelve months living together might work out. It's useful to involve the children too and let them come up with their own questions to ask potential au pairs. Over time, you learn what kind of things tend to bode well – for us, people who played team sports got a big thumbs up, as did people who had already travelled a bit. Although there may be many spreadsheets along the way, in the end, trusting your gut instinct about the right person works best.

Grandparents

When trying to come up with a magic solution to how you and your partner will manage life with children and jobs, it can be very tempting for one of you to innocently suggest, 'Do you think your mother might be interested in minding them?'

However, as several grandmothers I know have told me, they had no trouble articulating clearly that they had already done their time raising their own children and were not in the market for another ten years of it, thank you very much!

If you are lucky enough to have a grandparent in your life who is able – and keen – to play a helpful role in looking after your children on an ad hoc basis, that's marvellous for all involved. I know many families who benefit enormously from regular support from grandparents – perhaps where children are picked up after school to spend a few hours doing homework in Grandma's house until the parents get home from work, or where Granddad drives someone to piano lessons once a week. It's important not to take such valuable help for granted!

Short-term and impromptu childcare

When people who don't have children are going somewhere, they just grab their coat, phone and wallet and walk out the door, right? Well, once you have children, there are a few additional Lego blocks you need to add to this simple sequence. Whether there's a school meeting you have to attend or a tennis match you'd like to play or you just want to meet a friend for a walk in the evening, you cannot budge without first appointing someone in loco parentis.

For a hilarious narrative on the difference between leaving the house before and after you have children of your own, Michael McIntyre's video 'People without children have NO IDEA what it's like' (available on YouTube) is mandatory viewing.

Babysitters

You need to first identify a capable someone in your area who would be willing to babysit your children (in fact, ideally a whole network of *someones*). Then you need to arrange in advance for that *someone* to look after your child(ren) for a fixed time on a given date whenever you need to escape for an hour (or three!)

To find a babysitter you can trust, a little bit of networking will be required; it's a good idea to ask neighbours or parents from school to see if they can recommend anyone in the area. Ideally you want someone who lives nearby, firstly so that getting to your house is not too onerous for them, and secondly so you can get them home safely on foot if you have had a few drinks and can't drive them home. You will want someone you feel is responsible enough to look after your child/children and has a good rapport with them. If you have a baby, you may want someone who has looked after babies before. Arranging for you and your children to meet the babysitter together before he/she looks after them for the first time is a really good idea, as you can see if they have a good rapport. If so, your children are likely to be much happier to let you walk out the door when he/she comes to babysit.

Once you have recruited one or two people, you need to get good at forward planning, as babysitters (naturally) have a life of their own and will not always be available at short notice. To be efficient (but mainly to avoid realising at 7.30 p.m.

as you stand in the hallway with your coat on that you've completely forgotten to book a babysitter!), it pays to go through your diary every few weeks and make a list of all the upcoming dates when you and your partner will need a babysitter to hold the fort. Send the list to your favourite babysitter, asking which of them they are available to cover. For whatever dates Babysitter No. 1 can't do, try Babysitter No. 2 and so on.

Although obviously essential (and not very onerous), this job of arranging babysitters is often invisible to one partner, who may just think it's incredibly fortunate that Emma, Eleana, Sarah-Jane or another familiar face happens to arrive at the door at exactly the time you need to go out. So invisible, in fact, that I realised recently that my husband doesn't have the telephone numbers of any our babysitters!

Whenever you get a new babysitter, someone also needs to dedicate a little time to familiarising them with whatever they need to know to look after your children and feel comfortable in your home. This might include any medical details like allergies, asthma inhalers, bedtime routines and favourite teddies, and obviously what to do in case of any queries or emergencies. They'll also need to know practical things like where to find keys to the house, and how to log into the wi-fi network and work the TV. You may also want to warn them about 'fast ones' you suspect your enterprising children might pull on unsuspecting new babysitters ('Mommy says I don't need to brush my teeth before going to bed and always lets me have her iPad when she's not here.')

You also need to look after your babysitter if you want them to be available next time! Be sure to have snacks and drinks available and be mindful of times when they might be coming straight from work or college and therefore probably would be delighted by dinner. And obviously ensure you don't forget to have cash on hand to pay them when you come home.

Holiday camps

While children look forward to school holidays, working parents often dread them because there is a fundamental mismatch between the total number of weeks schools are closed each year and the number of weeks of annual leave that working parents have. Primary school children in the UK, Ireland, Norway, Sweden, Finland Poland, Austria and Switzerland typically get about fourteen to fifteen weeks of holidays from school each year. In France, Spain, Italy, Turkey and Russia it's even more (sixteen to eighteen weeks) (6). In the USA they are typically thirteen to fifteen weeks long and Australia's school holidays are among the shortest (about ten weeks). While these breaks are great for children, no country in the world offers Mommy or Daddy paid annual leave of equal duration! While EU employees are entitled to a minimum of four weeks of paid annual leave, in the US, paid leave is at the discretion of the employer, with a quarter of private US firms providing no paid leave whatsoever to employees. Many Americans consider themselves lucky to receive two weeks of holiday per year. This deficit means that working parents need full-time care for school-age children for about ten weeks of the year. Hence the mad scramble as parents search for camps to occupy their children during midterm breaks and school holidays.

Identifying suitable camps with activities you think will suit your child (or at least ones they will not refuse point-blank to attend), in a location you can manage to transport them to and from each day is a mission you would happily outsource to an MSF logistics officer. To say spreadsheets are required is an understatement. Really popular camps are booked months in advance by parents keen to fill their bingo sheet of holiday child cover and the whole process can involve hours of painful research. While there were occasional exceptions among the couples I spoke to, the strategic planning for this job almost always falls to mothers.

Managing holiday camps for your children involves several components and ideally whoever is doing this job would take responsibility for all of them, so that nothing falls through the cracks:

1. Identifying and booking suitable camps, including filling in enrolment forms and managing payment.
2. Being the contact point for all communication with the camp organisers from the time of booking to the completion of camp, including information on location, what to bring, and what to do in the event of any emergencies.
3. Arranging/providing transport to and from the camp each day – whether you do this yourself, lift-share with other parents or arrange for someone to do it for you. Co-ordinating plans with other parents to pool lifts is highly advisable, as it makes things much more efficient but obviously requires time to liaise and arrange.
4. Daily management during camp. Every day, someone also needs to ensure your child leaves the house with everything they need – water, snack, sunscreen, appropriate clothing, whatever equipment they need to bring – and attend to whatever delights await you in the backpack thrown on the floor on their return (muddy socks, smelly wetsuit, half-eaten lunch, etc.) Note that most camps tend to start later and finish earlier than an adult's working day, meaning extra hours of child supervision are usually needed in the morning and in the evening.

One friend of mine is a very organised Dad who researches and books summer camps for his two children by Easter each year and then helpfully shares his plans with all the other parents in the class – the idea being that if they book the same camps, the children will have some friends as company and the parents can share lifts.

6

Children's Clothes and Shoes

Someone needs to take responsibility for ensuring your children have all the basic clothes they need. This is an essential but surprisingly invisible job that your partner may believe is managed overnight by a benevolent pair of elves. There are moments when this job is very visible (and even very exciting!), for instance going shopping for baby clothes before your first child is born. The rest of the time, it is just another part of the mental load, like a satellite orbiting your brain, transmitting warning messages like, 'Tom's pyjamas are too small!'

BABY CLOTHES

Adorably cute and impossibly small babygrows made of the most huggable and cosy fabrics will fill you with excitement and anticipation of the little bundle about to become part of your lives. Everyone around you will be almost as enthusiastic as you about this baby clothes buying phase, meaning you will probably receive many gifts of gorgeous tiny dresses and dungarees from friends and family. You can't wait to see how these will look on your little boy or girl, images playing in your head of mornings spent mulling over which beautiful outfit you will put on your darling today.

The reality turns out to be a little different! Although your new baby may be the proud recipient of a wardrobe of frilly dresses, you quickly realise how completely impractical it is for small babies to live in anything other than a babygrow (sleep suit). They are cosy and comfortable to wear day or night and easy to change, which is convenient because they get soaked several times a day by collateral damage from milk, food and nappy spills.

The real multicoloured challenge starts when baby moves on to solid food. I have photos of my daughter sitting in a springy little rocker chair as I tried to feed her puréed broccoli. Everywhere is green – her mouth, her face, the bib round her neck, the babygrow, the rocker, the floor. And the damage zone gets even bigger when babies move on to feeding themselves – after most feeds you end up throwing the babygrow straight into the wash basket and grabbing another one.

The other nemesis of the pristine babygrow is the nappy, or rather what the nappy is valiantly trying to contain. Although you rigorously try to ensure that nappies are bombproof (by putting them on with the same degree of care you would apply when sealing emergency cyanide capsules), unfortunately this strategy will fail from time to time. (Well let's face it, even Durex don't promise 100% safety.)

I vividly remember my unfortunate friend holding my four-month-old baby on her knee for two minutes in a café where we'd met for a catch-up. Suddenly a very loud and long noise erupted from my baby's bottom. When I plucked up the courage to assess the damage, I found to my horror that this Krakatoan explosion had resulted in such a catastrophic nappy breach that the mustard-coloured liquid had not only extended halfway up the back of the babygrow, but my friend's lovely summer dress had also suffered a direct hit. Luckily, I had already learned the necessity of never leaving the house without a spare babygrow – I knew that in the event of an emergency, being able to locate one of those under my seat would probably be more useful than a yellow lifejacket with a whistle and a light.

This is why, even though your two-month-old's wardrobe may well be filled with beautiful dresses or gingham dungarees, your daily go-to will be the drawer full of babygrows and bodysuits. It is therefore imperative that when you open this drawer at 3 a.m., having just removed the umpteenth wet nappy of the day/night, you can locate a clean babygrow in the dark with one hand.

Eventually of course, you will get to put real clothes on your beautiful baby and yes, they are adorable. And best of luck with actually getting the baby dressed! Managing baby clothes is like a game where you are running on a treadmill, while scooping up clothes from the floor, the tumble dryer, the bottom of the buggy and anywhere else you spy them.

You also soon realise you need to proactively go through your baby's wardrobe every three months to make sure that all the clothes in it fit. Most children's clothes have the age written on the label (i.e. newborn, 0–3 months, 3–6 months, 6–9 months, and so on). If your baby is six months old, for instance, you might check all the clothes labels and remove anything with newborn and 0–3 months on the label. If you are planning to have another baby, it is a good idea to store the clothes Baby No. 1 has grown out of by age, because believe it or not, you are going to be even more busy next time round and you will be so grateful that you can find what you are looking for!

Sorting baby clothes by size is a bit more complicated than it sounds because different clothes manufacturers seem to have completely different ideas about what size a six-month-old baby is! The French company Petit Bateau make beautiful baby clothes. However, their sizing tends to be very small. Therefore, if the label says six months, you should read this as French for 'As soon as your baby reaches six months this will be too small!' Conversely, the Swedish company Polarn O. Pyret is exactly the opposite: if their label says six months this is Swedish for 'This will be way too big for any Irish/English six-month-old but will fit perfectly when they are nine months old!' But not to worry, soon you will be capable of accurately estimating the owner's age in a police line-up of baby clothes.

Having removed all the clothes that are too small, you then need to bring into circulation clothes that were too big three months ago (which you were therefore storing elsewhere). This will make it much easier to locate clothes for your child every day that fit.

While by no means an arduous job, somebody just needs to find time to do it every three months until your child is about two years old and after that, every six months.

CHILDREN'S CLOTHES

Buying

Although the rate at which children grow is more forgiving than babies, managing children's clothes also requires time and effort. Even if you buy online to be time-efficient, you will need to brave the cupboards from time to time to find out what you need to buy.

Sorting

Although you do your best each week to keep children's clothes in some semblance of order, because you are working against the scientific forces of child-powered entropy, this order is always transient. Sometimes, you may as well just throw everything off the shelves onto the floor and start from scratch, sorting clothes into piles of trousers, t-shirts, long-sleeved tops etc., while keeping an eye out for anything that looks like it probably no longer fits. After giving the shelves/drawers a quick dusting (it's now or never), you pop these neat piles back where they belong and admire the brief semblance of order in front of you. You may realise that your three-year-old owns seventeen t-shirts but only one long-sleeved top. And possibly no trousers whatsoever.

Mending

Whether you are an experienced seamstress or not, holes appear in children's clothes and create the dilemma: to sew or to throw. Within a few weeks of buying new school jumpers and tracksuit bottoms, huge holes can appear in the knees and the elbows of these otherwise pristine items. Although I have zero talent for sewing, throwing them out just seems so wasteful. The pile of Things that Need to Be Mended therefore grows until I eventually force myself to attack it.

SHOES

While you can get away with buying most children's clothes online, when it comes to shoes, you have no option but to bring your child to the shop, as it's essential they fit properly. This means shoe shopping at least twice a year. As children are in school Monday to Friday, this requires carving out some precious time on a Saturday amid the usual activities and birthday parties.

SCHOOL UNIFORMS

Each August, before the start of the new term, someone needs to go through all the school clothes and see what no longer fits or can't be located at all. (It is remarkable just how many items of school clothing your child will lose each year; school jerseys in particular seem to disappear without trace and you may spend many hours trawling through lost property at the school for missing coats, gloves, jumpers and sports gear.)

You generally need to bring your child with you to the uniform shop to buy whatever items are needed because uniform sizes can be a law unto themselves. But time your visit carefully. If you go too early the uniform may be tight by the time term starts but if you go too late you will likely join an interminable queue on a hot August afternoon only to find whatever size you need is out of stock, meaning you have to either send your child to school in a jumper that's too small or with no jumper at all (and come back to the shop again in two weeks' time).

Having procured all the various bits and pieces of school uniform, there is one final task: label them all. I know you are thinking, 'You must be kidding me!' but unfortunately it must be done, otherwise you stand little hope of making it one month in school without losing half the things you've just bought. You can simply write your child's name in permanent pen/marker on the label of each item but it might be easier to do a one-off order of printed nametags that you can either sew or iron on. The tag might simply be your child's surname (this will increase the odds of a missing jersey finding its way back to you by a factor of 1000) or better still, you can order tags featuring your surname plus your mobile number. Thanks to such labels I have received phone calls from many kind souls leading to the recovery of many items that would have been forever lost – from a man who found my child's coat on the floor in a toy shop in central London to mothers at school coming across stray jerseys at the bottom of schoolbags).

CHRISTMAS JUMPERS AND DRESSING UP

Dressing up is great fun for children. However, it can require a lot of work on the part of parents. For weeks leading up to Hallowe'en my children are preoccupied by what they will wear. I do my best to encourage them to be creative and resourceful (as well as sustainable) by creating an outfit from clothes/props we already have. Sometimes this works – but sometimes they insist that they absolutely need to buy something: 'Mommy there's no way we can make horns like Maleficent!'

Either way, your help may be required, whether to fashion something at home or locate a particular item/outfit from a shop. The key here is to be prepared in order to avoid disappointment.

However, you may be totally unprepared for the email from school announcing light-heartedly, 'Tomorrow all the children will be allowed to wear their Christmas jumpers!' Or, 'Next week we will be celebrating World Language Day with an Indian theme and would like your children to come to school wearing an outfit from the Indian sub-continent'. Such events are huge fun but without notice can be a source of considerable stress, especially for the working mum!

SPORTS GEAR

My husband is great at bringing our son to hurling practice and matches on Saturdays. While both are very good at articulating loudly at 8.30 a.m. if they can't find his club jersey or clean socks (usually because they are still in the kit bag after training on Wednesday), the invisible job of ensuring our son even owns a club jersey or socks the right size tends to fall to someone else. This entails keeping an eye out for the club email announcing it is placing its annual order for kit. You then have a few days to find out what kit your child currently has, whether it still fits and if there is anything they are missing. Unfortunately, as far as my son is concerned, there just never seems to be a good moment for this. While not having socks or a jersey was more important to him than climate change last Saturday morning, I now waste an hour trying to get him off Xbox for five minutes to confirm what gear he needs and stay still for sixty seconds so I can measure his height and waist.

7

Children's Toys, Games, Books and Art Supplies

Choosing children's toys, books and art supplies can be overwhelming. Someone needs to research what to buy and the choice and variety of educational value is immense. And someone needs to organise them at home so you can find them. I know, I know: the mere notion of a system for organising toys/games sounds like it would suck all the fun and spontaneity out of playing. But hear me out on why organising toys does makes sense.

Life is a lot easier and happier if children can locate their toys easily and if the toys are complete when found. Younger children in particular don't need – and often can't cope with – having to choose from too many options. For parents in a house covered in random toys, it can feel like a never-ending, losing battle trying to keep things even vaguely tidy, and the chaos will eventually wear you down. Even the best feng shui experts would be beaten into submission by the combined force of half a ton of Lego, the jumbled together pieces from fifteen jigsaws, several remote-control cars that don't work and a box containing pieces from two different Monopoly sets, where it appears that the street ownership cards, along with the top hats and irons, have undergone a poorly-negotiated merger.

Tempting as it frequently is to pile all the toys in the house into a box the size of a builder's skip just so that you can see the floor again, this would be a very short-term win. The next morning the contents of that box will be scattered all over the house again by your industrious children, eager to play.

Therefore, the best way to maintain a little sanity is to set up some kind of system to organise toys and games. Shelves, drawers and storage boxes are all great ways of doing this. Label them with words (e.g. 'cars', 'guns', 'Lego', 'dolls', 'jewellery', 'dinosaurs') or better still, with pictures of these things, so even small children know what they mean. Tidying up toys will still be time-consuming but having somewhere to put them makes it much less of a headache. It also means you can encourage your children to tidy away their own toys when they are finished playing. (While I would recommend low expectations regarding their participation in tidying up, I guarantee they will appreciate being able to find what they want to play with.)

Making art is a lovely activity. And I love nothing more than getting a hand-drawn card or picture from one of my children. Drawing or colouring is also therapeutic – allowing children to wind down while their brains unpick the day's hustle and bustle. So after school it's great to be able to whip out some paper and something to draw with and just let them at it.

To do this, though, you need to be able to locate some paper and something to draw with without an hour-long search of the house. We assigned a big drawer in the kitchen as a place to keep art paper and a series of coloured boxes – one each for crayons, colouring pencils, markers, sharpeners and pens and one for Blu-Tack, glue and glitter. It is great but, like everything else, it descends into chaos unless somebody puts things back where they belong.

Although children generally have little interest in establishing or maintaining order themselves, paradoxically, they really like things to be ordered. For instance, if they find a box containing a jumbled mix of markers (some working, some dried out and dead because the tops are missing), crayons (some perfect, some broken in half, some with the paper falling off), and Twistables (some working, some empty), they don't want to use them.

Children prefer to have a nice selection of pencils in front of them when trying to draw a rainbow, rather than getting frustrated searching for an orange pencil or marker that still works. Therefore, although it's tedious to do (and I realise it will appear neurotic to anyone who has never had to manage it), it is worth putting them all back where they belong. Which is why someone needs this on their job description!

CHILDREN'S ARTWORK ... AND WHAT TO DO WITH IT!

From the time they start kindergarten – if not before – children start to create things. Their first experience of art might involve dipping their hands in paint and making handprints on a page. Next, they might learn how to hold a crayon in their fist and scribble or make splodges on a page with a paintbrush. They experience the fun of sticking colourful things like feathers, glitter and chopped-up pieces of paper onto a page with glue and the excitement of cutting things with a scissors. They progress to holding a pencil – first in their fist and, eventually with a writing grip. And there's no end to the imaginative creations they will produce after that.

At each step along the way, you will be the recipient of a piece of art created by your proud child, for which you will shower them with praise and thanks before looking for a suitable place to display this masterpiece. Initially this is simple – the splodge of green paint, which your three-year-old daughter proudly tells you is a 'bootiful butterfly' – is immediately given pride of place on the fridge door and admired for weeks. As the rate of artwork production ramps up, although you remain equally enthusiastic about encouraging them, it gets harder and harder to find suitable places to display the growing collection. Not all are immediately presented to you when children come home, either; you will often come across more 'mature' art (crumpled up paper and stray glitter) at the bottom of the schoolbag while searching for your child's empty lunchbox.

Many of these creations are simply adorable – Valentine cards featuring a furry red love heart or a paper angel for the Christmas tree made from a toilet roll insert with a photo of your darling stuck to a pipe-cleaner halo. As the months go by, a formidable amount of art starts to mount up in the kitchen, with no obvious answer to what to do with it. I would sometimes fast-forward twenty years in my mind, to a time when my children would be all grown up and we wouldn't have a single memory of all the lovely cards, drawings and paintings that they had industriously and lovingly created. This made me realise the importance of keeping some as mementos (whether for them or for me I wasn't sure). I imagined opening scrapbooks or folders in years to come and showing my grown-up children their first painting, first fluffy snowman or any of the other gorgeous things they had created when they were young. However, the gap between my aspirations and reality was enormous: the most I could manage was to periodically gather some of the drawings and paintings into a big plastic folder (possibly scribbling the child's name and the year on the back) with wild hopes of one day sorting through them. At least this freed up space on the fridge and the walls for the next batch of lovely creations and avoided 'art' being thrown in the bin, having outlived its welcome on the kitchen counter.

Each time we moved house I'd encounter these plastic folders full of children's art, reminding me that I had still not found the time to do anything permanent with them. About five years after moving into our own home, our lives had finally calmed down enough that I had the time to open and sort through a four-foot-high cardboard box containing about ten years' worth of children's art and crafts. I had almost no memory of any of the creations in the box. Although I had often questioned my sanity when I'd found myself sifting through the stack of art on the kitchen table at midnight (rather than dump it all in the bin), I am so happy that these little mementos of childhood survived.

8

Children's Activities

Identifying, arranging and supporting suitable activities for your children might sound like a fun and relatively easy part of the Invisible Job Description but trust me, it's a wolf in sheep's clothing. It is deliberately vague in terms of scope because it is 100% up to you as a parent to decide what activities (if any) to get your child involved in. There is no rule about how many – or how few – they should take part in. Nobody will ever decree that your child must learn to play an instrument or play a sport or swim. Although parents are under constant external and internal pressure when it comes to their children taking part in various activities, in the end they decide whether they should and therefore are responsible for all the work that goes with it. So be careful what you wish for! Before your baby is even a few months old, ideas for exciting-sounding activities for your child will present themselves, often via word of mouth from an acquaintance whose child is already doing it. It starts off slowly enough. Someone might benevolently enquire 'Is your daughter doing Aquababies? Oh, you must sign her up for it; Lucy loves it!' So the next time baby goes down for a nap you might look up Aquababies on the internet to find out what it's all about and conclude that you must immediately sign your baby up for this apparently essential component of child development.

'When is it on and how much does it cost? 10.00–10.30 a.m. Tuesday mornings ... in a place about a 10-minute drive away. Yes! We should be able to manage that – perfect!'

So I phone up to join, only to be told, 'Sorry Madam, I'm afraid we are already three weeks into this eight-week term and you really need to be there from the start.' (Damn). 'There will be a new term starting in November ...'

'Great! I'll take it.'

'But I'm afraid it's already completely full. Would you like to be put on the waiting list?'

Or perhaps, undeterred, you might go back to the internet to try to find an equivalent to an Aquababies class that is less than a 30-minute drive away, is not already full and is not smack in the middle of baby's nap or feeding time. You get as far as page two of the Google search before baby wakes from her nap and you have to abandon your search. Frustrated, you add 'Finding an Aquababies class' to the long list of unfinished jobs flying around your head.

Up until school age, children's activities are relatively straightforward. There are lots of things you could potentially get them involved in but it's not really until they start school that you will find yourself swept away by a largely self-imposed wave of activities that you eventually have to learn how to surf. Financial resources and time will inevitably dictate what and how much you sign up for. If you are fortunate enough to have the means, you will have a huge choice. Whether it's sport or music or drama, there is something for you! Your child may help you decide.

For instance, does he go around the house singing all day or jump up on the piano stool every time you go to Granny's house? Does she spend hours trying to cartwheel in the garden or does she love kicking a football? And when your daughter announces that she wants to learn violin, does she have a genuine interest in learning music or is it just because the girl who sits next to her in school (who is learning violin) tells her that she gets sweets every week after her lesson?

There will be no shortage of ideas and options to choose from. The challenge is figuring out what a healthy and manageable number of activities looks like for the child and for the family (these may be different and compromise may be needed). To someone who has never undertaken this process, it may look deceptively straightforward. In reality, it is an enormous logistical challenge to create a weekly timetable that facilitates getting your child to and from whatever activities you/they have chosen to pursue, with the correct kit in tow. Potential feasibility will also depend on whether you or anyone helping you with childminding has access to a car (or even sometimes two cars!) and the constraints of school, homework, your job, sleep, and the millions of other responsibilities of the Invisible Job that you need to accommodate every day. As you'd expect, the complexity of masterminding this schedule is multiplied when you have two, three or four children to accommodate. Eventually, you will come up with a schedule that works (for now at least), probably tweaked many times through trial and painful error, and for a while some balance is established and life for becomes a bit more manageable for everyone.

Especially if it appears to function relatively smoothly, the other partner often has little appreciation of what it has taken to put this schedule together. And while they may take pride in their child's progress in a given pursuit, they often lack insight around how this progress has come about. They may even subscribe to the genetic theory ('I think she gets it from me.') At a particularly positive parent–teacher meeting evening, when my friend and her husband were asked who the historian was, the father beamed and conceded that it was probably him. True, he had considerably more knowledge of history than his wife, but it had been his wife who had made a considerable effort to teach their son history over the previous two years through endless trips to the museum and home-made posters!

Of course, these are the luxuries of the fortunate. They explain why privileged parents struggle with what are jokingly referred to as 'first-world problems', i.e. worrying about minor issues that only people who are reasonably well off have to worry about. There's a wonderful sketch by Irish comedians Dirt Birds about organising children's extracurricular activities, in which a south Dublin mother is explaining to a neighbour how this year they've 'decided to narrow things down a bit' because their daughter 'was doing a bit too much'. She explains, 'Literally, literally, all Saoirse is doing this year is cello, chess and swimming.

On a Monday. On a Tuesday, she does violin and Irish dancing, on a Wednesday drama and yoga, on a Thursday gymnastics and ballet, on a Friday piano and cello'.

'Oh, so she has the weekend free then?' enquires the neighbour.

'Oh no, no, no!' cries the mother. 'Saturday, she's doing abseiling, rock climbing and orienteering ... through Mandarin!'

For more from Dirt Birds, search for 'Eleanor and Eimear discuss extra-curricular activities' on YouTube.

Of course many activities are free and can be done at home. This point was brought home to me recently by a teacher and community worker in a very disad-vantaged area of Dublin, who was explaining to an audience how proud she was that so much of the current talent for spoken word poetry by young people in Ireland today is coming from disadvantaged areas such as hers. She explained that the reason for this is that it costs nothing to rap or to write a poem; it doesn't require having parents with enough money to pay for a violin or a tennis racket. Such activities can go some way toward reducing both financial and logistical stress for parents. Rather than signing them up for a touch-typing class that you need to drive your child to after school (with siblings in tow), why not try following a free online programme at home while the siblings do their homework?

MUSIC

Although many parents might be keen on the idea of their child learning music early in life, it may not be apparent at the outset exactly what this will entail. Everyone will undoubtedly feel very proud to hear their seven-year-old son playing a little piece on the piano at the end-of-term concert, but how much thought has been given to what is involved in the child reaching this point? In terms of musical icebergs, the piano performance at the concert is only the visible tip, while underneath lies an invisible mountain of ice comprising:

1. Researching and finding a teacher: When my daughter was about five years old, I started making enquiries through my parent network about learning piano. I discovered that there was a teacher with a good reputation who had classes in the afternoons at her school. (Perfect!)
2. Scheduling a class: I managed to get the piano teacher's number but she informed me she was fully booked but would keep me posted. She also explained it is essential that a parent attends each class in order to be able to help the child with their practice each week. (Oh.) I told her that the only day we could make would be Friday (as I was in work every other day). I then waited patiently for about nine months until one day the piano teacher called to say a Friday space had come up. Hallelujah!
3. Buying/renting an instrument: Oh God, that meant now we urgently needed to get a piano! I recalled that my mother still had the piano we learned on as children in the living room and that nobody used it. When I called her she said she'd be delighted to get rid of it. Marvellous! That just left the small matter of finding and booking a man-with-a-van who could transport the piano from my mother's house to ours. I also needed to arrange a piano tuner. Marc, the lovely French piano tuner, then informed me diplomatically that it might not stay in tune because unfortunately it did not have long left in this world. Before committing to investing in something better, I decided to wait and see if my daughter would stick with the piano. When, a few years later, it turned out that both my children quite liked the piano, I decided to bite the bullet and buy a decent one.

   But what constitutes a reasonable amount to pay for a piano? All I wanted was a piano that sounded good, stayed more or less in tune and was not a complete eyesore. Sounds straightforward, but like most things, it comes down to juggling time, cost and quality.

   After spending some time speaking to the assistant in the piano shop, I realised that I was positively clueless about pianos and beat a hasty retreat from the shop, despite her kind offers to let me play a selection of their pianos, 'to help you make up your mind'.

   After many more hours of desk research and trips to more piano shops, I eventually buy a (reasonably good, reasonably priced, secondhand) piano. Mercifully, this time the French piano tuner approves.
4. Attending classes: Every Friday, I collect my daughter from school and we run straight to the piano lesson. I do my best to arrange a playdate for my three-year-old but when this fails I have to bring him into the lesson with us and try

to keep him quiet doing jigsaw puzzles while keeping an ear out for whatever practice his sister is meant to do for next week.

5. Practising: The teacher recommends ten minutes of practice every day for a child her age and I walk out thinking this sounds perfectly manageable. However, I soon learn that trying to get my child to do ten minutes of practice each day is harder than I had envisaged.

6. Doing exams: Exams need to be booked and paid for and musical accompaniment may need to be arranged and paid for if they are playing something other than the piano. I remember sitting nervously outside the exam room one year, probably twice as nervous as my son, hoping that all the hours we had put in together would be enough to get him through. Afterwards, before going back to school (him) and work (me) we went to a special little café nearby for a treat to celebrate the exam being over. My son chose a delicious chocolate gingerbread man to have with his hot chocolate. However, when I reached for an almond croissant to have with my coffee, he looked at me indignantly and said, 'Hey wait a minute Mommy!', what have you done to deserve a treat?!'

SPORT

The same applies when it comes to sporting activities. While Daddy remarked approvingly the first time the four of us were finally able to play a little game of tennis together, he didn't seem to have any idea about what had preceded getting to this stage ...

- Finding a club
- Arranging membership
- Purchasing equipment
- Arranging and attending coaching/training
- Admin
  This point is particularly important, as each activity comes with its own mountain of administration: setting up log-ins on new websites to pay for membership or lesson fees; putting all the details of training sessions/matches/club days into your phone calendar; scan-reading and signing permissions about your children being included in photographs on the club website; staying abreast of emails, texts and WhatsApp messages telling you that the car park will not be available this week or that Sunday's football match has been moved to a different location. This may sound trivial but it is mentioned because it eats your time! You and your partner need to know this and take it into account.

The thing about WhatsApp

WhatsApp groups eat a disproportionate amount of time. All day you will receive new WhatsApp messages and you won't know whether they are relevant or require a response unless you periodically scan through the thread. Sometimes it contains vital or urgent information (e.g. the match you were just about to drive 30 km to has been cancelled). More often, though, it will be the fifteenth person in a row who has sent a thumbs up emoji acknowledgement to the whole group.

If everyone adhered to the following basic etiquette, it would dramatically reduce the admin time for everyone else in the group. And given that parents may easily be members of 30+ WhatsApp groups between school, sports and other children's activities, it might even restore an entire day per week to your life!

- When someone sends out an invitation that says 'Regrets only please' this means you do not need to send a message to the whole group saying 'Thanks! Jim will definitely be there!'
- When Hannah's mother sends a message to the group saying 'Hannah left her hockey stick at training last week. If anyone found it, could they please send me a PM. Thanks', this does not mean that all the people who know nothing about the whereabouts of Hannah's hockey stick should send a response to the whole group saying 'Sorry, we don't have it but hope you find it soon!'
- If you need to send a message to a specific person in the group: just look up their number in the group info at the top and send a message directly to that person, not to the whole group.

Volunteering

Many clubs will also require a parent to get involved with the club in a volunteering capacity, either on a regular basis or on one-off occasions. This may include coaching, providing lifts to matches, assisting on a committee, fundraising, or organising treats for a kids' tournament or party. If parent participation is a feature of your child's chosen activity, it is only fair that you pull your weight. Considering yourself to be a 'very busy person' is not an acceptable get-out clause. There will be something that you have the necessary skill to put your hand up to do and we cannot expect other parents to carry the load on our behalf.

9

Family Scheduling and Project Management

More than any individual task, the heaviest burden in the Invisible job is the 'mental load' that comes with being the project manager for the family. Like gravity, this responsibility seems to fall to women – meaning they are constantly noticing and prioritising things that need to be done, then either doing the thing themselves or assigning it to someone else to do (in which case, having to check that it was actually done). For many women, it can feel as if everything to do with the home or children is their responsibility 24 hours a day; schedules and priorities swimming around in their heads, constantly being updated. Because of this, they are never mentally 'off duty'.

Being a partner who only opts in (when asked) to do something is relatively easy; what really drains your energy is the mental load of being the co-ordinator of all the tasks 24 hours a day! This is what makes you:

- Turn the bedside lamp back on just after you've closed your eyes to write yourself a reminder about bringing swimming gear to school in the morning.
- Respond to a text message from the school (while in a meeting) asking you to urgently confirm your daughter has permission to go on today's school trip.
- Remember to get money from an ATM on the way home from to pay the cleaner.

- Notice that your child needs new socks.
- Take something out of the freezer before going to work in the morning as you know you won't have time to cook before driving the children to sports practice tonight.

When your child starts school, co-ordinating children's activities and needs can become a full-time occupation, which would be best managed by a small committee. The project management skills required would easily include:

- Competency in logistics and transport planning: i.e. figuring out whether it would be possible to still make it to tennis lessons at 5.00 p.m. on Thursdays now that your daughter wants to play basketball between 3.30 and 4.30 p.m. and your son has to be dropped off to scouts at 6.30 p.m. but needs to eat dinner beforehand.
- Ability to persuade and negotiate: (This does not even include negotiating with children – challenging as that is!) I'm talking about liaising with other parents to arrange lift sharing, gentle negotiations with teachers and coaches and discussions with benevolent grandparents you may need to rope in occasionally to make the impossible possible.
- Excellent administration skills: Even when you have finally created a feasible weekly schedule (accommodating the demands of work, school, home, and children's activities), don't congratulate yourself too much because nothing is set in stone. Frequently, children's activities can change or be cancelled for a million reasons. This may mean emergency measures are needed to avoid having a stranded child. It could include liaising with another parent to ask if your child might be able to tag along with them to the park for an hour after school now that neither your child nor theirs has basketball this afternoon. You will of course need to return the favour at the earliest opportunity (nobody wants to be the kind of parent who thinks it's acceptable to solve their own logistical struggles by passing them on to someone else).

While women don't consciously decide to become the project manager for the family, they often end up taking on this responsibility to enable the household to function.

Often, her partner seems to have no idea that she is doing this 24-hour project management job on behalf of the family, much less understand how exhausting and inescapable it is. In fact, it is the most invisible of all the elements in the Invisible Job. It never ends and therefore does not even offer the temporary satisfaction that comes with completing any of the individual tasks. Neither is it a job women get external acknowledgement for doing. Instead it usually is a thankless role that keeps their minds spinning all day, like an endless game of Tetris, with pieces descending at varying speeds all day, every day.

It must be highlighted that much of this family scheduling task is largely self-in-flicted. What I mean by this is that apart from making sure your child eats, sleeps and attends school, nobody said that you had to complicate matters by determining that they must do anything else. Child welfare will not lock you up just because your child does no sports, music or drama, has never been to the dentist or has no hobbies. So, in a way, we have only ourselves to blame for some of the project management that comes with child and family activities. The sudden freedom you experience when unforeseen events like a two-foot snowfall result in school and all extracurricular activities being cancelled is palpable. When you suddenly find you are not chasing your tail to get somewhere by 6 p.m. and that you haven't mentioned homework or piano practice to your children in days, the merits of a simple life can appear very attractive. The Covid-19 lockdowns magnified this for many people. For the first time in years – or perhaps ever – we experienced what it is like when so much of what we accept as unavoidable routine is suddenly stopped. To our surprise, the world itself didn't stop and this may have caused many of us to reflect on whether we should restart our too-busy world in a different way.

10

School

FINDING SUITABLE SCHOOLS FOR YOUR CHILDREN

Primary school

Education is a top priority for most parents, wherever they live in the world and whatever their financial circumstances. Most parents would therefore like their child to attend a good school. The definition of 'good' will mean different things to different people. I guess the bottom line is that a 'good' school is one which is logistically possible for your child to get to and from each day, and where, above all, you feel they will be happy and have an opportunity to reach their potential.

In an ideal world, there would be a lovely school in your neighbourhood, walking distance from your house, with smart, committed teachers and small classes. Better still, a couple of months before your child is the right age to start school, you could simply phone the school, ask if it would be possible for parents and child to have look around, maybe meet the principal and, assuming all is good, sign up. Unfortunately, it's not usually that straightforward. Schools generally have a maximum capacity and therefore the number of pupils they can admit each year is limited. They operate a selection system to determine which of the children who have applied to the school will be assigned places. In some schools, this might simply be a case of whoever applies first. I know a man who drove straight from the maternity hospital to a primary school near his home to enrol his one-day-old son for school (… in five years' time). The boy didn't even have a name yet! But others select according to geography, religion, sex, feeder-school status and other criteria.

At some point, someone needs to sit down and do the research to find out what primary schools are in your area, what the criteria for getting into them are and enrol for one that would be acceptable to both parents. Annoyingly, by the time this job makes its way to the top of your to-do list, you are likely to discover that the point at which you should have done this was usually some time ago. But most new parents are so busy just trying to survive day to day that even thinking about enrolling for schools will not be at the top of the priority list for at least a few years.

Once you have figured out what your best option is, someone needs to submit an enrolment application to the school (or several schools if you are not guaranteed a place in the first one). This might be a two-minute online job or it may be something much more involved, requiring copies of birth or Baptismal certificates, proofs of address, details of parents' occupations and a whole host of other information.

Getting a place in the school of your choice can be difficult. When applying for a place for his son in his neighbourhood school in New York, one man I know was quizzed on what specific skills he and his wife (as parents) could offer children in the school. Seeing the blank look on his face, the admissions clerk mentioned that, for example, they have one parent who provides free yoga classes to the whole preschool year, another who is a children's author who does periodic readings with children and another who is fluent in Spanish and gives free language tuition to four-year-olds. He realised that demand for the school was so high that rather than parents selecting a school, the process was more akin to the school selecting parents.

Secondary school

The same rigmarole applies to finding a secondary school, only this time everything is magnified. For a period, it can feel as if the only topic of conversation among parents is 'What secondary school is your child going to go to?' Decisions about future careers could scarcely be debated as much!

Just like primary schools, some research is required in order to establish which schools your child is eligible to attend. There may be open days (where children and parents get to have a look around the school, hear about their ethos and perhaps talk to students currently in first year to hear about their experience to date) and in some cases entrance exams to sit. Some secondary schools give priority to children from specific primary schools (feeder schools); others operate based on a geographic radius; some hold entrance exams – often assigning scholarships to one or two of the brightest applicants in fee-paying schools – while some allocate several places to children of past pupils or current teachers. In the UK, children in their last year of primary school sit an academic exam called the Eleven Plus, the results of which determine whether they get a place in specific secondary schools known as grammar schools. Although most children are only about ten years old when they sit the exam, competition for some of these schools is so intense that some parents spend hours coaching their children in Maths and English in advance of the exam or even hire tutors for extra lessons. I know one mother who gave up her job to focus on preparing her son for this exam.

Compared to primary schools, the enrolment process for secondary school is likely to be more involved, possibly requiring photos, copies of academic results from primary school, and other details. And since deadlines for submitting applications will usually apply, one of you needs to be on top of this. In the end, finding a secondary school will probably all work out swimmingly but it can suck up considerable time along the way for the parent managing this job.

ALL THAT SCHOOL ENTAILS

Getting to and from school

Time: Anything from minutes to hours
Frequency: twice a day, Monday to Friday
Flexibility around timing: Zero

Depending on their age, and how far from their school you live, your children may need to be accompanied or even transported to and from school five days a week during term (i.e. about 30 weeks each year). This may entail anything from a delightful stroll together, happily chatting to your child about the universe, to a stress-inducing drive across town during peak morning traffic with a car full of disgruntled children trying to kill each other in the back seat. In between are many possible permutations of scooters, bicycles, buses, taxis and trains.

The time this job takes up each day is dictated accordingly, ranging from minutes to hours. However, regardless of how you get to and from school, this is a job with almost zero flexibility as regards timing: your children must get to school on time and you must pick them up on time, regardless of whatever else is going on in your day.

One additional responsibility that comes with this job element is ensuring that on leaving the house, your children have with them whatever they need for the day, which includes any items needed for extracurricular activities during or after school.

Helping with homework

Frequency: Once a day, Monday to Friday
Flexibility around timing: Medium

For most parents, helping children with their homework is among the fundamental things they envisaged doing some day in the future, back when having children at all was still just a romantic notion. Seeing their child learn and develop throughout their lives is a source of great happiness to parents and being there to support them if there is anything they are struggling with is hugely helpful to the child. Indeed, teachers may insist that someone at home monitors homework, signs the homework diary in the evenings and acknowledges any notes to the parent. Whichever parent oversees this lovely job just needs a chance to dedicate some time to it each day ... ideally when they are not simultaneously trying to make dinner, hang up washing and unload the dishwasher.

Managing school communications

Frequency: Variable
Flexibility around timing: Medium

The amount of administration and communication associated with having a child in school comes as quite a shock to many parents. The following, while lengthy, is a genuine reflection of that reality. So please do read on to appreciate the scale of the work involved in keeping on top of daily school communications!

In the beginning, it's like a few thrilling drops of rain falling on dry ground: perhaps a welcome email from the school principal on Monday morning saying how delighted she is to usher your little five-year-old (and 59 others) into the school for what they hope will be the start of a wonderful relationship over the next eight years.

A second drop falls an hour later in the form of an email reminding parents that, 'To settle children in during this first week of school, we will be ending each day at 12.30 p.m., rather than the usual 1.30 p.m.'

OK.

This is followed fifteen minutes later by another email clarifying, 'Apologies, actually, the 12.30 p.m. end time for this week only applies today, Tuesday, Wednesday and Thursday. On Friday please can you collect your child at 12.00 p.m.'

Put note in diary.

As I search for yesterday's empty lunchbox on Tuesday morning before leaving for work, I come across an A4 page in my child's schoolbag, alerting me that Speech & Drama classes on Tuesdays, between 2.30 and 3.30 p.m. will be beginning on 20 September. If I wish to enrol my child, I should complete the form and return it to the school administrator with a cheque payable to the teacher. My mother always tells me she regretted not signing her children up for speech and drama classes. Perhaps we should put our daughter's name down. I wonder would she like it? I leave the page on the kitchen counter and make a mental note to get back to it.

That evening when I get home there's another form in the schoolbag, announcing that ballet lessons will take place on Wednesdays between 1.30 and 2.30 p.m. for junior infants and senior infants, beginning next week. Anyone wishing to enrol their child should complete and return the form with a cheque. Places are limited. Parents are also requested to note that children taking part in ballet should wear a blue leotard and either a white ballet skirt (girls) or shorts (boys).

On Wednesday evening, the first sports-flavoured raindrop falls in the form of another A4 page in the schoolbag. Football will take place on Thursday afternoons between 2.30 and 3.30 p.m. in a park not far from the school, run by a local football coach. Anyone interested should complete this form and return it with a cheque to Mr. Z. (I put it on the kitchen counter for now with the other pages.) There's another about music classes, which apparently take place in the school every Monday evening: if I would like my child to learn violin, tin whistle or guitar, fill in the form and return with another cheque. Thursday, there's a rain shower of sports notes: hurling will take place on Wednesdays after school between 2.30 and 3.30 (sounds great! But hang on, wasn't that the same day as the ballet? Did I already sign up for that one or not?); table tennis will be on Thursdays between 3 p.m. and 4 p.m. and basketball on Mondays between 3.30 p.m. and 4.30 p.m. starting from 29 September – cool! (Actually no, on closer reading I realise basketball is only for older boys and girls, so ignore that page).

The following week sees strong email showers from the school about additional payments due for photocopying costs and art supplies, child insurance cover and 'voluntary' contributions that all parents are required to pay to support the running of the school. (I make a note in my diary to attend to these tonight as soon as I get the children into bed.) There's also an announcement about the school AGM which will take place in two weeks' time – all parents kindly requested to attend (Oh no! I've got a work meeting that evening; I wonder if it would be possible to get away early and catch the second half of the AGM – or should we book a babysitter so my husband can attend instead?)

Hopefully (I tell myself), this deluge of information will surely die down to just occasional showers of scattered rain now that Week One is out of the way. But the WhatsApp groups haven't even got going yet! Before long, I am regularly doused with messages from the junior infants class representative about bake sales, recovering lost property from school, volunteering for a reading rota in my child's class each morning, attending the parents' night out and buying tickets for the school play. The same WhatsApp group will also be used every day by parents in the class to:

- Ask if anyone knows whether the kids are really allowed wear fancy dress to school this morning or if that's just a story their child has made up.

- Announce that Peter will be having a birthday party at 2 p.m. on Saturday the 19th and all the boys are invited. Even though the note specifically states, 'Regrets only', someone will immediately reply (to everyone) that 'Tom would be delighted to attend, thank you!' This will then be followed by fourteen more replies (to everyone in the group) over the next few days: 'Liam too!'; 'And Seán!'; 'Toby would love to come'; 'Ian really looking forward to it!'; 'Yes from Eoin!' and so on.
- In the lead-up to Peter's birthday party there will be helpful messages from Peter's mum about logistics for the party – maybe a link to Google maps or which exit to take if you're coming from the motorway – followed by fifteen messages of 'Thanks Nora, that's really helpful!' After the party, Peter's mum will probably send another WhatsApp message saying, 'Peter had a lovely day, thanks to all the boys for coming!' Which will be followed by fifteen responses along the lines of 'Thanks Nora, great party, Tom/Seán/Toby had a wonderful time!'

The long-term outlook for school-related communications from your child's school, whether via email, WhatsApp, text, a dedicated school app or simple notes in the schoolbag will remain at Force 5–7 for most of the year, bringing to your attention matters of varying degrees of importance and urgency daily. It may include things like:

- Today's football will be cancelled due to the rain. (Let au pair know.)
- Parents are requested to refrain from parking right outside the school gates. (Noted.)
- Fourth class are reminded that swimming is on tomorrow. (Doesn't apply to us.)
- The school is delighted to announce that all children in the school will be doing yoga once a week from now on.
- Class rep nominations for next year are now being sought.
- To celebrate the school being 100 years old tomorrow, children are encouraged to dress up in clothes from a bygone era. (What?!)
- The board of management is looking for a new treasurer, can anyone with accounting skills who is available to help please get in touch with the school ASAP.
- The bus returning from the school trip today has broken down and is therefore expected back at 5 p.m. instead of 3 p.m.
- Your child has forgotten to bring her swimming gear to school. The bus is leaving at 11 a.m., please can you drop the bag in before then or she will have to stay behind. (Mad scramble ensues to find swimming bag and get down to the school immediately.)
- A reminder that MMR booster immunisations for children aged six and seven will be administered by a nurse from the Department of Health tomorrow;

please ensure your child is wearing a short-sleeved shirt. (Put reminder in my phone for the morning.)
- An outbreak of foot and mouth disease has been reported; if your child develops the following symptoms, kindly keep him/her at home and do not let him/her come to school until symptoms have resolved fully.
- All parents requested to urgently check tonight if their child has headlice and treat immediately if detected. (Not again!)

No doubt, some of these messages serve a purpose. Opening, digesting (and where needed, acting on) them promptly can be quite an undertaking though, especially when you're at work, but leaving them all until later that evening can sometimes lead to disasters, like the time I didn't read the one about the forgotten swimming bag and spent the whole evening listening to my child tell me how terrible it was having to spend two hours sitting in the classroom while everyone else went swimming.

It probably does not make sense for both parents to process all these messages. Instead, a divide and conquer approach may be efficient – for instance if one of you is the contact for all school communication, the other could be the contact for whatever activities your children are involved in outside of school or at the weekends, along with the respective supervision/lift duties entailed.

Volunteering for school activities

Schools often rely to varying degrees on help from parents to help keep the world spinning. For instance, they may look for parents to volunteer on fundraising committees (helping to arrange events ranging from cake sales in the school yard to dinners in swanky hotels). All parents will be strongly encouraged to attend. Even if you are not actually organising the event, you may end up agreeing to bake cakes, sell tickets for the raffle or staff the 'Guess the weight of the teddy' stall. If you have any relevant skills in areas like design, PR or IT, you might be asked to design flyers for the event or arrange the AV system.

Volunteers may be needed for special events like school sports day – to hold the finish line tape for the sprints, announce the races on a loudspeaker, call 'Ready Steady Go!' in the egg and spoon race, manage car parking on the school sports field, paint lions and butterflies on the faces of enthusiastic six-year-olds or ensure there are no head-on collisions on the bouncy castle. Other events requiring parental input may include religious ceremonies like First Communion or Confirmation, where armies of parents are enlisted for duties ranging from covering the school in bunting to co-ordinating weekly rotas for children's readings in church.

Sometimes 'volunteering' is mandatory – for instance if your child is taking part in school swimming, as a parent you must commit to accompanying the children on the school bus once over the course of the term. A rota will be drawn up (usually by another volunteer parent) and each child is assigned a specific date on which their parent must accompany the class. If the parent doesn't show for their allocated slot, the class doesn't go swimming. Where volunteering is not mandatory, you will need to decide whether you will do it and make time accordingly.

One thing to bear in mind is that while the time taken up by the specific activity itself may appear relatively short, the associated administration and communication can often take up much more time. For instance, if you are responsible for supervising the Friday cross-country running, on paper this involves a 30-minute drive to a sports track, where you take a roll call and then hang around for 90 minutes as the parent in charge, ensuring no fights, toilet accidents or other major disasters occur. You will receive an email with a spreadsheet attached detailing which Fridays you have been assigned. Open the spreadsheet, enter the dates in your diary (checking whether you need to juggle around meetings or other commitments to accommodate) – job done!

Or so you'd think. More than likely there will be four or five updated versions of the spreadsheet circulated over the following weeks/months. Each time you'll have to go through the updated spreadsheet and check whether the dates in your diary are still correct. If you do not, you may rock up on the original date, three months from now, only to find another parent with a clipboard in their hand looking at you quizzically. Or worse, get a phone call one Friday afternoon from the cross-country coach urgently enquiring if you are on your way!

There will be an initial flurry of messages from people on the rota to try to swap dates they can't make. There will be a further steady dribble of emails and WhatsApp messages throughout the year: 'Hi, I'm meant to be supervising on 2 November but I've got a meeting I can't get out of. Would anyone be able to swap?' Following this, there will be twenty unfruitful responses along the lines of, 'Sorry I would definitely swap but I won't have the car that day', (usually copying the entire class), until eventually a solution will be found and world peace (in parent supervising duties) will be reinstated.

11

Celebrating

BIRTHDAY PARTIES

There is a wonderful episode of *The Bugle* podcast in which Andy Zaltzman and John Oliver postulate what might have been going through Osama Bin Laden's mind just before he was shot in his Pakistani hide-out by a crack team of US Navy Seals (https://thebuglepodcast.com, episode 193).

Reflecting ruefully about why he hadn't really achieved all his life goals, they surmise the most likely reason was that too much time was taken up by birthday parties (especially time-consuming when you have 6 wives and 22 kids). 'How was I supposed to destroy the West and Capitalism if every other fucking weekend [we have] ... birthday parties?!'

Other children's birthday parties

Frequency: Weekly to monthly
Flexibility around timing: Medium

Even if you don't have 22 kids, the amount of time that children's birthday parties will take up in your life is not to be sneezed at. In my son's class (of 30 children), there are eighteen boys, almost all of whom will have a birthday party every year, inviting all the boys in the class. In my daughter's class there are fifteen girls (and fifteen parties). So, from the age of about five onwards, that's up to 33 Saturdays or Sundays each year that one or other parent needs to drive their child somewhere for two hours of some fun activity, followed by food and fizzy drinks. Occasionally it is somewhere nearby but usually it's about a 45-minute drive away, meaning it's hardly worth coming home after dropping them off, because you'd be no sooner be in the door than it would already be time to go back. Mercifully, over the years, the parents have been amalgamating birthdays in the class into double or even triple parties, a move that has delighted parents by restoring about a week per year to their lives.

Your own children's birthday parties

Frequency: Annual
Flexibility around timing: Low

Back when I was a child, birthday parties were relatively simple affairs: they would always be at home, my mother would make a lovely cake along with yummy treats we wouldn't normally get too often, like Rice Krispies buns. There would be copious amounts of chocolate biscuits, crisps and popcorn. We'd play innocent games like musical chairs/statues (with my Dad in charge of turning Abba tracks on the record player on and off at random) and pin the tail on the donkey. And despite my friends turning up looking pristine in their best dresses, they never looked like that going home, as quite a lot of running around on the grass and tree-climbing usually happened, too. All my friends' birthday parties were identical.

So when my daughter had her first birthday party at school (age five), I knew no better than to try to emulate my parties from days of old. As we waved goodbye to fifteen little fairies at the end of the afternoon, I felt that while it had involved quite a bit of prep and Mummy and Daddy were badly in need of a big glass of wine, overall, it had all gone rather well.

Over the next few months however, I gradually realised that birthday parties had moved on from my childhood. These days, most parents wouldn't dream of having a party at home; instead, they usually book a dedicated venue where fifteen children can jump around on trampolines and inflatable slides, or shoot each other at Quasar, followed by chips and burgers served on paper plates in a brightly coloured zone with no decibel limits. If parties are at home, many hire professional entertainers like magicians or a zoological person to bring along all sorts of exotic animals to show an enthralled audience of six-year-olds.

Parents often don't bother preparing party food themselves, either; instead, they just order a tower of pizzas that are delivered by a chap on a motorbike. (Much easier!) Party bags are apparently essential these days, too and unless you buy these from a dedicated party planning shop, will require quite a bit of thought and coordination!

So, what's involved these days in having a birthday party for your son/ daughter? Is it now so simple that you can pretty much arrange everything online through a magical birthday company while you sip a glass of wine, or does it constitute a job that needs to be listed in the Invisible Job Description? Well, joyous as a child's birthday celebration is, the effort involved would suggest that it does. While partners might benignly remark – as you hand the last of the party bags to fifteen bouncy children and open a bottle of wine – that, 'It seemed to go well; Susie certainly seemed very happy anyway', more often than not, they have no idea of the preparation involved to have a birthday party run smoothly ... and get the all-important big thumbs up from Susie.

If you are time-deprived and cash-rich, then opting for an external venue may seem the best option. But be warned: while it involves considerably less work on the day itself, you will usually need to arrange this months in advance. And you will still have to organise the food (even if this doesn't mean preparing it yourself).

If you opt for a party at home, to keep a group of between fifteen and thirty children entertained for two or three hours, a central activity and/or a professional entertainer is advisable. You will also need to tidy your house (before and after), prepare party decorations, ensure you have sufficient chairs for little people and buy/prepare food and drinks. In either case you will need a cake, candles and party bags. And you will need to send out invitations, confirm attendees, send out a reminder and ensure any online permissions and insurance waivers for external venues are signed in advance. On the day, try to ensure no children have gone AWOL, manage any minor injuries/squabbles and hand them all back to their parents at the agreed collection time, having lost as few coats/shoes/children as possible. Capturing lots of fun moments with your camera as memories of a great day for your child is the icing on the cake. Tissues, plasters and the telephone numbers of all parents, in case of any emergencies, are always useful.

BUYING AND SENDING PRESENTS AND CARDS

We all love receiving presents. And many people get just as much, if not more satisfaction from giving them. That is, presuming we are talking about people and occasions that genuinely matter to us. When it is scaled up, by the addition of lots more people, present-buying can lose some of its allure, becoming just one more task to fit into in the ever-decreasing amount of time available to us.

Birthday and Christmas presents for family

There are all-important people in your life for whom you always want to have a thoughtful present wrapped and ready to give on their birthday or at Christmas, whether in person or posted in good time to wherever they live in the world.

Curiously, while women usually retain responsibility for choosing presents for people who were always on their present list, they often also take responsibility for buying most (or even all) of the presents for people on their husband's list. For instance, their mother-in-law. As one of the most important people to most men, you would think they would remember to get their mother a thoughtful, suitable present for her birthday. However, if it emerges that they haven't, their horrified wife/partner may do it for them. Why? Perhaps she just really likes her mother-in-law. In other cases, it's because she knows that when a husband/partner does not buy his mother a thoughtful birthday/Christmas present, it will not be viewed by the mother-in-law as her son's failing, it will be a failing of the couple. Or by mothers-in-law of a certain vintage, specifically as a failing of the daughter-in-law.

The origins of today's unjust distribution of responsibilities for the Invisible Job stem from generations before us. Thirty years ago the imbalance was even more profound than it is today. Many never questioned – and some still don't – whether this was acceptable; instead, they were conditioned to accept this as the natural order of things. These women may therefore have very low expectations when it comes to their sons' contributions as a home-maker/parent, believing deep down that this responsibility falls to women.

Once, when my in-laws came to stay, I had the guest room prepared and had been busy getting all the provisions in for their stay, but when they arrived I hadn't finished putting the new cover on the duvet. My mother-in-law uttered kind absolutions of, 'Not to worry,' and, 'We'll manage,' with conspiratorial empathy for how tough it is for 'us girls'. There was no suggestion of it being a job that a man might have been just as accountable for.

Your mother-in-law probably knows all too well what it was like to be the one who bought and wrapped all presents on her own and her husband's behalf – even the ones labelled 'To my darling wife'! So if your husband does not remember to buy a birthday present for his mother, she may be somewhat disappointed with him, but deep down may see his wife as the person ultimately accountable. Aware of this unconscious bias in older generations, women will often factor members of their extended family into their own present/card list. Having bought the presents, they will probably also be the ones to wrap them and, if needed, post them in good time to far-flung places.

Birthday presents for schoolfriends

At a guess, based on the birthday party mathematics from earlier, each of your children is likely be invited to fifteen to thirty birthday parties of schoolfriends each year between the ages of five and twelve. Let's suppose you have two children. That means 2 x 8 years x 15 (or possibly 30) parties, which is 240–480 birthday presents that someone in your house needs to buy and wrap for schoolfriends.

Each time you need to head to a toy/book shop to buy a birthday present for parties, this might take you at least 40 minutes (or even twice that) by the time you:

- Get to the shop with your child and park.
- Choose something suitable at a reasonable price (after asking your child for advice on what the friend is interested in – Lego? Reading? Art? Jigsaw puzzles?)
- Pay at the till while trying to remember whether you have wrapping paper at home that doesn't have Merry Christmas written on it.
- Then get home and wrap it. (Whenever you encounter a wonderful shop assistant offering to wrap the present for you, you will hug them.)

Multiplying the conservative estimate of 240 presents by this even more conservative estimate of 40 minutes means that a parent will likely spend at least 160 hours (i.e. 20 working days) of their life buying birthday presents for their children's primary school friends! And who does this job tend to fall to?

I remember one hectic Saturday trying to simultaneously make my son lunch, get him to write a birthday card and change out of his football gear, conscious that he needed to be at a birthday party in half an hour and we had yet to get a present. Tight for time and stressed, I quickly explained the situation to my husband and asked if he could please help. Bizarrely, the job he opted to do was to get the birthday present.

'OK ...' I said dubiously, morbidly curious to see what he would choose. Five minutes later, he reappeared in the kitchen, saying, 'Right, I'm ready to go. You just need to tell me exactly what present I need to get and where to buy it'.

Busy mothers can't afford to spend 160 hours of their life on school birthday presents. A well-stocked gift drawer and a stash of book tokens is one way efficient parents deal with this task! But it still makes up part of someone's mental load.

Santa

Santa is a remarkable and magical individual who brings much joy to children. His remit can get complex, as children make very specific (and sometimes sophisticated) demands. Expectations of Santa delivering the Lego Star Wars Kessel Run Millennium Falcon may be high, availability online and in shops may be low, and as ever, both the available time and money to procure them are finite. But Santa always seems to pull out all the stops to ensure that, come Christmas morning, a pile of eagerly awaited presents appears magically under the Christmas tree or in stockings. If only Mummy and Daddy weren't always so exhausted Christmas morning when woken up at 5 a.m. by excited children. How did Santa manage to think up just the right presents for everyone? It must have taken him forever. Good job he has all those elves to help, eh?

Presents for teachers

Whatever your thoughts on buying presents for teachers (an unnecessary expense, an inappropriate bribe, an appropriate token of your appreciation), your child will not want to be the only one without a present for their teacher. And don't forget music teachers, sports coaches and other people whose patience in putting up with your children every week you'd like to acknowledge annually.

Thank you cards

Whenever I see a handwritten envelope in my post box, it's definitely the first thing I open. Handwritten letters are a joy. Not only do they almost always say something pleasant but crucially, they are written by a person, not spewed out by a computer that doesn't know you from a widget. Sadly, they only represent a tiny percentage of my post. Sometimes these rare hand-addressed envelopes might contain a thank you card. It could just be a two-line note to say, 'Thank you for having us over for dinner last weekend; the lamb tagine was delicious and we had a great time!' but it is so lovely to receive. Although you felt the dessert you made was a bit of a disaster and you'd forgotten to chill the wine, it feels great to know that your guests had a good time regardless.

For the same reason, if someone sends you or your child a present or goes to the effort of having you over for dinner, you may wish to acknowledge this person-ally by sending them a handwritten note. It only takes two minutes to write. It helps if someone ensures you always have a box of nice notecards in the house, along with a supply of stamps. Then someone just needs to find the two minutes.

Birthday and Christmas cards

Who doesn't love receiving birthday cards? Remembering to send birthday cards to everyone who matters in your life just needs a little thought and planning. Prac-tically speaking, it requires putting in diary reminders a few days in advance of all birthday dates and keeping a stash of suitable cards (and stamps) to hand so that you can dispatch one that will arrive on time.

When sending birthday cards to people from you and your partner, does this job tend to fall to one person, with the partner (at most) scribbling their name at the bottom of a thoughtfully written card, already in a stamped and addressed envelope?

Writing Christmas cards to friends and family around the world can take up two full working days. Yet it can be a really great way of ensuring you touch base at least once a year to let them know what is happening in your life. If sending Christmas cards is still a thing in your house, is it a job you share between you?

If not, does the person who writes those cards redistribute other aspects of their Invisible Job that week?

I used to have a boss who gave a Christmas card each year to each member of our team ... written and signed by a wife who had never met any of us.

12

Being There Whenever Your Children Need You

The following are not jobs. These are the things you really *want* to dedicate your time to as a parent, except perhaps when a) you are mentally exhausted and dying for a G&T or a child-free ten-minute break or b) simultaneously attending to three other jobs.

However, if you are stretched too thinly across the Invisible Job (potentially in addition to your paid job), you don't have the time to focus properly on the parts of being a parent you really want to do. This is one of them!

LISTENING TO THE DAY'S WOES

Frequency: At least daily
Flexibility around timing: Low

When you're a big person, it's easy to forget what it was like being a small person. A handful of moments from our childhood, especially those involving strong emotions, may still play over and over in the dusty video libraries of our memories. Chances are, the memories are not even accurate because each time we play them, our brain changes them a little. But the emotions embedded in those memories might still capture some of what it felt like to navigate the highs and lows of being a child.

Over the course of every day, children encounter lots of tough moments. And it doesn't really matter whether they seem tough to you (an adult); what counts is how it feels to them. When your son comes out of school and says, 'Today was the worst day ever!', he doesn't want you to rationalise with him (or put his experience in context with the wider world by telling him that a day in the life of a child in war-torn Syria was probably worse); he just needs you to listen and to empathise with his woes and frustrations, such as, 'That boy wasn't playing fair today in the school yard!' or 'The teacher gave out to me for talking in class when it wasn't me!'

Often children don't even want to tell you what happened. But just knowing that you understand that they feel upset will affirm and reassure them; enabling them to deal with it better themselves. Twenty minutes later they may be out bouncing on the trampoline without a second thought for the boy in the school yard. This important activity requires time. And, crucially, this requires some 'give' in the routine because these issues arise unexpectedly and cannot be scheduled.

It is wonderful when children are lucky enough to have a parent or another trusted adult to talk to when they get home from school; someone who will pick up on their mood and notice when there's some little (or big) upset lurking under the surface. When working full-time, this was not something I could always offer my children; sometimes the best I could do was pick up the embers of any burning torches at 6.30 p.m. when I finished work. By that time, there may have been sibling fights or other outbursts (sparked by the earlier upset), meaning there were now layers of upset to be diffused and soothed. But it was still important and valuable, even at 6.30 p.m. Dinner would have to wait, we needed to just sit on the couch together until everyone had been listened to and felt better. That didn't mean that checking homework, music practice and finding the football gear for tonight's training could be completely ignored; it just meant somehow squashing all of that in afterwards.

READING

Frequency: Variable
Flexibility around timing: High

The benefits of reading are well known and undisputed. Instilling a love of reading takes time. You may want to read to your child daily from an early age. As your children start to learn to read themselves, being able to spend a bit of time with them each day to encourage their efforts and help them with tricky words helps instil a sense of achievement and hopefully a pleasure in reading that will grow year on year. Being comfortable with reading makes school more enjoyable and manageable, but the biggest win is giving them an activity in which they can forever lose themselves, where they can learn and stretch their horizons and importantly, giving them an outlet that ensures that their default downtime is not always spent using a tablet or in front of a computer screen.

PLAYING

Frequency: Variable
Flexibility around timing: Medium

'Mommy do you want to play Uno?' Or lightsabers?'

In an ideal world, I'd reply, 'Ooh yes, I'd love to darling! Whose turn is it to have the green one?'

But in reality, I have to finish peeling these potatoes. And hang up the clothes that are in the washing machine.

Brandishing two lightsabers, he asks 'Quick Mommy, which do you want to be: Darth Maul or Luke Skywalker?'

Buying myself two minutes, I ask 'Hmmm, Darth Maul, remind me, is he the one with the red and black face? Does he have the double-sided lightsaber?' as I quickly peel the last potato and put the lid on the pot.

'Right so. How about we have a quick lightsaber fight in the garden?' As it's 6.45 p.m. on a Thursday, almost dark, almost bedtime, and Daddy won't be home for at least another hour.

'No! A long one! And let's go to the park to do it!'

Finding time to play can be challenging, especially during the week. It's not that you don't want to play (although admittedly, you might not always be in the mood), it's just that there are so many other things you need to do too. Playing games in a hurry doesn't feel good – for anyone – but that's sometimes all you can manage. You're not the only person in the world your children can play with but, especially when they are small, Mommy or Daddy usually tend to be the No. 1 choice. And when they are very small, the only choice. Having a sibling is the ideal way to increase the number of play pals (at least there will be a conspirator keen to sit on the other end of the seesaw or make a witch's stew out of mud and sticks at the playground). As children get older, you reach a point of being able to play games that you can enjoy as a family, including loads of board games and sports. You may be completely useless at some of the games they want you to play – in my case, that includes anything on an Xbox – but my eleven-year-old seems to appreciate the effort, nonetheless.

Playing with children is not a job, but it does take time, so although both Mommy and Daddy are probably both very happy to spend time playing, when you are both trying to fit in paid work and/or the Invisible Job, be cognisant of the importance of freeing up a little time for one parent to play (while the other takes care of other things). Ensuring you both get a chance to play with your children regularly is important, as the following piece written by a father highlights: 'While I was playing with my daughter and continuing to be the fun one, my wife was stuck doing chores around the house, like dishes, laundry, etc ... It wasn't that she and I had a discussion and decided we would have those roles. We just sort of fell into it. And it's a feedback loop. The more I continue to play with my daughter, the more I am the "fun one", and the less my wife is, which results in my daughter asking to play with me the next time, making me more fun.' (7)

For parents who are at home full time, however, playing/keeping children entertained can be less fun. It's an 'area under the curve' thing: once you reach a certain point in the curve, your patience and enthusiasm for having sponge darts fired at you by one child while another upends a whole box of Lego pieces that you had just gathered up moments ago starts to waiver. Sarah Turner, author of *The Unmumsy Mum*, started a blog as way of letting off steam about the frustration and tedium of spending the whole day with her two young boys while her husband went out to work:

Adayathomejustfeelssoooooooooloooooooooooooooong!

She describes candidly her efforts to while away a day at home with two toddlers, in between watching episodes of *Peppa Pig* she'd already seen a hundred times:

> *Cars: This game is pretty basic. It's also pretty dull. You get down on the floor and 'drive' a tiny toy car while following the path of the toddler's tiny toy car. Sometimes, this will be a race. You will be required to make annoying engine noises. The only hard-and-fast rule is: you never win.*

As she puts it, 'Nothing is mentally as tough as confinement in the house with small people'. (8)

BEDTIME

Frequency: Daily
Flexibility around timing: Low

There's a certain routine attached to bedtime. It will differ in every house and evolves as children get older but between the ages of say, three and ten, it will include a lot of chasing around to try to shepherd tired (but suddenly hyper) little people up to their bedrooms, locating and getting on pyjamas, negotiations over brushing teeth, extended debates about which teddy gets pole position in the bed tonight and which book we're going to read (if you are reading to two or more siblings, reaching agreement on the book may involve NATO-level peace treaties), followed by arguments about whether the light/lamp can be turned off or must be left on (more peace treaties when one child wants complete darkness and one can't bear you to leave the room unless the light stays on), then finally snuggles and kisses goodnight. If you manage not to fall asleep on the floor in your child's bedroom, you emerge as a slow-moving sleepy shadow of the person who, thirty minutes ago, was all set to do this year's tax return as soon as you got the kids to sleep.

KEEPING THE BOWLING BALL FROM FALLING DOWN THE GULLEY

Every parent wants the best for their child, even if they can't fully articulate exactly what this means. As one mother I spoke to described it, perhaps it simply means ensuring your children get a chance to be their best. The child may or may not be academic, good at sports or drama or music. But you'd hate them to feel they were useless at everything or that they gave up every time something felt challenging. Above all, you want your child to like and believe in themselves, to have at least one or two good friends and be kind to others. While they will frequently encounter setbacks, you want to ensure they develop resilience so they will be able to cope. You want them to not care so much about what other people think of them and instead to learn to understand themselves and what they believe in and to not be afraid to live in accordance with this.

As an adult, you have a long-term perspective on life that your child won't develop for years. While they live in the moment, you can see the bigger picture. And while you want to let them find their own way and figure out their own solutions, you don't ever want them to make mistakes that there's no coming back from. You can't – and shouldn't even try to – live their lives for them, but there will be times when you will be very tempted to intervene. I sometimes picture a child navigating their way through life's challenges like a bowling ball rolling down the shiny wooden alley towards the skittles standing at the end. As parents, we should not expect the result to be a perfect smash, knocking all ten skittles down. The ball may not even reach a single skittle, or even if it does, have the power to knock it down. Yet we must refrain from jumping in and throwing the ball for them. As we watch the ball wobble slowly down the alley, if it teeters on the edge of the gulley, our job as parents is to gently nudge it away from the edge, keeping it in play long enough for our children to figure out for themselves how to knock down a skittle or two.

Crucially, this requires time and attention. If we are rushed off our feet it is much harder to spot the ball approaching the gulley. And sometimes that little nudge may require some serious effort (e.g. identifying a professional who can help your child and engaging in that process). This is very much part of the mental load of the parent who takes primary responsibility for the day-to-day wellbeing of the children.

CREATING STRUCTURE AND SETTING LIMITS

Although children will strongly disagree (just ask Calvin from *Calvin and Hobbes*), it is generally considered important that their lives feature some structure and limits. For instance, it is useful to have some intelligent guidelines about how much time they can spend watching TV or using a tablet or games console every day, what time they need to go to bed and how much access they have to money. Establishing healthy routines for doing homework, playing, getting fresh air and reading is important, as is downtime to just daydream or be bored. And assigning children responsibility for contributing to chores at home in small ways also helps them understand that everyone in the family has a role to play. It enables them to become more independent and begin to understand interdependence.

Negotiating these limits can be challenging and scores *nul points* in the Popular Parent League Tables: 'What do you mean I can only have one hour of Xbox every day? That's so unfair!! My friend Tom is allowed play as long as he wants!'

'I am not going to bed at 8 p.m., that's way too early!'

'Why *can't* I have a bag of caramel popcorn as my lunch?'

Equally unpopular with older children are all moves to curtail access to phones/screens or limit the places and times they are allowed out: 'It's so unfair; everyone else in my class is allowed to go to this disco.'

(When you ask the other parents, it usually turns out they're not).

'Why can I not bring my phone to bed with me? You are the meanest parents ever! What's wrong with chatting to people online that I don't know? Seriously! You are ruining my life!'

Somebody (or better still *two* somebodies) needs to consider what might be age-appropriate limits for things like bedtime, screen time, internet access, eating sweets and going out (either alone or with friends). While often invisible work, it requires consideration and therefore time: it is much less time-consuming to just let children have what they want without boundaries.

Both parents need to agree on these limits, then explain them clearly to their children, including why they are being set in the first place. After that, both parents need to consistently enforce them and back each other up whenever children push these limits (as they inevitably will).

13

Family Holidays

Frequency: The more the better!
Flexibility around timing: Medium

BOOKING THE HOLIDAY

Going on holiday sounds fabulous. A break from the routine of work and house-work and minding children and constantly rushing around all day. Whether you fancy a fortnight by the sea in a nice cottage close to home or flying overseas for a bit of guaranteed sun or to experience the culture of a new city, plans need to be made. There is no shortage of enticing options; someone just needs to find and commit to one that matches the picture in your head but at the same time, doesn't break the bank.

Whether you fancy a cottage in Kerry, an Airbnb apartment in Rome or a hotel with a pool in the Algarve, it takes time to search through the available options to find something that you like, that can accommodate you on the dates you need and that you can afford. The internet has transformed how we book holidays, turning it almost exclusively into an online exercise. The myriad review sites appear, at first, to make the whole job easier – we all like to be reassured that it's going to be good. However, the more we trawl through reviews, the more impossible it becomes to find a place with a clean bill of health.

If you're going to a completely new country, you might first need to do some reading to get the lie of the land. You may also need to look up visa requirements, health risks and which months are best to go. Once you've figured out all that, there will be diaries to cross-check, tickets to book and accommodation to arrange. As you try to work out the best value/timing/availability, you may find you have ten tabs open on your computer and a spreadsheet on the go. Booking a holiday will typically take several hours at least and may take several days, especially if you are doing it at night after the kids have gone to bed or sandwiched in between work and everything else in your Invisible Job.

Of course, for the lucky few for whom money is no object, booking a holiday is much less time-consuming. You can just hand responsibility for the whole thing to a bespoke holiday booking agency that will listen to what you want and come back to you with a tailor-made holiday with all the travel, accommodation, transfers and pick-ups arranged, along with reservations for eating out, tours and whatever else you fancy.

PACKING FOR THE HOLIDAY

It is the day before we head off on a family holiday to France. The thought that next week we'll be in a gîte somewhere in the Alps sounds like heaven. I'm imagining mountain hikes, sunshine, fresh air and lazy afternoons in the garden consuming vast amounts of French wine, cheese and pastries. The only thing between us and French utopia is 24 hours ... and the small matter of packing. My husband tells me he's 'good' on the packing front – in other words, all the stuff he wants to bring on holiday is already on the bed in the spare room. Apparently, the only thing left to do is to take the pedals off his bike before putting it on the car rack. I spy neat piles of his cycling shorts and tops, merino base layers, spare tyres, bike bars, socks and chamois cream, alongside more neat piles of shorts, t-shirts, boxer shorts, swim togs and sunglasses. Good for you, I think. Are you going to France alone by any chance?!

I see no sign of neat piles of clothes for two small children that will cover two weeks of (hopefully) sunny (but possibly wet) days, the odd mountain hike with small people in woolly hats and gloves carried on our backs in MacPacs – come to think of it, there's no sign of the MacPacs, either. I calculate how many nappies and wipes we will need for two weeks and am flabbergasted by the tower this creates on the bed. How will this fit in the car?! Would it be risky to assume there will be a local supermarket that sells nappies? Sunny days at the municipal outdoor pool means we will also need towels, UV swimsuits, sunhats, swim nappies, armbands, the little shaded tent for the eighteen-month-old to have a nap in and, oh yes, a picnic blanket. As the gîte is self-catering, there's a big box of kitchen things we'll also need to bring in order to be able to meet the culinary demands of two small people: a decent sharp knife, potato masher, garlic press, whisk, baby bottles, Heinz ketchup and a travel steriliser for baby bottles.

We will also need a few more child essentials, like sun cream, Calpol, tooth-brushes, baby toothpaste, my daughter's precious blankie (and a spare, as if it goes missing nobody will get any sleep for a week), soothers, some toys, crayons and favourite books. After a quick look at the list I jotted down last year, I am happy we're now more or less there so at last I climb into bed, conscious we'll need to be up early to pack the car before driving to the ferry. Just as I'm about to close my eyes, I remember I haven't yet packed any clothes whatsoever for myself.

And not to forget, when you get home, there is also the whole unpacking thing – and the mounds of clothes washing that goes with it – that somebody needs to attend to.

14

The Place We Call Home

Most couples will live in rented accommodation at some point, perhaps for a few years or even their whole life. This often requires lots of time-consuming research to find somewhere suitable and affordable to rent, and once you do find a place, someone needs to take care of rental contracts, the deposit and monthly rental payments as well as being the point of contact for the rental agency/landlord. And each time you move, you start from scratch again.

MANAGING UTILITIES

Frequency: Monthly/Quarterly
Flexibility around timing: High

Like the air we breathe, utilities are something we just take for granted: access to high-speed internet, phone, electricity, water and gas. Only when the supply is interrupted do they enter our consciousness at all. But for anyone lucky enough not to know, there is quite a bit of invisible work needed to ensure that they are available and that you're not paying a fortune for them unnecessarily.

Gas/electricity

Once someone in the house has signed up to a gas and electricity provider, it's easy not to give these a second thought. Setting up payment via direct debit means you can even avoid the hassle of opening bills that come by post and paying them online or over the phone. You will receive emails every couple of months asking you to go look up the meter readings and submit them online. Admittedly, not a huge job, it's just that someone needs to do it.

While you're logged in (especially if it's for the first time in ages), you might look up your recent bills, as happened to me, and discover that you seem to have been paying a fortune for gas or electricity for the last twelve months. As customer services was already closed, I stuck a reminder in my phone to try to ring them the next day. After a frustrating number of automated telephone options and waiting online for ten minutes, eventually I was speaking to a person. He told me (something along the lines of), 'Yes Madam, these crazy bills are correct because the 20% discounted contract you originally signed up for ended months ago and we therefore switched you automatically to our standard contract rate'.

What he didn't say (because 'this call may be recorded for training and monitoring purposes') was, 'That is what happens to all idiots like you who don't monitor their bills or remember when their contract is due to expire. Unless you ring us to specifically state that you don't want to be fleeced for the coming year, we are perfectly entitled to do that because that is how our business model works.'

I learned that the previous year we had paid out an additional €800 for electricity that could have been avoided if we had phoned them up after twelve months to say we wanted to continue getting the discounted rate.

'Well can you please put us back on the discounted rate now?' I asked, keen to dig my way out of this financial blunder.

'Unfortunately not, Madam', he told me, 'because that rate is now only available to new customers'. He then added, 'However, if you were to switch to one of our competitors, then you'd be eligible to switch back to us in a year at the 20% discounted rate'.

'What?!' I said. 'Do you mean that every twelve months I need to switch suppliers just to avoid being overcharged by €800?'

'Essentially yes, Madam', he confirmed, acknowledging that the system is crazy but that is the game you have to play. So I put a calendar reminder in my phone that someone needed to cancel and switch our gas and electricity contract on 17 September next year (and every year after that forever).

'Just one last thing', the Customer Billing Enquiries man said. 'Is there a specific reason that your gas consumption is twice as high this year compared to last year?'

'What?! No! Is it seriously? How?'

'Yes, about six months ago it jumped up considerably and has been really high ever since. Do you perhaps have any new gas appliances?'

'No! Actually, we've spent a fortune getting the roof insulated so if anything, our gas consumption should be much lower this year compared to last'.

'Hmmm, strange', he says. 'Perhaps you'd better get an engineer to look at your boiler.'

I then spent an hour trying to track down an engineer to service our (apparently unusual) make of boiler and book an appointment. After inspecting everything, he identified the problem: a small valve at the top of the boiler had blown, meaning that it had been heating water 24 hours a day for the last six months. That was why the gas bill was more than double what it should have been.

While we tend to focus most of our financial efforts on earning money, when we don't have time to attend to the mundane things like electricity and gas bills or contracts we may find we are leaking money almost as fast.

Internet, phone and streaming services

The same contract issues apply when it comes to internet, phone and streaming services like Netflix and Apple Music. When you moved into your house/flat, somebody probably researched who offered the best high-speed internet, phone and streaming services for a reasonable price. Since then though, it's possible that nobody has thought twice about it and that you are now paying twice as much as the deal you originally signed up to. If you had five minutes to spare, you could look up a comparison/switching website that would tell you instantly which provider to switch to in order to pay 40% less than you currently do. If you had twenty minutes, you could dig out all the necessary paperwork and switch providers. But even though we know it could save us money, these are the kind of tasks we just wish happened automatically – or failing that, that they were part of someone else's Invisible Job Description.

MANAGE THE IT NEEDS OF THE FAMILY

While anyone aged over forty today grew up in a world where the internet did not yet exist and home computers were only used for playing *Space Invaders*, now it feels as if the sky is falling if our broadband stops working for an hour. Whenever we have a hardware, software or network issue at work, we can just call the IT guys. At home though, it feels like a disaster on the scale of Chernobyl. Unless someone takes responsibility for being the surrogate IT guy/gal. Whether this involves farming the job out to a network provider or literally sorting it all yourself will depend on your IT skills. Either way, it will require a bit of time and attention.

For starters, someone will need to ensure your house is properly set up to deliver whatever broadband and wi-fi capabilities you need. Having systems that back up your data is also essential. There's also the job of setting up devices whenever you buy a new computer, tablet, phone or printer. And not just for you/your partner;

some of your most time-consuming IT clients may be children (where much of your efforts may go on regulating access to devices) or grandparents (not too many grandads know how to transfer their contacts to a new phone).

Perhaps the busiest part of the IT job is sorting things out whenever something goes wrong – with the wi-fi, a computer, tablet or phone. Very frustrating for Grandma when her printer stops working or when Grandad keeps getting emails saying he has run out of iCloud storage. Head-wrecking for most of us when our computer appears to be on a go-slow or a program is no longer supported by our operating system. And Armageddon-level panic when we lose access to essential files.

Some people are naturally gifted at calmly figuring their way through the most likely causes and resolving such problems themselves. To others, even figuring out whether it's a hardware or software issue is akin to deciphering Mandarin symbols and the only option may be to call in the professionals. No shame in that, but it still needs *someone* to arrange it. In our house, all IT credit goes to my husband.

HOME MAINTENANCE

Wouldn't it be great if things never went wrong with houses? If drains never got blocked, toilets always flushed properly, doorbells always rang, taps didn't leak, doors closed fully, roofs didn't leak, alarms always behaved, the washing machine worked perfectly and nothing ever blew the electric fuse box. Sadly, these things do happen, prompting us to say, 'We need to get the X fixed'. I say 'we' because that's always the phrase used. By saying 'we', one partner can highlight to the other that something is broken and needs to be fixed, but without necessarily taking on the responsibility for getting it fixed.

It's a delicate dance, though. When it is mentioned a second time, the phrase uttered is often, 'We really need to get the X fixed', i.e. publicly communicating with a little more gravitas the urgency of getting the job done, while still avoiding any responsibility or commitment to personally tackle the tap in the bathroom that has been dripping for months.

'We' is also a very popular word when discussing a job that has been success-fully completed, regardless of whether you had any hand, act or part in completing the task. Such as when my husband says, emerging from the bathroom one morning, 'I'm really glad we got that new shower put in'.

I'm thinking, 'What do you mean 'we'?!

We are all quick to highlight when a job needs to be done, as well as to congratulate ourselves when a job has been successfully completed but possibly less visible when it comes to the bit in between (the invisible bit). Instead, we might hope that some benevolent elves will quietly take care of it, like that clever pair who made all the shoemaker's shoes.

When something is broken, we can either try to fix it ourselves or get a profes-sional to do it. The former obviously takes time and usually requires at least a modicum of expertise, but in this era of YouTube, we are all capable of much more than we credit ourselves with.

For example, even if you have never attempted to unblock a blocked toilet, after ten minutes of Googling, you will have five possible strategies for tackling this problem. None of them pleasant, all of them requiring rubber gloves, but at the same time, inexpensive and not requiring any plumbing qualifications. Just your time. If you decide you simply can't face this job, of course you could just call an emergency plumber – no rubber gloves required (at least, not by you!) Obviously, while this takes up less time, this privilege comes at a financial cost.

Sometimes fixing things yourself can save a lot of money. However, many jobs require professional expertise and competence to even attempt – and certainly to do them properly. From time to time, we need to engage plumbers, electri-cians, drain specialists, carpenters, painters and other specialists to solve various problems in our homes, often urgently. But even when we are getting a tradesman or other expert to fix a problem for us, it still takes time to manage. Identifying a reliable person or firm that is available to do the job at a reasonable cost takes time. Someone also needs to arrange to be home to let the person in, monitor the job and take care of payment. It's very easy not to appreciate that this is all time being subtracted from someone's day, compressing whatever time they have left to do everything else.

There is also a certain amount of basic house maintenance that must happen periodically and someone needs to take responsibility for either doing it themselves or arranging for a professional to take care of it. Home maintenance projects mate-rialise periodically like comets, demanding some TLC. They're usually not urgent at first but slowly assert themselves over time. They include things like:

- Changing water filters
- Servicing and testing the house alarm
- Cleaning chimneys
- Testing and changing batteries in the smoke and carbon monoxide alarm

STORAGE

We all have large items that we only use occasionally – suitcases for instance – or only need at certain times of the year (like Christmas decorations or wetsuits). Along with things that we don't need right now but which may be useful in the future (such as children's clothes that are currently too big or spare light bulbs/ printer cartridges). Not to mention tons of things that we acquired at various points in our life. And while we don't currently use them, we can't bear to throw them out, either because they have sentimental value or because we plan to get round to doing something with them eventually (e.g. the boxes of photographs sitting in my attic from a trip around the world in my early twenties, which I remain convinced I will make into an album one day). To have any hope of making it in the front door, owning all this stuff means you need to have some kind of storage system. Whether this is a brilliantly organised system of labelled, airtight boxes in the attic where everything inside is protected from damp, moths and mice, or a vaguely ordered set of shelves in the shed, is up to you. But someone needs to know how it works in order to have any hope of locating the item you need without spending a whole day searching for it.

HOME IMPROVEMENT PROJECTS

While it is very satisfying to review the result of home improvement projects, the time involved in managing or doing them is easily overlooked. One couple I know recently completed major work to a lovely (but very old) house they had recently bought as their family home. It involved liaising with an architect, obtaining planning permission and having builders being on-site daily for almost a year. During this period, the wife (who worked part-time) was the main point of contact for the architect and builder for on-site decisions, as well as handling unforeseen setbacks with potentially huge costs. This frequently involved several hours of careful review in the evenings after the children were in bed, but thanks to her intelligent and timely intervention, hold-ups were avoided and the potential cost was also reduced by tens of thousands of pounds.

HOME FURNISHING

This relates to selecting and purchasing the following items when you move into a new home or replacing them as they become worn or get broken:

- Curtains
- Sofas, chairs and cushions
- Beds, duvets, sheets, pillows and blankets
- Plates, dishes, glasses, cups and cutlery
- Pots, frying pans and baking trays
- Light fittings and lamp shades
- Wardrobes, drawers, tables
- Carpets and rugs
- Towels and bathmats
- Bathroom fittings
- Mirrors and pictures

OPENING MAIL AND RETRIEVING PACKAGES

Someone needs to stay on top of opening and dealing with mail – not the exciting hand-written envelopes, but the boring typed ones that can pile up on the hall table. This job is mainly a triage exercise – while all mail needs to be opened, much of it can be shredded/go straight in the bin. Some mail items will require action – such as paying a bill, making an appointment or sending a response. These should be directed to whoever is in charge of that particular element. But there can also be all manner of unexpected items. Someone just needs to flag things that need attention and ensure they are not missed by both of you.

As more and more of our purchases arrive by post, you may also find a steady stream of notes about packages that the postman or a delivery company tried to deliver but there was nobody home. Someone needs to go pick them up from the sorting office or whatever nearby location they have been left or arrange for them to be redelivered.

CARS AND BIKES

Car servicing and maintenance

As we move into an era of all-electric vehicles, cars will thankfully require less and less maintenance. With no combustion engine, hopefully all we will really need to monitor will be tyres and windscreen wipers. In the future, service visits won't even involve bringing the car to the garage; we will be able to log in for a remote assessment from our driveway! In the meantime, cars need to be regularly serviced. They also require an annual MOT/NCT. These need to be booked, someone may need to drop and collect the car at the (hopefully nearby) garage and someone may need to make alternative arrangements for transporting children or getting to work without the car.

Cleaning the car

When you have children, it is not unusual for the inside of your car to be frequently (and generously) covered in crumbs, spilt drinks and more. The seats and windows may feature permanent sticky handprints. With young children, upside-down milk bottles and the occasional throw-up incident will happen. And if you ever go to the beach (even once!), the car will mysteriously spout sand for weeks afterwards like *The Magic Porridge Pot*. Therefore, every so often the car will need a clean, inside and out.

Motor tax and parking permits

A straightforward but boring job, someone must remember to renew the motor tax each year or risk a hefty fine. It does not take long, especially online ... provided you can locate or remember the log-in details. When the new disc arrives in the post, just pop it on the windscreen.

If you live in an area where you need a permit to park your car, someone needs to remember to arrange this – whether this involves signing up for annual or quarterly permits or ensuring you have a stash of temporary permits for you and visitors to your home to use. In some cities, particularly in the US, the local councils only permit residents to park their car on the street on certain days or within specific time windows, meaning you must remember to move it again at the end of this period. Having experienced it many times myself while living in London, I sympathise sincerely with anyone who has every woken up in the morning to find their car clamped, having forgotten to move it the night before.

Bicycles

A bit like cars (but without the paperwork), bikes also need some regular love to ensure they will last you well and are safe to ride. Inner tubes pumped, tyres checked, brake blocks replaced and chain oiled. And as little legs get longer, saddle heights on children's bikes will need to be raised and bigger bikes bought, with the too-small bikes put up for sale or passed on to younger family members. Children will need your support as they progress from a balance bike onto one with pedals and to learn how to ride safely and independently. Someone will also need to see to it that they have the right size helmets (properly adjusted), bike locks and, if they will be out in the dark, reflective clothing and lights that work.

15

Finance and Life Admin

INSURANCE

While this would be financially impossible, it would be marvellous if insurance was something we could sign up for only if/when we needed it. The rest of the time, we could simply exist in an insurance-free (but also admin-free) nirvana. Unfortunately, however, unless you are really good at seeing into the future, someone needs to do the boring but necessary work to ensure you are covered for the unexpected as far as home, car, health and travel insurance are concerned.

Choosing a policy

When taking out any kind of insurance, some research will be required. Not only because the cost varies considerably from one insurer to another but also because there can be important differences between what the various policies will cover.

There may be information you need to gather. When taking out buildings insurance, for instance, you may be asked how much your house would cost to rebuild if it were burned to the ground. If you have no idea, some research may be needed to establish the approximate amount. Similarly, you may have no idea what the contents of your house/flat are worth. Many people underestimate this and simply opt for the lowest level of cover (e.g. <€10,000). However, if you are a couple in your thirties and have never calculated how much everything you own would cost to replace, it's an exercise worth doing for the peace of knowing you are realistically insured, should the worst come to the worst.

Having decided which company/policy to go for, there will be forms to complete, which is always tedious, whether you do it online, on paper or over the phone. You may be asked for various pieces of documentation, such as No Claims Bonus Certificates and vehicle registration certificates for car insurance or serial numbers and photographs for 'high-risk items' (such as laptops, expensive cameras, bicycles or jewellery) when taking out home insurance. However, once you have eventually received and filed away your policy documents, your work is done!

Renewals

But only for twelve months, at which point, the policy needs to be renewed. It's not good to discover that your insurance is out of date when you need to make a claim! Yet it is dangerously easy to forget to renew, so guess what? Yes, someone has to have renewals on their task list. Automatic renewals avoid this danger but be warned: loyalty is not always rewarded. Knowing that many people have not got time to scrutinise them, frequently automatic renewals do not represent value for money. If the premium has gone up wildly, somebody may find themselves back at the drawing board, searching for a new policy (probably armed with a large glass of wine).

Claims

If you ever need to make a claim, you will be hugely relieved that you did take out insurance, but someone still has to submit the claim. This will involve phone calls, completing forms, negotiating, obtaining quotes and submitting evidence of the actual damage/loss. While this ensures the costs will be covered, someone also needs to arrange for whatever has been damaged/broken/lost/stolen to be repaired/replaced. Not insurmountable by any means; it all just takes time.

Frustratingly, while insurance is very useful, its purpose is just to get us back to where we were before someone crashed into our car or the living room ceiling collapsed. A lot time and effort, without any net progress to show for it. Definitely a job to delegate to the shoemaker's elves if possible! (Of course, when you are not the one managing it, you can wonder in blissful ignorance why someone is plastering the ceiling or why a rental car has suddenly appeared in the driveway).

ORGANISING AND FILING

When managing household administration, locating the right paperwork is often half the battle. A straightforward job, like completing an application form for a new school, can take hours if it involves first tracking down your child's birth certificate and most recent school report. While we all like to be able to find things when we need them, let's be honest, nobody finds filing exciting! When life is busy with young children, managing documents and forms that we either need to act on or file is challenging. Sometimes the best we can do is try to put them somewhere safe, with a view to attending to them when we can. This may include everything from that letter from the bank about your overdraft to the football kit order form you need to complete. Creating a filing system at home is worthwhile, as it will ultimately save you time. It involves buying folders with labelled dividers where you can file (and find!) documents like utilities, insurance, motor tax, tax returns, school reports, medical expenses and so on. While it takes time to set up and some ongoing effort to maintain, it will ultimately reduce the hassle associated with managing household administration.

Identity documents and professional certificates

We start amassing important documents from the time we are born – birth certificates, school/university certificates, professional qualifications and marriage certificates. When children come along, this generates a whole new cycle of paperwork documenting their existence on the planet. We know these are important not to lose (as they're a pain to replace) but unless someone in the house bothers to store them somewhere recognisable, they can easily be misplaced or even thrown out in a house move.

Similarly, someone needs to attend to keeping identity documents, such as children's passports, up to date.

Warranties, receipts and instructions

When you've spent lots of money on things that come with warranties or guarantees, these are certainly worth keeping, but only if you can find them! Someone needs to devise a system and try to ensure important things get put in it.

These next items are some of the longer-term elements in the job description; important but time-consuming things that are few of us find fun and are easily left on the very long finger!

MORTGAGE

Being able to buy your own place as a couple is very exciting. Assuming you are taking out a joint mortgage, this is a job that both of you will be involved in. That means going to the bank together to discuss and sign all the paperwork. Before that, someone needs to go through the various mortgage offers available to figure out which bank/mortgage would work best for you. Someone will also need to arrange a solicitor to get the legal ball rolling ... and keep it rolling until all the paperwork has been signed and the place is finally yours.

After that, happily, there is not too much to do for the next 20–30 years, aside from keeping an eye on the mortgage payments and related paperwork. But since taking out a mortgage may be the biggest financial commitment of your life, it's a good idea if someone checks periodically for opportunities to switch to a cheaper one, as this may save you thousands of pounds.

LIFE ASSURANCE AND FINANCIAL PLANNING

If you haven't taken out life assurance before you have children, you may well consider doing so when you become a parent. Worrying about how your family would cope financially should the unthinkable happen might put life assurance or critical illness cover on our Invisible Job Description, but getting around to doing it is a different matter. Ironically, it's precisely because we have young children that we don't have time to do it. During this busy phase, parents are usually stretched so thinly between work and home responsibilities that it can feel like treading water in a sea of never-ending chaos. Just staying on top of urgent things each day is such a challenge that finding the time to attend to less urgent things (even if they are really important) can feel impossible. When you finally get to speak to a financial adviser, you will probably need to have calculated things like what annual income you think your family needs. After that, the adviser can review your financial profile and pension arrangements and advise you whether any further provisions are warranted.

WRITING WILLS

Which leads us directly to another important-but-not-urgent job that nobody in their twenties would dream of: writing a will. Couples with children obviously know that writing a proper will is really important but carving out time to get to it can be difficult. Important topics, such as potential guardianship of your children and their financial welfare, are tough to discuss but with guidance from a solicitor, it is not as complicated as you may fear. Being able to finally cross this job off your list is a huge relief.

16

Taking Care of Pets

Pets can be wonderful. Especially for children. Coming home from school after a bad day, it can feel much easier to snuggle up with the cat or dog than to talk to an adult. Pets don't ask questions or expect explanations; instead they offer uncomplicated empathy and physical reassurance that is worth its weight in gold. Pets also make brilliant social crutches for children – 'No I'm not hanging out by myself in the park, I'm bringing my dog for a walk'. As well as perfect conversation icebreakers: 'Oh your kitten is adorable! Can I please stroke her?'

Most parents will come under enormous pressure from children to get a pet at some point, especially if friends have one. While there is no doubt about the many positives associated with having a pet, they do add another element to the Invisible Job Description, as I explained to my children. For some aspects of pet minding, they assured me they would take full responsibility. Following detailed discussion about what this would entail, this commitment quickly got watered down to partial responsibility. In the end, it turned out that all they were willing to commit to was opting in (where have I heard that phrase before?) to pet minding when it suited them. This excluded whenever it was wet outside, when they were 'busy' (i.e. watching TV or playing Xbox) or whenever dog poo, cleaning or anything smelly was involved.

Exercise/interaction

Different pets need this more than others. Dogs, especially bigger ones, need plenty of exercise. If you have a huge, safe garden where they can run around all day without escaping out onto the road, marvellous. If not, someone needs to make time to bring them for a decent walk at least once a day, whatever the weather.

Feeding

There was great enthusiasm from my children for this job, especially after a trip to the pet shop. Both were very keen to be the *chef du jour* for a hamster or a tortoise (which basically involves collecting dandelion leaves from the garden and chopping up carrots and celery) yet, while willing to fill up a cat or dog's bowl with dry biscuits, they refused to handle wet food pouches ('because they stink'). On the other hand, fights broke out over who would be in charge of the kitty treats that cats love so much they will endure endless challenges to obtain.

Cleaning

For all animals, cleaning of any kind got minus marks from both of my children. The notion of cleaning the animal itself was OK – for instance, they thought brushing the dog's hair or giving it a bath sounded like fun. Their enthusiasm for anything more was tested when they looked after a friend's cat for a week. They proudly filled up the litter tray on Day 1. However, it was quickly evident that they were turning a very blind eye (and nose!) to the existence of any cat poo in the litter tray. When challenged on this, they indignantly told me 'it didn't count' if the cat had buried the poo under the cat litter; you only had to scoop up the ones on the top. There were also disputes about who was responsible for incidental cleaning e.g. when the cat sent the contents of its dish and water bowl flying across the floor. (Two more tasks delegated to parents.) Their dog enthusiasm was also put to the test when they agreed to look after our neighbour's dog for a few days. When it came to scooping up dog poo, although they agreed it was a dog owner's responsibility, neither of them were willing to do it!

Pet Health

Obviously not one of the responsibilities you can expect children to take on, but someone needs to attend to pet health. Whether it's taking a cat/dog to the vet for immunisation shots or treatment, scheduling appointments, giving it worming tablets or sorting out fleas, looking after an animal's health takes time.

GOING ON HOLIDAYS

Getting away can require a bit of planning when you have a pet. If you are lucky enough to have someone who loves pets and doesn't mind adding another dog (or iguana!) to the household for a fortnight, brilliant. If not, someone will need to arrange to have your pet looked after in kennels or at the vet, pet shop or elsewhere. And then transport your pet (with all its kit and caboodle) there and back.

17

Connecting with Friends, Family and Each Other

SOCIAL LIFE FOR ADULTS

In the words of singer/songwriter Christy Moore, 'Everybody needs a break; climb a mountain or jump in a lake.' If neither of these options floats your boat, fear not: the range of options that can make us feel rejuvenated, through specific activities or simply connecting with others, is limitless. Going out for a meal together, seeing that new film everyone is talking about, attending your favourite artist's gig, inviting friends over for drinks or dinner – it's all great. These are the things that make life fun. But even fun things require a little advance planning when your life is busy and coordination with others is involved. Note that arranging social activities exclusively for yourself (either of you) is not part of the Invisible Job but you do need to co-ordinate with one another whenever going out requires the other person to stay in (e.g. to look after children/pets). However, to keep the spark in your relationship alive, it's important to carve out time to do fun things together as a couple, either just the two of you or with friends. What form that might take is limitless – whether going out for drinks, a meal, a gig, a show, a game of tennis or a weekend away, it's up to you. Or rather up to one of you to arrange it! (Along with a babysitter).

SOCIAL LIFE FOR CHILDREN

Perhaps surprisingly, social diaries of younger children also take time to manage. Until they are old enough to take themselves to the park or a friend's house to play whenever they feel like it, parents need to be the social secretary (and often taxi driver) who makes this possible. For instance, while your eight-year-old may announce that his friend is coming over after school, unless the friend lives very close by, usually this can't actually happen until you ring the friend's mother/father, find out if they know their son is apparently coming over to your house (usually not), check if that's OK (often it's not as the child may need to be elsewhere at 4 p.m. today) and arrange the logistics of getting them from A to B and back (possibly with dinner thrown in).

FAMILY EXPERIENCES

There may also be lots of interesting things or places you'd like to take your children to at weekends, such as plays, musicals, educational centres, interactive museums, fun parks or the zoo. While these are all wonderful family experiences, they usually require a little forethought and perhaps advance booking. In other words, someone needs to take care of it. There are also tons of activities you might like to do with your children that don't require any booking, just some thought – like going for a picnic or a walk in the woods. Or playing a game/watching a movie together.

FOSTERING CONNECTIONS WITH RELATIVES

Family get-togethers can be lovely. Creating opportunities to meet up regularly, whether for Sunday lunch or a stroll in the woods on a good day, is important. If you have nephews/nieces of a similar age to your own children, afternoons playing on the lawn with cousins while parents and grandparents have a few beers are great opportunities to maintain close family connections.

There are often specific individuals within families who facilitate such gatherings. It just needs someone to exercise their initiative, perhaps by sticking a date in the diary to meet up somewhere or offering to host everyone at their house. Ideally, multiple people would take turns to be the social organiser. Sometimes grandparents are the ones who ensure families don't let months slide by without getting together, which can easily happen when everyone is busy. The benefits of ensuring this doesn't happen are that siblings stay in touch better; cousins can grow up being friends and grandparents have expanded social opportunities as well closer relationships with their grandchildren.

TAKING CARE OF OLDER DEPENDANTS

As our parents get older, they may start to need help in a range of areas. Their health may deteriorate, requiring medical intervention, which they may or may not be able to arrange themselves. They may already have advanced medical needs, such as physical or mental disabilities necessitating help from family and/or professional carers. Or they may be in reasonable health but just need occasional advice on technological or legal problems or life admin issues. Things that may take you a fraction of the time to resolve compared to them doing it themselves. Perhaps you both have parents who need help or maybe only one of you does. Either way, remember to make allowances for the time this important activity can take up.

PRESERVING MEMORIES AND MOMENTS

Throughout your child's life, there will be memories and milestones you will probably want to capture: pictures they drew, stories they wrote, happy days and successes. So much of it we will forget, as will they. Therefore, although it's not always easy, it's worth trying to capture some of these moments so that one day, many years from now, we can be reminded of them through diaries, photographs, videos, pictures, treasured items and other memories.

I've often heard older and wiser people (i.e. grandparents) describe how time passes when you are a parent: apparently, the hours go by like weeks but the years flash by in seconds. So even if right now you are submerged in the daily grind of parenting a toddler, dreaming of the day when you'll be able to pee without an audience, apparently one day (when the kitchen floor is no longer covered in Lego) you will be nostalgic for the days when you howled with pain after stepping on yet another piece of indestructible plastic with your bare feet.

Although there is still a lot of Lego in our house, my children are no longer toddlers and I must admit I am starting to see what the grandparents mean. Whenever I pass photographs on the wall at home of one of them on a lap or playing in puddles, it is hard to believe my children were ever so small. In fact, if it wasn't for all the wonderful photographs and videos that my husband has taken over the years, so much of their childhood would be little more than vague images in my head.

It doesn't matter whether photographs are printed on paper or stored some-where electronically, what matters is that someone has created these memories so that they are not forever lost. Even better is when someone has done the pains-taking work of sorting these precious images into albums so that whenever we get a moment to enjoy them, we can. When asked what they would grab from their burning house, it will come as no surprise that many people state it would be their photographs. Therefore, it is worth ensuring that all your precious photographs are backed up on hard drives.

Not all memories are captured in photographs, however. There are other milestones that our babies/children experience that we want to remember – such as their first tooth or first word. Or we may want to capture funny things they said or did. Wonderful moments for parents, which at the time, we think we will never forget. When my daughter recently asked me expectantly what her first word was, she looked truly underwhelmed when I replied I had no idea! Thankfully, when the children were little, I kept a diary for each of them where I tried to jot weekly notes about milestones like this, along with little everyday experiences like songs they loved, places we went and tasting ice cream for the first time. The frequency with which I managed to write in their diaries fell disappointingly short of my aspirations. I can see from the detailed pre-birth entries of my thoughts, hopes and concerns that things were going really well before my first child was born. However, the first post-birth entry isn't until my daughter is three months old and begins, 'I cannot believe this is the first time I have managed to write in this since you were born!'

Sadly, it also ends there – with no explanation for this truncated entry. It was another month before the next attempt, which at least was a bit longer. Most of the entries are written during rare moments of having nothing to do – like sitting on a plane without a child on my lap. Each entry sounds incredulous that I have not managed to find a minute to write anything for weeks/months (followed by an attempt to summarise whatever remnants of the preceding period were still in my brain).

Finally, there are also the mementos that baby shops and the Supermoms on Instagram guilt you into feeling you should be creating – such as framed pictures of your newborn baby's handprints/footprints next to their photograph. They range from simple paint prints on a piece of paper to more adventurous ones made of clay framed on pink or blue backgrounds or (I kid you not) professional 3D bronze images. As I am less than gifted in the art department, it was stupid of me to consider attempting even the simplest of these but one day I naïvely succumbed to feelings of maternal inadequacy. How hard can it be, I thought, to dip my baby's foot in poster paint and make a print on a A4 page? What I failed to appreciate is that no self-respecting warm-footed baby would let anyone put cold paint anywhere near them! The outcome was, unsurprisingly, a wooden floor covered in red poster paint, an emergency bath for both baby and Mommy and a washing machine hastily loaded with every stitch we had on.

PART II

THE BURDEN OF THE INVISIBLE JOB ON WOMEN

18

Who Actually Does the Invisible Job?

Adisproportionate amount of the responsibilities that make up the Invisible Job are borne by women. A major global report by the International Labour Organisation and Gallup found that women actually do 76.2% of all unpaid caring work (9). On average, women spend 4 hours and 25 minutes per day on unpaid caring activities – defined as looking after children and older relatives and doing household activities – while men spend on average 1 hour and 23 minutes on these activities. These averages encompass many underlying variables, which it is important to unpick by country, employment status, income and education.

Fathers typically spend longer hours engaging in paid work than mothers, an activity that is also of enormous benefit to the family, as it provides necessary income. Therefore, in a family unit where a father is the breadwinner and the mother is not engaged in paid work, one might surmise that perhaps, overall, men and women in such an arrangement spend equal numbers of hours working – only that they contribute in different ways. However, the ILO–Gallup report shows that this is not the case. When the total number of hours spent on paid work and unpaid caring work are combined, women's working days are still longer overall, at 7 hours and 28 minutes on average, while for men the figure is 6 hours 44 minutes.

While this might not seem like an egregious imbalance at first glance, the figures firstly ignore the vital question of whether gender differences, in terms of time spent on unpaid versus paid labour, occurs by choice; i.e. whether women would rather do more paid work and less unpaid work (the short answer is yes).

Second, the figures obscure what kind of activities men and women are including when they respond to these surveys on time spent on household or parenting responsibilities. Mothers tend to spend more time (and a greater proportion of their time) than fathers on the more onerous and less flexible tasks, such as routine housework (e.g. cleaning, laundry and cooking) and on the more routine care of children (e.g. feeding, bathing, and changing nappies). Fathers tend to invest more time in more rewarding and enjoyable tasks that involve engaging with children, such as playing and talking, accompanying them to sports classes, as well as on non-routine household tasks (such as DIY and gardening). These usually allow a degree of flexibility/choice around when the task needs to be done, along with greater variety in how to do it. This à la carte approach by many men of choosing the activities they contribute to is a key factor in women feeling dissatisfied with the gender imbalance in their relationship.

Studies have shown that for most women, it is the type of task their husband chooses to do, rather than the actual amount of time he spends on the task that determines whether she feels he is contributing equally to their joint parenting and household responsibilities. For both men and women, when asked whether housework is being shared equally between them and their partner, the concept of 'fairness' relates specifically to how the boring/repetitive jobs are shared (i.e. cleaning, cooking, laundry), not the total number of hours each person does (10). In fact, perceived fairness in how the Invisible Job is shared among couples is what leads to a happier and more stable relationship. Where this division is perceived as being fair, couples report better quality of the relationship, with better and more frequent sex (11). The actual proportion of work done by each person matters much less. It is not necessary for the workload to be split 50:50, as this fails to allow for relative differences in the preferences, capabilities, desires and availability of each person. An Italian study of 404 dual-earner couples with young children found that even where men did approximately a third of the total work, a majority of both men and women reported this felt fair to them. (12) Therefore, the goal is not for couples to judiciously divide the Invisible Job between them 50:50; instead, it is to honestly and generously figure out what feels 'fair' and then engage in this collaboration willingly.

Many people feel that being a parent is one of the best but also hardest things we do in life. While there are many highs, they would ideally like to engage in slightly more à la carte parenting. What does that mean? Obviously, we love our children and want to be there to encourage, comfort, support, teach, protect and look out for them always. It's just that on a day-to-day basis, if truth be told, not all of it is riveting stuff. In addition, we frequently encounter conflict between something we want/need to do right now and a parenting task that also needs our attention this minute. If we could choose to 'opt in' to the aspects of parenting that we want to do, at a time that suits us (in other words, à la carte), it would be ideal. But that's not how parenting works. It's a job for which you have permanent and constant responsibility – except when you temporarily entrust your children to the care of someone else (be it your partner, a childminder, babysitter, teacher or grandparent). These 'temporary staff' then hand them back to you. While mothers fundamentally understand that they are part of the 'permanent staff', fathers sometimes act like part of the temporary staff, i.e. willing to opt into child-care responsibilities for specific periods or activities but at the same time, keen to maintain the freedom of being able to hand them back afterwards.

Returning to the number mentioned earlier (that 76.2% of all unpaid caring work is done by women), the third point to highlight is that it tells us nothing about why there is such an imbalance between the sexes. This has barely changed over the last forty years, despite the enormous increase in the numbers of women in the workforce during this period. And most importantly, numbers alone tell us nothing of the deleterious impact that shouldering the majority of the Invisible Job has on women throughout their lives.

Women today are led to believe that gender imbalance is largely a thing of the past; that we live in an era where women are free to achieve their potential on an equal footing with men. Yet the reality is that we are still miles away from gender equality. This is true both in low-income and high-income countries and the main reason for this is the time women are obliged to spend daily on the Invisible Job (i.e. unpaid caring and household responsibilities). Between 1997 and 2012, the time spent per day has only decreased by 15 minutes, i.e. 1 minute per year. At this rate, the International Labour Organisation estimates that the gender gap for unpaid caring responsibilities will not disappear until the year 2228, i.e. 207 years from now.

Doing the Invisible Job is important in all families, as it ultimately benefits everyone in the household. Conversely, if nobody attended to it, all members of the family would suffer. When the details of what the job encompasses are understood clearly by both partners, both appreciate its importance. However, where the majority of the Invisible Job is conducted by only one partner (and this is often the woman), the true extent of what it entails, and the value it brings to the family, are markedly underestimated. So too are the negative consequences for women.

Even when men do have an appreciation of what the Invisible Job entails and understand the challenges associated with it, globally they are still not taking on their fair share of it. And at a societal level in many countries, welfare systems continue to be designed based on the assumption that the Invisible Job is a woman's responsibility, regardless of whether she has a full-time paid job of her own.

GLOBAL DATA

A pivotal report published in 2019 by the International Labour Organisation called *A Quantum Leap for Gender Equality* (13) reveals that across the world, the people who carry out unpaid work on a full-time basis are almost exclusively women. Globally, 606 million women of working age (21.7% of the total number) are engaged in unpaid caring work on a full-time basis. In sharp contrast, only 1.5% (41 million) of all working-age men are. This obligation to undertake unpaid caring work is the main reason that so many women globally are currently outside of the workforce. In fact, there is a strong correlation between the gender imbalance in unpaid work per country and the likelihood that women in that country engage in paid work, either on a part-time or full-time basis. In other words, where men do not share the burden of unpaid caring work with their partners, they are preventing women from taking part in paid employment.

The Organisation for Economic Co-operation and Development (OECD) conducts global analyses of how much unpaid work men and women do. Its most recent findings indicate that the average overall time per country ranges between 136 and 253 minutes per day (see Figure 18.1). The greatest proportion of this time is spent on routine housework, as depicted in Figure 18.2, which breaks this unpaid work down by category, using the UK as an example.

The research also identified that in all countries, women do more unpaid work than men, with Figure 18.3 showing how many minutes more per day.

Figure 18.1: Minutes of unpaid work per day by country (14)

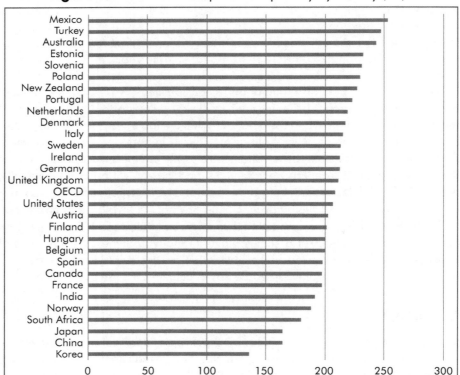

Figure 18.2: Minutes per day spent on unpaid work in the UK by category (14)

Average mins/day spent on unpaid caring work, UK (total time 211 mins/day)

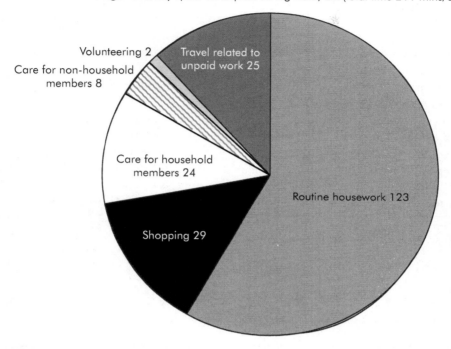

Figure 18.3: Additional time per day (in minutes) women spend on unpaid work compared to men (14)

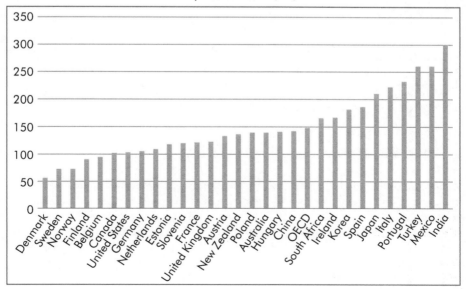

EUROPEAN DATA

The European Quality of Life Survey (EQLS) is a major piece of research carried out every five years by the European Foundation for the Improvement of Living Conditions. The most recent data set is from 2016. An excellent piece of analysis on this data was carried out in 2019 by Prof. Helen Russell and her colleagues at the Economic and Social Research Institute (ESRI) who looked at how unpaid caring work (which includes housework, caring for children and caring for older adults) is carried out in European countries (2).

In line with the ILO and OECD data, they noted that a gender gap in unpaid work existed across all 28 countries in Europe. It varied in size from 7.2 hours per week (in Sweden) to 20.2 hours in Greece, see Figure 18.4. The gender gap in unpaid work is narrowest in the Scandinavian countries where policies (i.e.

Figure 18.4: Modelled gender gap in unpaid work hours across Europe (2)

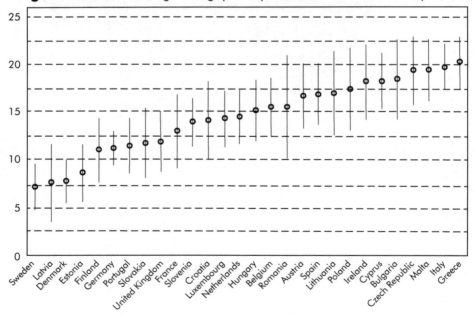

Notes: ESRI analysis of the European Quality of Life Survey 2016

Model controls for gender, country, age, education, paid employment hours, partner's employment, and age of children. An interaction effect between gender and country is included.
The data only includes responses for those who are involved in care responsibilities at least once a week, which makes the data more relevant when comparing men and women by not having the average data diluted by those who are not involved in these activities at all. Vertical lines indicate 95 per cent confidence intervals.

social services, tax, welfare and employment) have attempted to promote gender equality in both paid and unpaid work. These countries are closest to achieving a balance for men and women to engage in both paid and unpaid work (known as the 'dual earner/dual caregiver model').

Ireland was seventh in Europe when it comes to the size of the gender gap between men and women in caring responsibilities, at about eighteen hours per week. The UK performed much better, with a gender gap of approximately twelve hours.

Compared to the rest of Europe, Irish women are close to the top of the table when it comes to hours spent per week on unpaid caring and household responsibilities. As indicated in Figure 18.5, they spend close to a whopping 40 hours per week on unpaid work. Despite the strong cultural similarities between Ireland and the UK, the time spent on unpaid work by women in the UK is considerably lower (by about 25%), suggesting the availability of much more social infrastructure for caring responsibilities in the UK.

Note, too, that Irish men also rank one of highest in Europe relative to other countries when it comes to time spent on unpaid caring and household work (Figure 18.6). Together, these findings indicate a lack of available and affordable state or private infrastructure in Ireland to reduce the burden of caring and household work for families. While participation by women in the workplace has increased in recent decades, this has not been matched by the creation of adequate infrastructure supports for family caring and household responsibilities. This leaves the onus on individual families to manage these responsibilities themselves, or, if they

Figure 18.5: Modelled unpaid work hours per week per country, women (2)

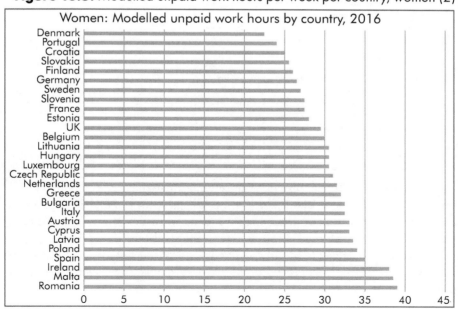

can afford it, to outsource (e.g. to cleaners, minders, carers) some of them. Due to this relative lack of support, combining paid work and caring remains challenging, with most of this unpaid caring work falling to women. The authors flag that this is partly because policies in Ireland (at the state and employer level) to encourage men to take on caring responsibilities are underdeveloped. As a result, far more women than men opt for reduced hours at work in order to shoulder unpaid caring and household responsibilities at home.

Figure 18.6: Modelled unpaid work hours per week per country, men (2)

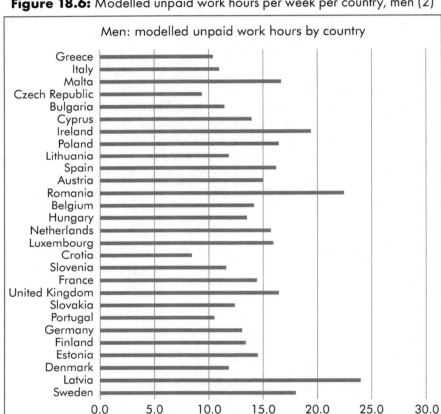

The countries with the greatest gender gap are southern European countries like Malta, Italy and Greece, where these responsibilities are largely left to families. There is very low provision of state support and instead women are expected to be the primary providers of unpaid care and household labour.

The two major elements of unpaid caring responsibilities are childcare and housework. The ESRI report looked at the male vs female contribution to each of these in Ireland.

Childcare

It found that 40% of women in Ireland are involved in childcare on a daily basis compared to 26% of men, a significant difference.

Involvement in childcare also differs between age groups. The age group most likely to be involved in childcare is that aged 35 to 49 years, with 70% of women and 48% of men in this age bracket providing care for children daily. Among those involved in regular childcare (i.e. at least once a week), the average weekly hours spent caring are significantly higher for women (42.6 hours) than for men (25.2 hours).

A really important point to appreciate is that hours spent on childcare are strongly influenced by the age of the youngest child in the household. Parents with a child under the age of five spend an average of 50 hours per week on childcare. In comparison, the average time is 41 hours for those whose youngest child is primary school age (five to twelve years) and 30 hours for parents whose youngest child is aged between thirteen and eighteen. When it comes to caring responsibilities, having a preschool child adds, on average, 34.9 hours per week to care time, compared to not having any children aged eighteen years or younger. Little wonder that life can feel like such a struggle for parents of preschool children!

Housework

Figure 18.7 shows the involvement of Irish men and women in housework by age category (2).

It found that 81% of women in Ireland report daily involvement in housework, compared to 44% of men. And not only do a higher proportion of women than men participate in housework, but they also spend much more time per week doing it than men: on average, women do almost twenty hours of housework per week, while men do seven hours (note that the reported median and mean figures are almost the same).

Figure 18.7: Daily involvement in housework by gender and age group

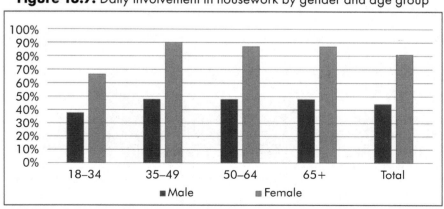

Data based on the European Quality of Life Survey (2)

Some might argue that it is reasonable for men to do less housework than women because they are spending more time in paid employment, thereby contributing equally but in a different way. Some 42% of women and 60% of men in this survey were in paid employment. Consequently, the average number of paid working hours for all women (19.6 hours per week) is significantly lower than for all men (31 hours per week). Among those in employment, men's hours are also significantly longer than women's (44 hours and 33 hours, respectively). Therefore, to test this theory, the authors modelled the time spent on housework (by both men and women) according to the hours they spend in paid employment to be able to compare them on an equal basis. As Figure 18.8 indicates, hours of paid employment do have a bearing on hours spent on housework. Men who are not in paid employment typically spend three hours per week more on housework than men who spend 40 hours per week or more in paid employment. And women who are not in paid employment spend six hours more per week on housework than women who spend 40 hours per week or more in paid employment. However, at each level of paid employment, women spend more time on housework than men. (The only category where this difference did not reach statistical significance was among men and women who both do more than 40 hours paid work per week.) This analysis therefore refutes the idea that men are contributing equally to the household but just in a different way.

Figure 18.8: Modelled housework time for men and women by employment hours (2)

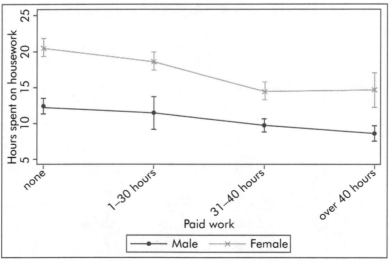

Analysis based on data from the European Quality of Life Survey 2007–2016. The interaction between gender and paid work hours is not significant, showing the gender gap is the same in all categories.

The authors also investigated what factors affect the volume of household work. The findings are very interesting:

1. *Having preschool children* leads to an increase of 7.9 hours per week spent on housework (11 hours for women and 6.5 hours for men).
2. For women, *having a partner*, whether they are employed or non-employed, increases time spent on housework. However, for men, having a partner who is not in employment lowers the time the spent on housework per week (compared to single men) by 2.2 hours. Does this fascinating observation imply that, in Ireland, a man goes from being looked after by his mother at home in his youth to being looked after by a partner, after transitioning briefly to a period of independence as a single man (presumably outside the family home)? Note that it is not possible to conclude this is indeed the case because the EQLS doesn't compare or collect data for individual couples.
3. *Level of education* is also an important variable: women with third-level education do 4.6 hours per week less housework than women with secondary school education, independent of age and of hours of paid work. This could either be due to differences in gender equality expectations or reflect the fact that women who have completed university have higher levels of disposable income and can therefore outsource housework to cleaners. The authors point out that if higher education was associated with greater sharing of the domestic workload in couples, we might expect more highly educated men to do more housework. However, they found that men's housework time also decreases the more highly educated they are.

Summary of total unpaid caring and household responsibilities in Ireland and UK

- Women in Ireland spend, on average, 21.4 hours more than men on total unpaid work per week. Even when you correct for age, level of education, hours of paid work and family structure, women still do an average 15.9 hours more unpaid work in the home per week than men.
- Unsurprisingly, the presence of children (particularly younger children) correlates strongly with total unpaid workload.

Data from the Office of National Statistics reveals that in the UK women carry out, on average, 60% more unpaid household work than men, typically doing 26 hours per week, compared to 16 hours for men (16) – see Figure 18.9.

Women in the UK do roughly twice as much as cooking, childcare and housework and vastly more laundry than men. The only area of unpaid work where men spend more time is in the provision of transport. However, this measure includes all time spent driving themselves or others around, as well as commuting to work. Not quite the equivalent of time spent doing laundry for the whole family!

Figure 18.9: Average hours of unpaid work done by men and women in the UK by category

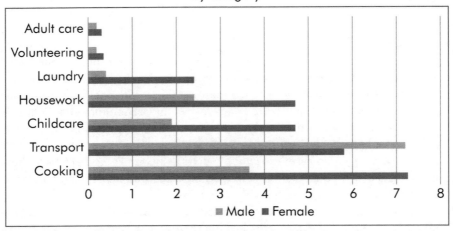

Data based on UK Harmonised European Time Use Survey 2015 (16)

Analysing the data further shows that in the UK this imbalance between women and men in time spent on housework exists across every age category (Figure 18.10).

However, the people carrying by far the greatest burden are women on maternity leave, who spend an average of 60 hours a week on unpaid household and caring work. This includes 37 hours engaging with their child/children, 8 hours cooking, 7 hours on housework, 2 hours on laundry and 6 hours transporting themselves or others.

At the other end of the scale are full-time students, who only spend 12 hours a week on unpaid work, half of which involves simply getting from A to B. Ah, the good old days!

Figure 18.10: Average hours of unpaid work done per week by age, UK (17)

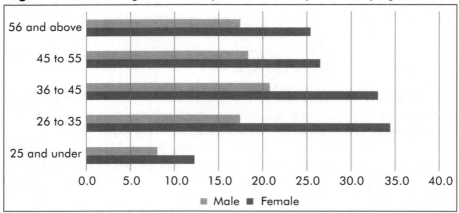

Eurostat

This second large set of European data (18) broadly echoes the findings of the EQLS. It found that, across all member states, women are doing a much larger share of childcare, cooking and general housework than men. In the EU, 93% of women aged 25–49 (with children aged under 18) looked after their children on a daily basis, compared to 69% of men. Figure 18.11 illustrates the pattern of gender imbalance by country very neatly. The longer the line separating the darker circle (men) from the lighter circle (women) for each country, the greater the imbalance in responsibilities.

As in the EQLS, differences were most marked in countries associated with more rigid gender roles such as Greece (where 95% of women did this work vs. 53% of men) and Italy (where the figures were 81 % and 20 % respectively). However in countries with the most egalitarian outlooks on parental roles, these differences were much smaller – for instance Sweden, where 96% of women and 90% of men respectively were involved in daily childcare and education.

When it comes to cooking and housework (Figure 18.12), the same patterns were observed but with even more marked differences between men and women. Overall, 78% of European women cooked or carried out housework on a daily basis, compared to just 32% of men. The greatest discrepancies were seen in Greece (85% of women versus 16% of men) and the most equal countries were Sweden (again!), where the figures were 74% of women versus 56% of men, and Latvia, which recorded 82% of women versus 57% of men.

Figure 18.11: Proportion of adults aged 18 and over (with children) engaging in the care and education of their children every day (18)

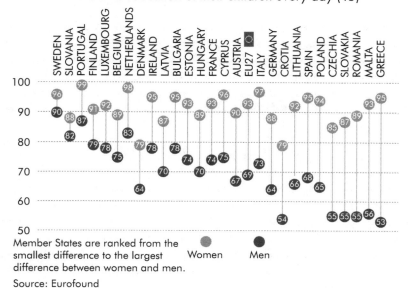

Member States are ranked from the smallest difference to the largest difference between women and men.

Source: Eurofound

Figure 18.12: Proportion of adults aged 18 and over cooking and/or doing housework every day (18)

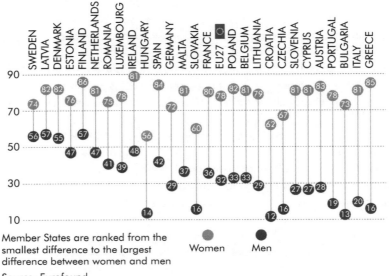

Member States are ranked from the smallest difference to the largest difference between women and men

Women   Men

Source: Eurofound

US DATA

For the past few decades, the US Bureau for Labor Statistics has been conducting regular population surveys that are a very useful source of data on the distribution of household and caring responsibilities in the US. The American Time Use Survey (ATUS) is conducted by telephone, with respondents asked to provide information on how they spent the previous 24 hours according to a broad range of specific types of activities – e.g. in paid employment, sleeping, eating, playing sports, relaxing, looking after children, watching TV, doing housework, travelling etc.

Using the data from the period between 2003 and 2007, an economist named Rachel Krantz-Kent quantified how much unpaid household work is carried out by people every day in the US (19). She defined 'unpaid household work' based on the following criteria:

a. *Unpaid* – i.e. any activities associated with one's paid employment or for which one would receive any kind of income are excluded.
b. *Economically productive* – i.e. 'activities that can be accomplished using readily available market substitutes'. This means that rather than doing the activity yourself, you could in theory have paid someone else to do it – for example, picking your child up from school, unblocking the toilet or vacuuming the car.
c. *Done for one's own household* – i.e. activities done for the benefit of someone who is *not* a member of your household, e.g. looking after your neighbour's child for an hour, are excluded.

As an example, time spent painting your own home would be included in the definition of unpaid household work because the activity is not done for pay, someone could have been hired to do it and it is done for the benefit of your own household.

Her report grouped activities into four main categories:

1. *Household activities*, which covers a very wide array of activities done to maintain a household, including meal preparation, household planning and organisation, laundry and sewing, lawn care, looking after pets and vehicle maintenance.
2. *Caring for and helping household members*, which includes all activities associated with looking after children and their welfare, health, education and activities, as well as looking after the needs of any adults in the household.
3. *Purchasing goods and services*, which includes a very broad range of activities, from grocery shopping to selecting and arranging insurance, security, veterinary, medical, maintenance and childcare services for the household.
4. *Travel related to unpaid household work*, which covers all travel time involved in the set-up, oversight and execution of the above activities. Travel is included as part of total unpaid household work when it meets the three criteria (a–c) above. For instance, time spent driving to the dry-cleaner's to drop off your husband's suit to be cleaned is eligible because it is a) unpaid, b) economically productive (you could otherwise paid have courier to drop off the suit for you) and c) done for the benefit of someone in the household.

They looked at how unpaid household work varied according to several interesting factors, such as gender, age and children – and reached some significant conclusions, as can be seen in Figure 18.13.

Figure 18.13: Average hours per week spent on unpaid household activities by sex and type of work done, US non-institutionalised population aged 15 and over, 2003–2007 (19)

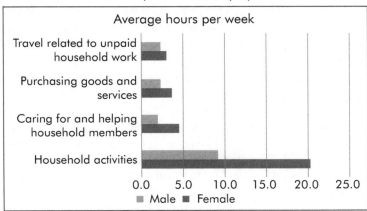

Women spend more hours per week across all four categories of unpaid household work, compared to men

They also found there were clear gender-specific differences within the category of household activities. For instance, women spent more time than men cooking and doing laundry, while men spent more time than women on tasks like mowing the lawn and doing household repairs.

Note that the data collected on time spent on unpaid household work simply reflects the answers respondents provided on the phone. It does not take into account factors that are likely to affect the time someone might spend on these activities, such as:

- Whether the person is skilled at a particular activity, e.g. repairing a broken shelf, and can therefore do it in a shorter time than someone unskilled in that activity
- Whether the person is motivated and/or capable of doing the activity well, for instance someone preparing dinner for the family might spend two hours cooking something elaborate and nutritious while someone less capable or less motivated might just put a frozen pizza in the microwave

The time people spend on both paid work and unpaid household activities varies importantly according to age

The percentage of adults in paid employment begins to increase sharply from the age of sixteen (the youngest age of respondents included in this survey) and reaches a stable plateau in our mid- to late twenties. Participation in paid employment then remains quite stable until after the age of 50, when people begin to exit paid employment for retirement. Between the ages of about 25 and 55, we see the period of highest participation in paid employment, at around 80% of the population surveyed (see Figure 18.14).

As would be expected, the number of hours per week people spend in paid employment almost mirrors the percentage participation in the labour force – i.e. across the population from the age of sixteen onwards, we devote increasing numbers of hours per week to paid employment, until reaching a steady state in our late twenties. This is maintained for about thirty years, decreasing gradually after the age of 50. The 35–44 age category represents the period in our lives when our engagement in paid employment peaks, with 82% of people in paid employment, working an average of 34.4 hours per week. The number of hours per week spent on unpaid household work lags behind the curve for paid employment. It rises steadily from young adulthood as we get progressively more involved in unpaid household work (probably corresponding with young adults moving out of home and taking on household responsibilities previously carried out by parents). Yet it

Figure 18.14: Average hours per week spent doing unpaid household and paid work and proportion employed by age, 2003–2007, US (19)

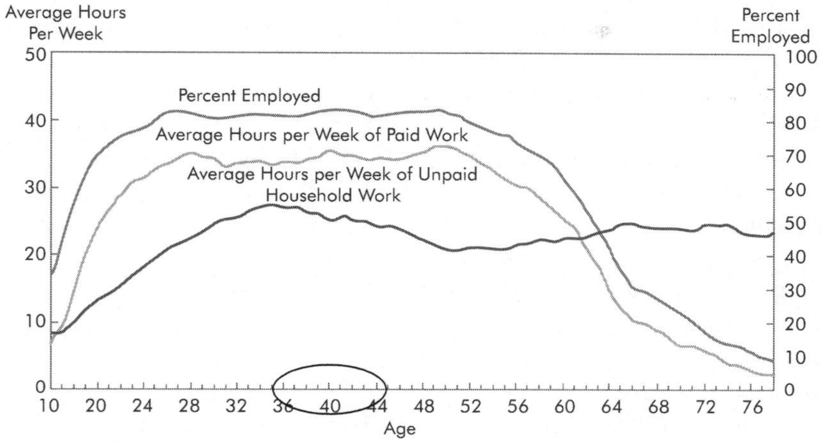

Note: Circle on X-axis added by author

only really reaches its highest demands on our time in our mid- to late thirties (which corresponds to the time many couples are caring for one or more young children). Given that this overlaps with the period when we are also devoting the most time to paid employment, it is not surprising that this is often the point where couples start to feel the pinch of not having enough time to get everything done. For both men and women, the total amount of time spent doing unpaid household work plus paid work peaks between ages 35 and 44, at about 60 hours per week for both men and women. This period (age 35–44) can therefore be particularly stressful for parents.

While people in this age category spent longer on several kinds of household work compared to other age groups, the activity that varied most was childcare. Women aged 35–44 spent an average of 33.1 hours per week doing unpaid household work, which is more than women in all other age groups. Men aged 35–44 spent an average of 18.3 hours per week on unpaid household work. For women in their late thirties and early forties, this period therefore potentially represents a time of peak stress, due to the double demands of professional work and unpaid household work. Based on conversations with many women I have spoken to, this also corresponds with an age when women begin to review their values and priorities in life, with many previously career-focused women switching their focus more towards family and children. Whether this represents a true change in their goals or is simply a mechanism for dealing with the growing demands on their time is worth exploring.

The presence/absence of children in the household strongly influenced the number of hours spent on unpaid household activities

To understand the impact of gender imbalance on caring and home responsibilities at the point in our lives when it impacts us most, it helps to look specifically at data representing men and women living with children. For individuals aged 25 to 44, the data shows that a major component of the total time they spent on unpaid household work was caring for and helping children in their household. The time parents spent doing several unpaid household activities also increased with additional children, e.g. time spent on food preparation, cleaning, laundry and sewing, caring for and helping children and travel related to unpaid household work. Parents living with four or more of their own children spent nearly eleven additional hours per week doing unpaid household work than parents living with one child. Looking specifically at the data from parents with children living with them, women spend an average of 38.1 hours per week on unpaid household work, while men spend an average of 20.9 hours. That's a difference of 17.2 hours per week! By comparison, the overall US population data for this period indicates that women only spent an average of 10.8 hours more per week doing unpaid household work than men. While still a significant difference, the additional work generated by children living with you is considerable. Another fascinating insight from this data is that the time mothers spent doing unpaid household work increased in accordance with the number of children they had; with the greatest increase observed between one child and two – an average of almost six additional hours per week. (While it increased for third and subsequent children, the incremental difference per additional child was lower.)

By comparison, the time fathers spent on unpaid household work didn't really change following the birth of second or subsequent children. In other words, although the total amount of unpaid household work increases with more children, the additional work appears to be done exclusively by mothers. (Fathers of two children spent 2.5 hours more per week doing unpaid household work than did fathers of one child, but fathers of three and four or more children spent about the same amount of time as those with two children.)

Fathers with one child spent an average of 40.8 hours per week on paid work (i.e. they are working close to a normal 40-hour week at the office). Having two, three, four or more children didn't really result in any change to their paid working week. In other words, having children doesn't really make any difference to the number of hours a man spends at work.

The picture is very different for women, however. Let's assume that before having children, women work similar hours to their male colleagues – i.e. a 40-hour week. Following the birth of their first child, the average number of hours worked by women goes down to 26.2 hours per week. This means that women either work fewer hours or drop out of paid employment completely. As this is an average figure, it is unclear what is predominantly driving the reduction – i.e. are all women reducing their working hours to a three-day week or do some women continue to work full-time while other women give up work completely (to stay at home looking after children and managing the home)? The reality is likely to be somewhere in between.

As the number of children in the family increases, the average time mothers continue to spend in paid employment decreases significantly. Mothers with four or more children spend an average of only fifteen hours a week in paid employment, while fathers with four or more children carry on working 40 hours a week in paid employment, as before. This begs the question: why do women with multiple children participate less in the labour force – or drop out of it completely? Since most of the incremental unpaid work associated with having children is done by women and since this workload gets progressively higher with each successive child, could it be that for many women eventually it just becomes too much? Krantz-Kent's analysis of the US Labour Data found that while 73% of mothers with one child were in paid employment, this declined steadily as the number of children in the family increased. Only 50% of mothers with four or more children were still in paid employment. On the other hand, the proportion of fathers in paid employment saw no such trend (where 84%, 90%, 89% and 87% of fathers with one, two, three and four or more children were in paid employment). Some men would see nothing wrong with this disparity between the paid employment status of fathers and mothers. Traditionalist men (as described in *The Second Shift*, Hochschild, 1989) view their role as being the breadwinner for the family and feel that, ideally, women should stay at home to manage the home and children. Traditionalist men believe that if they are successful enough financially, their reward is that there should be no need for their wife to work. Some women share this traditionalist outlook, viewing such an arrangement as the ideal harmonious family balance. Many more would view it as sexist, rejecting the assumption that a woman's place is 'ideally' in the home. Few parents would disagree with the idea that children benefit enormously from having a parent at home to provide emotional, social and educational support. While a range of childcare options exist (for those who can afford them), most children love the feeling of having a parent at home. However, it should not be automatically assumed that this parent must be the mother. Many men would love to be more involved in their children's upbringing and daily support and some, given the choice, say they would much rather be a primary caregiver to their own children than go out to work.

It is important to also consider the time spent by mothers and fathers on paid employment, because when total time spent on paid *and* unpaid work is aggregated, the data appears to suggest that fathers are dedicating just as much time as mothers to work overall.

Unsurprisingly, the data for the total US population indicates that men spend more hours on paid work in general and that women do more unpaid caring work (see Figure 18.15). When paid and unpaid work are combined, however, it suggests that men and women do an equal number of hours of work overall. It is important to establish, therefore, whether the imbalance discussed above simply reflects a split in how couples choose to share the demands of household responsibilities and the need to earn money for the household. Might it mean that men and women are contributing equally towards their household, only in different ways?

Figure 18.15: Average hours per week spent on unpaid and paid work by sex, US non-institutionalised population aged 15 or older, US, 2003–2007 (19)

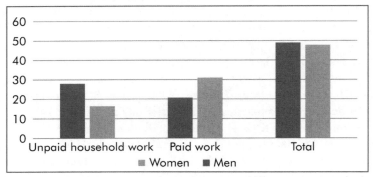

The problem with the population data collected by Krantz-Kent and colleagues is that it represents the average data for all men and women aged fifteen or over, i.e. it mixes up people who are working full-time, part-time or who are not employed at all. However, in many households today, both parents are in paid employment. Therefore, what we really need to know is how household responsibilities are split within couples where both people are in full-time employment. Luckily, insight into this can be found elsewhere in the US Labour Bureau statistics. Using the most recent dataset (2018), Table 18.1 specifically represents married men and women in full-time employment, living with own household children (aged under eighteen and six years, respectively). It shows the average time per week spent on household activities, caring for children and leisure activities.

This is more relevant, as it compares the contribution of men and women in similar situations, i.e. those who work full-time in paid employment and fit in any caring/household responsibilities around their paid job. If both parents are working full-time, it would seem fair to expect both to contribute equally to the Invisible Job.

Table 18.1: Average time spent on household activities in the US by married men and women in full-time employment, with a child aged under eighteen or under six years, respectively

Activity	Hours per week; household with child under 18 years		Hours per week; household with child under 6 years	
	Women	**Men**	**Women**	**Men**
Household activities*	13.1	8.6	12.2	8.4
Purchasing goods and services*	3.4	2.3	2.9	2.1
Caring for and helping household children*	9.6	6.2	15.9	9.4
Travel related to caring for and helping household children	1.8	0.9	2.1	1.0
Combined household/caring responsibilities	27.8	18.0	33.1	20.9
Leisure and sports	20.2	24.4	17.6	23.2

Data adapted from Table A-6A American Time Use Survey, Bureau of Labor Statistics 2020 (20)
*Household activities: Housework, food prep and clean-up, lawn and garden care
*Purchasing good and services: grocery shopping, consumer goods purchases excluding grocery shopping
*Caring for and helping household members – children: physical care, education-related activities, reading to/with children, playing/doing hobbies with children.

However, as Table 18.1 shows, among couples where both are in full-time paid employment, this responsibility is not shared equally. Mothers spend between ten and twelve hours per week more than fathers on unpaid caring work in the home, while fathers spend between four and five more hours per week on leisure and sports than mothers. And just as we saw with the European data, for both men and women, having a child aged under six years in the home markedly increases the total time spent on caring for children compared to older children (20).

19

How Do Men Feel?

Research carried out in the US in 2011 found that almost two-thirds of fathers felt that being a father was harder than it was a generation ago (21). However, it also found that the public has mixed views on whether today's fathers are making a good job of it. Only about one in four adults felt fathers today are doing a better job as parents than their own fathers did. Roughly one-third felt they were doing a worse job, and 40% thought they were doing about the same. Fathers themselves have similar opinions: 26% believe that today's fathers are doing a better job than their own fathers did. However, when asked specifically about the job they are doing raising their own children, nearly nine out of ten said they were doing a very good (44%) or good (44%) job; 11% classified themselves as 'okay' fathers, and less than 1% said they were doing a 'bad' or 'not very good' job as a father.

The outlook of fathers is definitely changing. The results of another survey conducted with 2,200 mothers and fathers across the US in 2015 found that fathers and mothers today share very similar feelings and aspirations about parenting (22). Some 90% of millennial and Generation X fathers say that parenting is their greatest joy and 86% say they work hard at trying to become a more effective parent. But they also feel they need better information and support and 60% would welcome information on how to be a better parent. Perhaps ensuring that men get access to guidance on being an effective parent may help them become more proactive in sharing responsibility for caring for their children with their partners.

A survey carried out in the UK in 2015 called 'The UK Dads Study' (23) looked at shifting opinions and values between fathers who are part of the so-called Millennial generation (i.e. aged 18–34) and Generation X (i.e. aged 35–44). It reported a trend towards increased involvement for fathers between the two most recent generations and prioritisation of their role of caregiver. Millennials stated that spending time with children was 1.3 times more important to them than providing for their family financially. Nine out of ten millennial dads claim to be at least partially responsible for shopping for the needs of their family (unfortunately, no further details are available regarding the actual extent of this participation relative to their partners!); 55% more millennial dads claim to be actively involved in this activity, compared to Generation X dads. Indeed, Figure 19.1 reflects an overall improvement in men's participation in many aspects of caring for children and taking responsibility for household chores between these two generations. On closer inspection, however, while it suggests that things are improving, the distribution of responsibilities between fathers and mothers is still far from equal. For instance, only 30% of fathers leading today's egalitarian charge claim even partial involvement in their children's morning or bedtime routine! And indeed, the nature of survey questions may not be conducive to painting a true picture of how much men are doing: having 'partial' responsibility for an activity may simply mean opting in whenever it suits them.

Figure 19.1: Which of the following do you have complete or partial responsibility for when it comes to taking care of your children? (23)

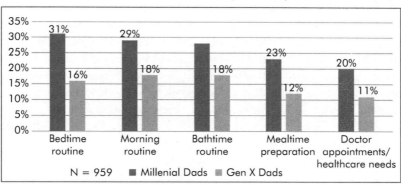

Many people would agree that today's young fathers are a different breed to men thirty years ago. While both my father and my father-in-law proudly profess never to have changed a nappy in their lives, many mothers today would not tolerate such a thing from their partners. And anyway, many fathers today wouldn't dream of behaving this way. Research carried out in the US in 2015 found that fathers were just as likely as mothers to say that parenting was extremely important to their identity (57% and 58%, respectively) (24).

20

What Is the Invisible Job Worth?

I nvisible work is notoriously hard to value. In her book *GDP: A Brief but Affectionate History*, the economist Diane Coyle estimates that if unpaid household work were included in the measurement of a country's GDP, the true measure of the UK's economy would be 74% greater than the figure currently used by economists. As to why it is not included, she ventures that, 'Generally official statistics agencies have never bothered – perhaps because it has been carried out mainly by women' (25). In recognition of this important omission in assessing the contribution that unpaid household and parenting work makes to the economy, the Office of National Statistics (ONS) introduced a new measure called the UK's Household Satellite Account, which accounts for and values unpaid production activity. This includes childcare, adult care, household services, as well as unpaid nutrition, transport, laundry and volunteering services, each of which is an important aspect of people's lives, and is largely missing from regular economic statistics such as gross domestic product (GDP) (17).

In fact, the ONS now officially refers to two measures: GDP and Extended GDP (e-GDP) – GDP plus unpaid household service work – and has updated its methodology to ensure this previously ignored data is now captured annually. In 2016, it estimated the value of UK unpaid household services at £1.24 trillion, which is larger than the UK's non-financial corporation sector and equivalent to 63% of the UK's GDP.

Figure 20.1 shows what this unpaid work comprises. While unpaid childcare and transportation accounted for the largest sections, at £352 billion and £358 billion respectively, note that laundry services in the home alone account for £89 billion unpaid pounds each year!

Figure 20.1: Value of unpaid household services UK, 2016 (billions)

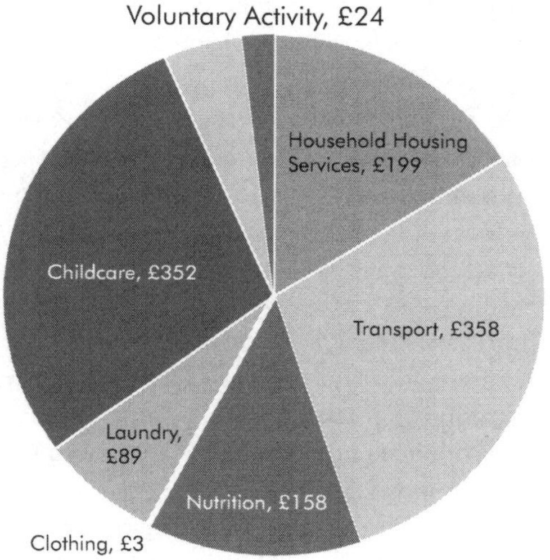

Figure created by author using published ONS data (17)

Until we understand the full extent of the Invisible Job, we cannot begin to estimate what its financial worth to an individual household is. Based on national data, the ONS quantifies its value at £18,832 per person. However, at the level of an individual family, where this benefit comes largely from one person's hard work, it can be hard to fully appreciate how valuable this contribution is to the welfare of the whole family. When estimating the hours of unpaid work carried out each week by women on maternity leave, the UK Office of National Statistics calculated the economic value of this work in 2015 as £762.75. Strange, therefore that the same government deems a weekly maternity benefit of £148.68 to be adequate (and less if this equates to more than 90% of the woman's previous weekly income)!

Perhaps the best approach to quantifying its value is to consider what supports you would need to put in place if the person currently doing the Invisible Job in your home became seriously ill or died. In households where it is largely done by the mother, this means estimating the financial cost of replacing the work a mother does for her family. This is an exercise a couple I know carried out to calculate how much life insurance they would need for life to continue as normal should one or other of them become seriously ill or die.

Estimating the required value of the husband's life insurance policy was straightforward: he worked long hours as a barrister but had limited involvement in either the care of their three children or household responsibilities. He left the house early each morning to go to work, returning typically around 9 p.m. to eat dinner, after which he often continued working late into the evening. From time to time, he also had to travel to courts in various parts of the country. Therefore, for the purposes of this financial exercise, his main contribution to the household was his (not insubstantial) salary. If he died or became unable to work, they would need an insurance payment equivalent to his annual salary every year for his wife to continue meeting all the family's financial outgoings – mortgage payment, school fees, food, clothes, holidays, etc.

What took longer to figure out was the required value of the wife's life insurance policy. She worked from home fifteen hours a week as a lawyer but the rest of her time was taken up with parenting and household responsibilities. If she was to suddenly become ill or die, they realised that the husband would no longer be able to continue doing his job because he only had the freedom to do so because she took care of everything else on behalf of both. She got the children up each morning, prepared breakfast and lunch for the children, drove them to school, ensuring they had with them whatever they needed for that day's school and after-school activities. After clearing up the breakfast things, three days a week she did five hours of paid legal work from home, with the other two days devoted full-time to parenting and household management.

After lunch she picked up the youngest child from school and kept him occupied until the older two finished school. Once home, it was full-on childcare for the afternoon (after-school snacks, homework, music practice, and keeping the youngest occupied) while cooking dinner for the children and staying on top of all school communications. There was also bath time, teeth to brush, nails to cut, stories to read, fights to referee and night-time hugs. After that there was laundry, cats to feed, litter trays to empty and household admin to attend to before preparing dinner for herself and her husband, who came home around 9 p.m.

While the financial contribution of her part-time job as a lawyer to their income was easy to quantify, they worked out that this was worth far less financially than all the unpaid work she did. Without her, the husband would not be able to leave the house at 7.15 a.m. to go to work and be missing all day, safe in the knowledge that his children's emotional, physical, educational and developmental needs were being met. He also didn't need to spend his evening cooking and attending to household chores and life admin.

If his wife was no longer there, he would need others to attend to all the things she did on behalf of the family. They realised this would involve hiring multiple people, as childcare alone would span a period from early morning to 9 p.m. five days a week (not even counting overnight cover needed whenever he had to attend court in other parts of the country). It would also require people with quite specific skillsets, not all of which you could expect any one individual to possess. For instance, the ability to cook, manage meal planning and food shopping, drive, understand and help children with various school subjects and provide guidance on practising piano and violin. It would also require the experience of being able to empathise with children, attend to minor mishaps and, more importantly, recognise if a child was really ill and manage things accordingly. And ideally, the energy and creativity to inspire/encourage children and make their days as fun as possible. Not to mention the kind of insight needed to recognise if a child might be struggling emotionally or academically and support them as needed.

Hiring someone to attend to all the housework would be straightforward enough but finding a person you could trust to manage all the household and life admin – insurance, utilities, banking and bills, repairs, arranging holidays, buying presents, etc. would be trickier. Ideally this person would also manage scheduling for children's activities, which would involve being the full-time point of contact for all school and extracurricular communications.

In the end, the couple concluded that it would be almost impossible to find an individual with the necessary skills who would be willing to take on this job. And that while it could be done by hiring several people to manage it between them, the resultant cost would be enormous. If you're in any doubt about the true value of the Invisible Job in your own home, this is a financial exercise worth doing.

Alternatively, you might like to try using the UK Office of National Statistics online calculator for a quick estimate of the annual worth of the unpaid household and caring activities you currently undertake. Follow this link and scroll down to the bottom of the webpage: bit.ly/valueofunpaidwork

21

Something's Gotta Give – The Impact on Women

Figure 21.1: Spinning plates, age 35 (Saverio Campione)

The total time women spend working each day mushrooms once children appear, between paid employment (which most women return to after maternity leave) and their unpaid parenting and home responsibilities. As simple mathematics dictate, the hours remaining for attending to every other aspect of their lives therefore progressively shrink. Women in this situation are too busy trying to keep all the plates spinning to realise how this time is being continuously eroded.

Mothers seem to develop a deep sense of obligation to their children and to their families that forces them to somehow continue to pile on more straws, even when the camel's back is clearly at breaking point. Something inside them simply can't bear the thought of their children or their family suffering. They will therefore ignore more and more of their own needs in order to meet those of others. In the tale of King Solomon, when the king announces to two women squabbling over a baby they both claim as their own that he will cut the baby in two and let each woman have half, it is the baby's real mother who shouts 'No! Stop! Let her have the baby!' Regardless of whether this ever really happened, the tale expresses an ancient understanding of motherhood and the sense of responsibility it evokes in women towards their children. Men also develop a sense of responsibility to their children when they become fathers, but it is often evident to a much greater degree in the daily actions and sacrifices made by mothers.

Mothers tend to put everyone else's needs first. Despite the cabin crew warning, 'Before attending to anyone else, please put on your own oxygen mask first!', mothers fail to prioritise their own masks. As a friend of mine once remarked, 'Now I know why Momma Bear's porridge was cold.' The family benefits in myriad ways from all the things a mother does every day. While this is great for everyone else, unless someone is in turn taking care of the mother, in the long term this is unsustainable. The singer-songwriter Imelda May puts this perfectly in the song 'Should've Been You': (26)

> I could tell you all the things I do for you
> But it's no surprise when you just roll your eyes
> And say 'Here we go again,
> She's gonna moan again.'
> But who takes care of me? ... It should've been you.

Women are not robots, though; machines that can keep going indefinitely. Eventually, something's gotta give. Unless women can offload some of the Invisible Job, whether their partner takes on more of it or they outsource some to a professional or simply decide with their partner that certain things will no longer be done, women's only option is to steal time from other areas of their lives. The areas frequently compromised are careers, financial security, health, personal goals/commitments, relationships and ultimately, mental wellbeing.

IMPACT ON A WOMAN'S CAREER

Before becoming a mother, women are free to work late or come in for early meetings as needed, to put their hands up for extra assignments, challenges and promotion opportunities or to participate in additional training to expand their expertise – just like their male colleagues. When they become mothers, women are often more restricted because they may need to finish work at a fixed time in order to take care of children. On top of this, taking work home must be juggled with the mountain of unpaid household responsibilities awaiting them.

Sheryl Sandberg may believe that the reason women fail to excel or reach their full potential at work is that they fail to believe in themselves professionally and 'lean in' at the boys' table. However, what she fails to acknowledge adequately is the impact of all the additional responsibilities outside of work that the majority of working women have to manage. It's not easy to put your hand up to be on the first flight to Madrid tomorrow for a meeting if this means arranging childcare at short notice. Equally, evening meetings that run overtime when you have child-care commitments are a real issue. Not to mention the challenge of taking work home when you know your evening will be taken up cooking, cleaning and getting children to bed.

If a woman has very strong support on the domestic front, whether in the form of capable professional help or family support from a spouse and/or grandparents, there is little she cannot handle professionally. Sheryl Sandberg herself had formidable support, not only because her husband took responsibility for much of the Invisible Job, but also because she benefitted from having a small army of assistants at work. Without such support, many women are tethered by an invisible cord that prevents them from leaning in.

The report *A Quantum Leap for Gender Equality* (13) reviewed data from around the world to assess how the gender imbalance of women shouldering most caring responsibilities in the home affects their career prospects. It found that, globally, women only hold 27% of managerial positions, a figure that has only improved by about two percentage points in almost thirty years. In higher-income regions, the proportions were greater: in Europe and Central Asia, the figure was 34.4% and in the Americas, it was 39.0%.

When you look specifically at data for men and women who are parents, it is clear that mothers of young children (aged under six) are penalised additionally, being the most under-represented group in management and leadership positions. Of managers who have young children, only 25.1% are women, while 74.9% are men.

However, this is not due to women being any less capable or qualified than men. In fact, the opposite is true: female managers tended to be better qualified than their male counterparts. Globally, 44.3% of female managers have an advanced university degree, compared with 38.3% of male managers.

Furthermore, women reached managerial levels faster than men. In middle- and high-income countries, female managers were typically a couple of years younger than male managers and in lower-income countries the difference was even more marked (about six years younger) (see Figure 21.2). One of the reasons for this is women's tendency to focus on accelerating their career as much as possible in the period prior to having children, conscious of an impending decrease in opportunities for career advancement later. The authors state that this 'faster-achiever' trait is also supported by LinkedIn profiles, which indicate that women reach director level positions at a younger age than men.

Figure 21.2: Median age of managers or leaders by sex (13)

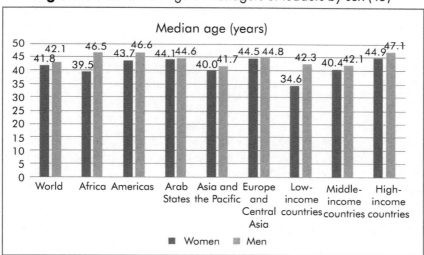

Notes: Age group 15 and older. Global, regional and income group estimates weighted by the male and female population in managerial and leadership positions. Percentage of employed population: World: 82%; Africa: 63%; Americas: 80%; Arab States: 33%; Asia and the Pacific: 89%; Europe and Central Asia: 82%; Low-income countries: 65%; Middle-income countries: 88%; High-income countries: 69%

It is also interesting to investigate gender imbalance at different levels of management. A survey of 347 Irish businesses conducted by the Irish Business and Employers Confederation (IBEC) looked at what percentage of managers in different types of companies at the junior, middle and senior management level were female (see Table 21.1).

It shows firstly that some career areas typically attract much higher proportions of either male or female employees – a phenomenon referred to as 'horizontal integration'. For instance, engineering and distribution companies typically employ many more men compared to women and therefore it is not surprising that there

Table 21.1: Proportion of women in management roles in Ireland (27)

Job Title	Junior Management	Middle Management	Senior Management
Finance/Accounting	59%	53%	39%
HR/Personnel	79%	80%	72%
Manufacturing	25%	17%	3%
Materials	45%	32%	20%
Sales and Marketing	43%	43%	28%
IT	24%	22%	17%
Financial Services	51%	45%	36%
Customer Services	67%	46%	53%
Environment	17%	23%	20%
Distribution	23%	22%	7%
Engineering	11%	18%	6%
Other	48%	37%	48%

are more men than women at every level of the organisation. Conversely, other career areas such as HR/personnel typically attract far more women than men and therefore there are naturally more women than men found at all levels in these organisations.

However, the interesting part is what happens over time to the proportion of women in management roles. Even where women represent a reasonable proportion of managers at junior management level, in almost all the industries profiled above, by the time they reach middle or senior management level, the proportion of women has dropped considerably. We know from other data that many women leave the workforce or reduce their roles to part-time ones in order to become primary care givers at home when their children are young. Some never return. Unless they have access to good but affordable childcare and household help, those who remain in work full-time end up in a compromised dual role of having a career while simultaneously managing the majority of the Invisible Job. They are therefore not as free as many of their male counterparts to compete for the top jobs in their organisation.

This view is supported by the results of a global survey of companies on barriers to women's leadership conducted by the International Labour Organisation in 2015, see Table 21.2. While many barriers were identified, the unequal burden of family responsibilities borne by women compared to men was number one, and the roles assigned by society to women and men was number two. Both have existed for decades and it is high time this changed.

Table 21.2: Barriers to women's leadership (13)

1. Women have more family responsibilities than men

2. Roles assigned to society by men and women

3. Masculine corporate culture

4. Women with insufficient general or line management experience

5. Few role models for women

6. Men not encouraged to take leave for family responsibilities

7. Lack of company equality policy and programmes

8. Stereotypes working against women

9. Lack of leadership training for women

10. Lack of flexible work solutions

11. Lack of strategy for retention of skilled women

12. Inherent gender bias in recruitment and promotion; management generally viewed as a man's job (both factors at joint twelfth position)

13. Gender equality policies in place but not implemented

14. Inadequate labour and non-discrimination laws

At higher levels of management, women are even more poorly represented. Across G7 countries, women only account for a tiny percentage of board members. In the US in 2016, only 16.4% of people on company boards were women. Research shows that this situation is only being rectified in countries where governments/organisations have put compulsory measures in place, e.g. quotas to increase female representation on company boards. Such countries include France, Germany, Italy and the UK, which have all seen dramatic improvements in short periods of time, as shown in Figure 21.3.

Being appointed to a non-executive board position is about having the relevant skills and experience, but is also a vote of confidence. It represents status, power and access to networks, and, for that reason, excluding women from boards reduces all of these for women.

The proportion of women who chair company boards is critically low; in 2019 it ranged from 0% in Germany to just 4.6% in the US. (13)

The board composition of employers' organisations don't embody gender equality either, with the majority having fewer than 10% women (13).

When it comes to the top of the tree, women are a very rare species indeed, with fewer than 5% of chief executives in the USA, Canada, the UK, France, Germany, Italy and Japan being female (13).

Data for Ireland compiled by the Central Statistics Office in 2019 reveals a more positive picture: for companies with 250 employees or more, one in nine CEOs were female (27).

Figure 21.3: Share of women sitting on company boards, 2010–2016

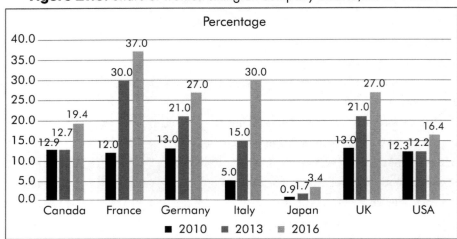

Source: OECD data 2018, based on data from largest publicly listed companies (13)

Several initiatives have tried to address the gender imbalance at the senior management, board and CEO level within organisations. One common approach has been to introduce quotas, such as the government initiative mentioned above in the UK, Italy and Spain requiring companies to ensure a specified percentage of their board members are women. Where such measures are supported by penalties or legal consequences for companies that fail to meet targets, the evidence shows that they are effective in this singular outcome, i.e. if they set a target for a minimum of 20% women on the board of a company, and there are significant consequences for this goal not being met, then it usually will be met.

There are also global initiatives being led by pioneering individuals and groups to try to address the gender imbalance in voluntary ways. One of the leading efforts is The 30% Club, a worldwide association of CEOs and chairs of medium to large organisations who are committed to achieving greater gender equality at senior levels in their organisations. Started in the UK in 2010 by Dame Helena Morrissey, with the aim of achieving 30% female representation on the boards of FTSE 100 companies, the movement now includes many country-level chapters around the world.

It was hoped that increasing the representation of women at the board level would automatically have a positive impact on gender balance throughout an organisation, i.e. that having more women at the board level would increase the likelihood of the CEO being female, along with the proportion of women at director level and so on, down through the company. But this hasn't happened. Why? Because this approach misses the point in two important ways:

1. While having more women at board level will encourage women to aspire to the most senior positions in an organisation, as we know, lack of role models is not the biggest barrier preventing women from occupying these positions, at least for women with caring responsibilities. At every level of management and leadership, the real issue facing women is the unfair expectation that caring responsibilities are women's responsibilities. Until these are shared equally by men, and until men and women are adequately supported through a social infrastructure that enables them to equitably manage both caring responsibilities and paid employment, women will never be free to achieve their potential and workplaces will never be equal.

2. Secondly, having a quota that only applies to women is an imbalance itself, one that will (rightly) be resented by men. Even though there is nowhere in the world where men are currently under-represented at the board and senior management level, introducing female-only quotas may lead people to feel that women are being appointed to senior positions to meet a quota obligation, regardless of whether they are the best candidates for positions. A more balanced and sustainable quota approach would be one that ensures that neither sex predominates, such as the system that was introduced in Norway in 2002 (and became mandatory in 2007), whereby no more than 40% of any company board should comprise either men or women.

IMPACT ON YOUR FINANCIAL SECURITY

If a couple decide to manage the Invisible Job by one parent working reduced hours or taking a career break for several years, this has a significant financial impact on the person doing so. In the vast majority of couples, this person tends to be the woman. And while she will doubtless appreciate the impact it has on her earnings in the short term, she may not realise the full extent of the financial penalties she will incur in the medium and long term.

Reduced income – the gender gap

The gap between male and female incomes across the world (a discrepancy known as the gender pay gap) persists to this day, despite efforts to ensure that men and women doing the same work are paid equally. In 2019, the gender pay gap globally was 18.8%. In lower-income countries it was less pronounced, at 12.6% and in higher-income countries, where men earn on average 20.9% more than women, it was more pronounced (13).

EU data shows that in 2017, when comparing average gross hourly pay, women earned 16% less than their male counterparts, an improvement of just 0.2 percentage points on the previous year. The figures vary considerably across Europe, with high differences observed in Estonia (25.6%), Germany (21.0%) and the UK (20.8%) but quite low differences in Romania (3.5%), Italy and Luxembourg (both 5%) (18).

In the UK, the Office of National Statistics data report that the gender pay gap has been closing, slowly but steadily, over the last twenty years. In 1999, the median gross hourly pay for women in full-time work was 16.4% lower than men's (the mean was 20.5% lower). In 2019, the median difference was 9.0% and the mean was 13.1%. The gender gap for all employees (full- and part-time combined) is also narrowing but remains higher, reflecting the fact that pay for part-time work is typically lower than full-time work and that fewer women are free to work full-time due to other commitments. In 1999, the median difference between men and women's pay for all employees in the UK was 26.9% (the mean difference was 25.0%). By 2019 it had fallen to 17.4% (the mean difference was 16.3%). This was no doubt helped by the UK government making it a legal requirement in 2017 for firms with over 250 employees to publish their gender pay gap figures annually, after years of feminist campaigning.

Clearly it is important to ensure we are comparing like with like, given that certain types of work are better paid than others. When specifically comparing jobs within the same professional categories, an analysis of UK salaries in 2014 found that men still earned more than women working in the same category in each of the nine categories studied: managers, professionals, technicians and associate professionals, clerical support workers, service and sales workers, craft and related trades workers, plant and machine operators and assemblers and elementary occupations.

There is another kind of pay imbalance that also contributes to the gender pay gap: fields of work that typically predominantly employ women tend to be worse paid than fields in which men are typically highly represented. According to ILO 2019 data, simply working in a company that consists predominantly of women versus one where men predominate is associated with a 14.7% wage penalty (13).

Some of the reasons postulated for large differences between areas of work that are male- versus female-dominated include:

- The fact that men are more likely to belong to unions (note that where women bargain collectively through a union with senior female representation, their pay is significantly improved)
- The practice of using an applicant's previous salary to determine their joining salary in a new organisation, which perpetuates the salary gender gap

In some fields, such as nursing or primary school teaching, average earnings have steadily decreased as the proportion of people employed in that field shifted from being predominantly male to predominantly female. The highest-paid jobs globally are currently in the STEM (Science, Technology, Engineering and Maths) fields, where, according to LinkedIn, women are under-represented relative to men due to a lack of digital skills.

Why does the gender pay gap exist? Are women less well educated, less qualified or less able than men? The number of Europeans completing primary, secondary and tertiary education continues to rise year on year. At secondary school level, on average, girls in the EU outperform boys academically and at present, more women in the EU have completed third-level education than men (33% versus 30% respectively) (18). Therefore, women are certainly not entering the labour force any less qualified than their male counterparts. However, as their careers progress, men earn progressively more than women and, as seen earlier, occupy 66% of all managerial positions in Europe. Why? The ESRI identifies that breaks in employment to attend to caring responsibilities are a key component of the gender wage gap. Part-time work, which is often undertaken to accommodate this, is also typically associated with lower wages and poorer promotion prospects than full-time work (2).

The motherhood pay gap

While women globally earn less than men, mothers also earn less than women without children, a further imbalance known as 'the motherhood pay gap'. As the most recent research on this conducted by the International Labour Organisation (depicted in Figure 21.4) shows, it affects women in different countries to varying degrees. In South Africa for instance, becoming a mother only reduces your pay by 1% compared to the average for women without children, whereas in Turkey the impact is an almost 30% reduction. In most cases, for women the financial effect of becoming a parent is negative (19 of the 23 countries listed below), whereas for men it has the opposite effect (positive (in 15 of 23 countries).

The motherhood pay gap is affecting an increasing proportion of women because more and more women are becoming mothers. According to 2018 US Census figures, 86% of women in the US aged between 40 and 44 (i.e. nearing the end of what is perceived as their reproductive period) are mothers (28). This has increased from 80% in 2006, as more women in this age group make the decision to become a parent. The greatest increase has been observed among women with advanced degrees and those who have never married: two decades ago it was almost unheard of for a woman in her forties with a postgraduate degree, who had never married, to be a mother. By 2016, a quarter of women in this category had one or more children. While the increase in motherhood has been most acutely observed among the most highly educated women, today more than half of US women currently in their forties who have never been married have at least one child. (28).

Figure 21.4: Motherhood and fatherhood wage gaps for selected economies (13)

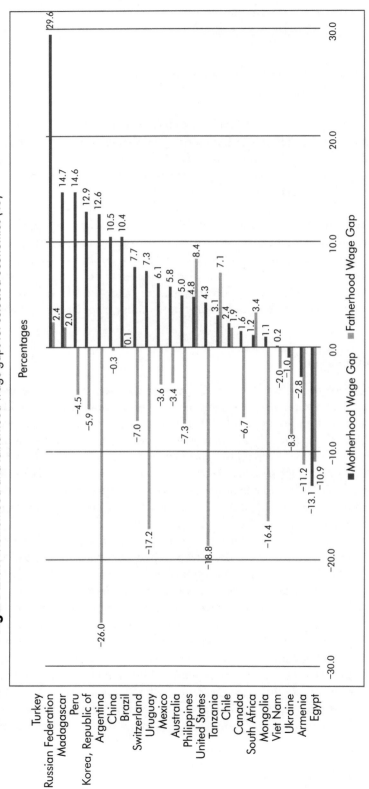

Percentages

Turkey
Russian Federation
Madagascar
Peru
Korea, Republic of
Argentina
China
Brazil
Switzerland
Uruguay
Mexico
Australia
Philippines
United States
Tanzania
Chile
Canada
South Africa
Mongolia
Viet Nam
Ukraine
Armenia
Egypt

■ Motherhood Wage Gap   ■ Fatherhood Wage Gap

Therefore, the motherhood pay gap is hugely relevant. There are several reasons for the motherhood pay gap, including:

a. *Reduced working hours,* as some women switch to part-time work to look after children.

     Often this diminishes women's professional image in the workplace, with some people identifying them more as carers than as key employees. This can be reflected in casual, even seemingly well-intentioned comments, e.g. when a woman is greeted by a senior colleague with 'Hi Eve, how are the kids?', rather than 'Hi Eve, how is that project coming along?'

b. *A temporary cessation of work during maternity leave,* when most men do not take similar paternity leave.

     Some women miss out on promotion opportunities during maternity leave, while others are overlooked as being 'not really promotion material', even after their return to work. This might be because they are viewed as less committed to their job if they have opted for flexible or reduced working hours to accommodate childcare responsibilities. Or it might be that they are considered by management as highly likely to have another child (and go on maternity leave again). Note that even women who never have children are unfairly impacted by employer bias that simply presumes that they will do so.

Curiously, the opposite is found for men, i.e. becoming a father seems to result in increased earnings, a phenomenon known as the 'fatherhood pay gap'. Why? It seems that becoming a father is a sign of maturity and stability in men; an indicator of a person likely to be committed to his job in order to support his family. In other words, 'ideal promotion material'.

A fascinating 2018 study in Sweden attempted to get to the bottom of when and why the gender gap develops (29). Researchers tracked the careers of highly skilled men and women in high-earning sectors, measuring their earnings by age to identify possible factors that might account for differences in earnings. Specifically, they chose to study business and economics graduates working in the private sector in Sweden, starting at age 25 and followed them up over twenty years.

By focusing on men and women with similar qualifications working in the same industry sector, they could accurately investigate whether differences were gender-based or whether other factors, such as the kind of firm men and women choose to work in or a tendency to switch firms more frequently in search of higher salary might account for it. The authors also specifically examined the impact that becoming a parent had on the earnings of both men and women, using childless men and women of the same age as controls in their models. They discovered several things: As expected, the data confirmed that even within a tightly defined industry, among men and women with the same qualifications and experience, a clear gender pay gap existed, as Figure 21.5 shows. It represents the change in

Figure 21.5: Profile of [log] wage by age, men and women (29)

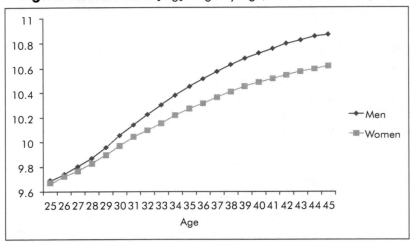

their wages over time, using a log scale on the Y axis, instead of a normal linear sale. This makes it easier to meaningfully interpret the percentage change in wages over this long period.

While the starting wage for men and women was effectively the same at age 25/26, by age 45 there was a large difference between men's and women's salaries. This confirms the general gender pay gap pattern seen in broader study populations. But what the researchers wanted to get to the bottom of is the critical question: *what* is driving this wage divergence over this period? How do wages change as these men and women accumulate experience in their roles and might it have anything to do with the arrival of children?

Their findings are very interesting: as shown in Figure 21.6, while the birth of a first child had little impact on earnings for a man, for women it was associated with a marked drop in earnings.

The authors therefore analysed the salaries of men and women over time, with reference to the year their first child was born. As can be seen from the two curves in Figure 21.6, beforehand there is little difference between the salaries of men and women – in fact, women were seen to earn slightly more than their male counterparts and work more hours, especially in the period shortly before having their first child. The authors believe this represents women's attempts to get as far as they can in their careers before making the decision to have a child, knowing that afterwards they will be forever playing catch-up with their male colleagues. What is fascinating to observe from the curves, however, is the dramatic impact that having a child has on women's earnings: one year after the birth of their first child, women's salaries had nose-dived. Conversely, there was no noticeable downward impact on men's salaries when they became fathers – in fact, a small but sharp increase was observed in the first year. It was also striking that for the next ten

Figure 21.6: Profile of [log] wage according to time (in years) from birth of first child (29)

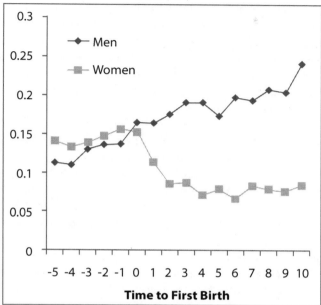

years the salaries of mothers remained on average at the low level they fell to after having a child, while fathers' salaries continued to increase steadily as if nothing had happened. This reveals that the critical point where the gender gap starts is shortly after the birth of a couple's first child. It is no coincidence that this is also the period where women take time off work to attend to childcare.

In a more egalitarian society, both men and women would be free to reduce their hours or take a short career break in order to be able to meet the demands of being a parent during the years when these demands are at a peak. In today's society however, few companies show such progressive attitudes to assisting employees in achieving a feasible work–life balance. And we are even further away from a society where men who elected to do so would not have their dedication to the job questioned by their employer.

Reduced pension and long-term financial security

Obviously, women suffer financially in the short term if they work fewer hours per week or take time off for a period to manage family and household responsibilities. It is less well appreciated that women's lower salaries and shorter working lives also bring lower lifetime earnings, reduced pension entitlements and a greater risk of poverty in old age, relative to men (30).

One could argue that in a committed relationship where a couple shares total household income, perhaps this shouldn't matter. However, it can leave women in a vulnerable position later in life. If the relationship ends, for instance, the woman may end up being reliant on only her own pension to support herself in old age and if this pension is very small, she may struggle financially. Equally, the woman may feel unable to leave the relationship for the same reason – lack of financial independence. This situation may be used by some men to wield power over their partner, creating an unequal relationship. If a man has a generous pension amassed over forty years of full-time work, he is not only financially secure but in theory also an attractive catch in the older dating game.

Frequently, the solution to coping with the demands of the Invisible Job is for a woman's career to take a back seat – or no seat at all – i.e. for her to focus instead on children and the household. However, although this may have been a joint decision, made at the time in the best interests of a young family, years later it can end up coming back to bite her. Meanwhile, things work out just dandy for the husband, who neither had to pull his weight doing the Invisible Job nor put his long-term financial security at risk.

The design of pension schemes heavily influences whether the short-term income penalties suffered by women who reduce or cease paid employment (to take up caring responsibilities) continue to impact them in old age. Many employer private pension schemes are based on defined contributions, meaning that if a woman stops drawing a salary to attend to family responsibilities, whether for a few months, a few years or half of her life, she also stops accumulating pension contributions (both employee and employer) during this period. Therefore, her resultant pension on reaching retirement age will be markedly lower than it would have been had she remained in her job throughout this period. One way to remedy this unfair outcome, at least in the case of lost pension earnings during maternity leave, would be for employers to continue to pay both the employer and employee share of a woman's pension contribution during her maternity leave. In the longer term, the financial situation of women who give up work to attend to family responsibilities could be protected through pension schemes that facilitate the husband diverting half of his pension to his wife's pension fund.

In recognition of the years we are likely to live beyond retirement age, and the need for everyone to maintain a minimum standard of living during this period, a more equitable approach to pensions overall would be for the state to ensure all citizens receive an adequate pension in old age, funded through social insurance. This should take into consideration both paid work and unpaid caring work carried out by men and women throughout their lives.

IMPACT ON THE BODY

Physical health

If all your time is taken up with your job and home responsibilities, it leaves little room for looking after yourself physically, both in terms of maintaining your fitness and attending to personal grooming. The former is important because if you don't allow time for at least a few hours a week of cardiovascular exercise, your body will start to fail. Even over the course of a few months, lack of exercise will mean your muscles will lose their tone and strength and your fitness will decline. This makes all the daily running around you do, both at work and home, harder. On top of this, depriving yourself of regular exercise means your overall energy levels will be lower, which is exactly what you don't need when you are already working flat-out. Even small regular doses of cardiovascular exercise, like a fast twenty-minute walk to work every day, bring significant benefits in terms of energy levels and alertness.

Having even a small window in the week to exercise also provides important mental and physical respite from a tightly packed schedule. It represents a chance to just let your mind switch off and wander; to reflect absent-mindedly on the events of the day/week/month and process how you are feeling – which is especially important if nobody else is enquiring about this! We get some of our best ideas when we are not consciously trying to come up with solutions. Instead, the answer might just appear while standing in a warm shower or walking along the canal watching the ducks. Getting out for a run or a bike ride without hearing 'Mum!' for 60 minutes also goes a long way towards recharging your mental batteries, making you better able to deal with the weekly challenges.

The other downside of allowing your work and family commitments to consistently get in the way of your weekly exercise is that your body won't look or feel the way it used to. Lack of exercise means you may not like what you see when you look in the mirror – that dress that doesn't look good on you anymore because your stomach is too big or your arms have no tone whatsoever. These unwelcome discoveries can make some women feel less attractive and undermine their confidence.

Feeling less attractive also impacts people's relationships with their partners and may reduce their interest in sex. Men, please note that suggesting to your wife/partner that she should therefore get to the gym more often is not a good idea, however well-intentioned. However, what many women would welcome is the offer to create space for her to have regular time to herself each week – for instance by the man holding the fort for an hour or two at a regular time during the week and managing whatever child-related activities/housework that may entail. Important point: do not tell your wife/partner what she should do with this window of time to herself. Chances are, she will jump at the chance to finally do some exercise/yoga. Or she may also use the time to attack things on her to-do list that she has been dying to get to for months. Sometimes, though, she might just choose to stick on some headphones and listen to music in bed or go for a quiet walk – simply enjoying not having to be available to anyone for an hour.

Pelvic floor exercises

I know this is not at the top of anyone's list of favourite conversation topics, but I'm afraid there's just no way we can ignore the leaking elephant in the room. I never gave the pelvic floor any thought before attending an antenatal class, where the instructor mentioned that looking after your pelvic floor is very important. If this gave me pause, however, it was probably only to ask myself if I knew what the pelvic floor is. Pelvic floor muscles (I now know) are a band of muscles that run like a hammock from the pelvic bone to the tailbone, supporting the bladder, uterus (womb), and colon (bowel). At the time, however, I was more interested in finding out what a water birth was and whether getting an epidural meant childbirth could be 100% pain free!

Talk of pelvic floor muscles surfaced again in antenatal class as our bellies grew to the point where various parts of our anatomies were being pushed down or out and trips to the loo were becoming more and more frequent. But we all just blamed it on the baby and presumed that close calls were just par for the course in pregnancy.

The pelvic floor may have been mentioned at my postnatal visit by the midwife, but I think I had bigger problems to contend with at the time. The first time I remember it coming up properly was at the free postnatal physiotherapy classes provided by the public hospital in London where my babies was born. By then, I was definitely receptive to hearing about pelvic floors, because mine was in need of some TLC, having recently pushed out a small cannonball. At that stage you are loath to discuss it openly but suspect that your pelvic floor is less reliable than it once was and needs to be fixed.

Even if you don't have access to physiotherapy sessions to help your pelvic muscles recover, there are plenty of useful books and DVDs available. And in theory, it all looks very doable – just do some exercises with names like 'the bridge' and 'tabletop' six times a day and apparently your pelvic floor will soon be as robust as an Angry Birds catapult. The problem is that new mothers at home with a small baby simply don't have the luxury of being able to get out a yoga mat six times a day to do any kind of exercises; for many, just finding time to eat and shower every day can be challenging enough. Therefore, the all-important pelvic floor exercises may get bumped off today's schedule, and tomorrow's ... and may not get a look in the day after, either. Having realised all too late myself just how important it is to somehow make time (or more accurately, demand time!) for pelvic floor exercises after having a baby, when my sister had her first child, I bought her a copy of the exercise DVD I got from my physiotherapist. Although I had completely failed to dedicate time to this important activity, I hoped that if I impressed upon her just how important it really was, she would fare better than me. However, it appears not: when helping her pack up for a move to Australia with her four children nine years later, I came across the pelvic floor exercise DVD, still unopened.

So why should women (or their partners) care about pelvic floors? Well, although this important health matter is not given nearly enough airtime, the first reason is that a weak pelvic floor (and damage that may occur to this area in childbirth) can result in urinary (and bowel) incontinence, debilitating and embarrassing conditions that no woman wants to live with. While it is more likely to affect women as they get older, it can affect women of any age. The actual prevalence of urinary incontinence among women is uncertain, but a review in 2013 of all the published studies involving European women found it ranged from 13.1% to 70.9%, increasing with age (31). Urinary incontinence is also among the most common reasons for women aged over fifty in the UK to be admitted to hospital for elective surgery.

The second reason is likely to be of equal interest to men and women: While the pelvic muscles are important for controlling the flow of urine from the urethra, they are also vital when it comes to contracting vaginal muscles during sex. As a country that believes firmly that good sex is as essential as good wine, the French are not shy when it comes to safeguarding important elements of female anatomy. For this reason, after childbirth, all French women are provided with a vaginal probe that they bring with them to a series of free postnatal physiotherapy sessions. The physiotherapist connects it to a machine that emits electric waves, stimulating the muscles of the vaginal wall. These strengthen the pelvic floor muscles, ensuring that French vaginas return to peak sexual performance as soon as possible and avoid organ prolapse. So, for men, ensuring that their wife/partner gets protected time to focus on her pelvic floor exercises may be a very wise move indeed.

Personal grooming

Even if reluctant to publicise it, women like to look good – at least sometimes! They also know that looking good requires a bit of effort. Following childbirth, for a while your expectations of what 'looking good' means will plummet to a point you might never have envisaged back in the day. Leaving the house without both shoulders of your jumper smelling of sick or your leggings smeared in snot is now considered a result. In the dark days of being a new mother, weeks may go by without you glancing at yourself in the mirror and when you do, you may not recognise the dishevelled mess looking back at you. But fear not, things improve. Chances are, you may never again get to devote an entire evening to 'getting ready' to go out – since getting out at all is quite the achievement – but as your babies start to sleep through the night, you will begin to believe that it may be possible to look (and feel)

– like yourself again. And while few women would ever put themselves in the 'high maintenance' category, we all need time to do whatever we deem to be 'essential maintenance'. Time to stick a 'Women at Work!' sign on the bathroom door for an hour and emerge feeling sexy. Yes, believe it or not, men, many women in their thirties and forties like to dye their hair and wax and groom themselves in various ways every few weeks (the finer details of which there is no need to elaborate on further here).

Having no time to attend to self-grooming is a bad thing for women. It's important to us to feel presentable, both in terms of our professional image and our personal/social life. You feel like a million dollars when you finally get a chance to leave conditioner in your hair for more than a microsecond or rediscover what a loofah does. And dare I push the boat out by mentioning possibly even painting your toenails occasionally?!

However, listen up men: although you may not be personally bothered about whether your partner has made it to the hairdresser in months or when her skin last encountered body moisturiser, trust me, it's in your interest to care. If you find yourself saying you wish your wife was more interested in sex, hold this thought: when a woman has had a little time to dedicate to personal grooming and feels ready to walk down a runway in a bikini, that's also when she is open to sharing every inch of her beautiful body with you.

IMPACT ON YOUR PERSONAL GOALS, KNOWLEDGE, INTERESTS AND COMMITMENTS

When all your waking hours are spent working and looking after family, there may be no time left for things you might like to accomplish for yourself.

Before having children, we have so much time, although we may not realise it. In our late twenties, we always feel we could do with more time for the things we love doing – like socialising, sports, travelling, reading, watching films or going to gigs. As well as those things we keep meaning to do – organise our flat, write a decent CV, do a photography course, file our tax return. After the birth of your first child though, it's as if someone has vacuum-packed the world and removed 95% of the hours in it. (A further compression of universal time happens when your second child arrives.) For a while, making choices about how to spend your free time becomes a distant memory. Wandering past a photo of yourself on the wall, it can be tempting to lean in for a Robin Williams moment and whisper 'Carpe diem' to younger, child-free you. But you adapt; you learn to focus in order of strict priority on the things you absolutely must do until eventually you start to gain ground and keep your chin above water. While this allows you to function, there are some casualties.

No clue what's going on in the world

You know how there's always two minutes to have a quick look at newsfeeds at work each morning to make sure you haven't missed anything important going on in the world? Or a few minutes during the day to click on a link someone has just sent you on WhatsApp? Well, for mothers of new babies trying to survive maternity leave – as well as mothers who have now returned to work – those minutes just don't exist.

One thing that often goes out the window when you become a parent is keeping up with current affairs. If you're lucky, you might catch the news on the radio on your commute to/from work but you will probably have no time to read newspapers, watch TV or look up news websites. If something huge happens in the world it may filter through to you in quick conversations at work or with a taxi driver, but otherwise there's every chance you will not know about the massive volcano that erupted in Iceland four days ago and only realise there's a national election taking place because of the posters on your road. This does not imply a lack of interest in politics or world affairs, simply that you don't have time to listen to commentators debate it. You'd love to sit and read a newspaper but when it comes to choosing what to do with any time left after work and attending to the needs of a family, keeping up with current affairs usually doesn't make the cut. You may also have 2,000 unread personal emails. You are not proud of it, but that's just how it is for now.

No time to pursue personal interests

Remember all those things you had on your bucket list before you had children? Like finally taking up the piano, which you 'temporarily' gave up when you were fifteen, brushing up on your language skills or joining a hillwalking club? If you are a new parent, even maintaining your closest friendships and social connections can be tough. Therefore it might be best to tip the contents of your bucket into a Ziploc bag, seal it up and put it in the freezer for a decade. You may be interested in exploring new personal goals or using your skills to contribute to society in a meaningful way, perhaps by using your professional expertise/experience to assist as a volunteer or by becoming politically active. However, if you have zero time, as Austin Powers would say, it just ain't gonna happen baby!

It can take a while to finally accept this new reality. You can feel very defeated/ cheated by the fact that there never seems to be any time left over for you. Determined to carve out time to do something for myself when my oldest child was about seven, I joined a local tennis club. However, in two years I only managed to play one game.

Before having children, my husband and I used to see a lot of plays. When we moved to Dublin I was really excited about the Dublin Theatre Festival. While we spotted the posters each year, for many years getting to it remained wishful thinking. For a decade, even reading books or watching TV became something that only other people did. I would sadly eye the bookshelf in the living room, full of books I would love to read if ever I had a free hour to sit on the couch.

Caring for others

While all these things would of course be very nice to do, they don't really matter. At least not compared to things that really do count, which you can never postpone or make up for later. Like when people we care about are ill or need our help but we don't have time to cook them a meal or do something kind to let them know we are thinking about them.

IMPACT ON YOUR SLEEP

It can be tempting to try to 'fit it all in' by getting out of bed earlier every morning like some self-help books advocate, or staying up until 2 a.m. to finish everything on your to-do list. When we have so much on, sometimes it can feel like there is no other option. Compromising our own sleep is often easier than saying no to demands at work or in other areas of our life as it doesn't create any visible conflict with others. However, most of us dangerously underestimate the consequences of not getting sufficient sleep, both in the short and long term. The ground-breaking book *Why We Sleep* by Professor Matthew Walker, a neurologist and neuroscientist, reveals just how critical sleep is to our wellbeing (32).

Why does sleep matter?

Lack of sleep limits our ability to learn, to remember things and make logical decisions. Getting sufficient sleep each night is also critical to our capacity to cope emotionally and calmly with everyday social interactions and psychological challenges. Insufficient sleep can lead to overeating, weight gain and diabetes. It can reduce fertility (in both men and women), increase the risk of stroke, heart attack and cancer, as well as weaken our immune systems and even trigger mental illness.

How much sleep do we need each night?

According to Professor Walker, scientific evidence clearly shows that all humans need between seven and nine hours of sleep every night. Margaret Thatcher famously claimed she routinely slept only four hours a night as Prime Minister of the UK and that this was sufficient. Professor Walker would disagree. In fact, he concurs fully with the findings of Dr Thomas Rath, who says, 'The number of people who can survive on five hours of sleep or less without any impairment, expressed as a percentage of the population, and rounded to a whole number, is zero.'

What are the short-term consequences of not getting enough sleep?

After sixteen hours of being awake, the human brain starts to fail and urgently needs sleep. If we don't get it, a series of physical and mental consequences will impact the body.

Poor cognitive performance

We need at least seven hours of sleep to maintain cognitive performance. This includes our ability to concentrate, learn, recall information we have taken in and create memories. When we are awake, the electrical activity going on in our brains resembles a series of individual shallow, rapid and uncoordinated movements. When we fall asleep, however, these uncoordinated electrical signals start to synchronise in a highly regular wave pattern called NREM (Non-Rapid Eye Movement) sleep. NREM is a deep phase of sleep, in which the brain carries out many essential restorative functions every night. While we sleep, our brain switches in regular cycles between NREM and REM (Rapid Eye Movement) sleep, the phase associated with dreaming. Each phase of sleep is important for different reasons.

One of the key functions of NREM sleep is learning and remembering. We use a part of the brain called the hippocampus to store short-term memories, for example a password we created today, the name of someone we met for the first time, or which level of the car park we parked in. The hippocampus has two limitations, however:

1. It is only a temporary storage area; unless we convert the information it holds into a more permanent type of memory, after a period it will just be wiped, much like images are cleared from a CCTV loop that is being re-used day after day.
2. There is a limit to how much information our hippocampus can hold, a bit like a maximum storage amount on a smartphone. Once we reach this limit during the day, we cannot remember any additional new information without deleting other information that is being temporarily stored in the hippocampus.

But good news: humans have an ingenious mechanism for transferring short-term information (from the hippocampus) to a long-term storage area of the brain (called the neocortex), where they are preserved carefully as memories. It's called sleep. During light NREM sleep, electrical pulses shuttle back and forth between the hippocampus and the cortex, emptying the hippocampus of short-term electrical information and preserving it as long-term memories in the cortex instead. NREM sleep therefore benefits us in two important ways:

1. It enables us to retain information we were exposed to before we slept – i.e. we learn and remember things more effectively. Several clinical studies have demonstrated how simply getting eight hours of sleep can enable people to

remember 20–40% more information compared to spending the same period awake.

2. Emptying the hippocampus while we sleep means that when we wake up, it is ready to take on a full load of new information– i.e. our brain is better able to absorb and process new information the following day (32).

Benefits can even be observed after a 90-minute nap, but the full benefits are reaped during a full night's sleep (i.e. seven to nine hours). The period in which most NREM activity occurs is towards the end of our sleep, in the early morning hours. Consider what this means for people who regularly get up early to catch a train/ flight or those who try to cope with the never-ending demands of housework by getting up an hour earlier to do some before going to work.

If we deprive our brain of a minimum of six hours of continuous sleep, it misses out on an essential and one-off opportunity to learn and create permanent memories. Little wonder, then, that mothers of newborn babies feel they are suffering from 'baby brain' – i.e. being incapable of remembering even the simplest things. Instead of recognising this as an inevitable physiological consequence of persistent sleep deprivation, exhausted new mothers berate themselves for feeling stupid and unable to think clearly. They fail to realise just how potent a torture tool sleep deprivation can be.

I have almost no memories of the three months following the birth of my first child. Luckily, I managed to jot down some notes in a baby diary I was trying to maintain at the time and my husband took lots of wonderful photos. However, without these, I would have almost no recollection of anything that happened during this unique period. While this is sad, understanding why it happened lets me view it more rationally. Given how sleep-deprived I was throughout this period – like all new mothers – my brain simply never got enough NREM sleep each night to turn each day's images and experiences (sitting temporarily in my hippocampus) into permanent memories (stored safely in my neocortex); in other words, the CCTV tape in my brain was just wiped each night.

Loss of creativity

This is another consequence of not getting enough sleep, highlighted in Walker's book. During NREM sleep, the brain combs through ideas and information and often combines them in unpredictable and creative ways. We experience this as dreams. While we sleep, our brains act like experimental pots where facts, situations and experiences can intermingle in uninhibited ways. How to arrange the periodic table came to the Russian scientist Dmitri Mendeleev in a dream. For years he had been convinced there was a logical way of ordering all the elements but the solution had eluded him. It wasn't until he fell asleep at his desk that his brain was free to piece the answer together in a pattern he had been unable to see while he was awake; 'I saw in a dream a table where all the elements fell into place as required. Awakening, I immediately wrote it down on a piece of paper'.

Especially for people whose work might involve coming up with creative ideas, missing out on the rich dream-filled periods of sleep comes at a cost.

Poor mental health

When we are sleep-deprived, we are less able to handle social interactions and psychological challenges. Prof. Walker considers REM sleep an essential commodity that facilitates our 'coolheaded ability to regulate our emotions each day'. There are several reasons why:

1. REM sleep increases our ability to interpret social signals like facial expressions and hand gestures and to gain insights into group behaviours. When our brains get insufficient REM sleep, we are less able to function at a high level in inter-actions with others, a skill important to all of us in our daily lives, but vital for remaining calm under pressure and being able to negotiate with others.

2. Sleep also helps us process traumatic experiences. When our brains dream about stressful or painful experiences we have suffered, it acts like a therapy session where we can relive the experiences, putting the events into perspec-tive. Crucially, during REM sleep we can do this without experiencing the hurt/anxiety/fear that accompanied the event. Professor Walker explains that this is possible because during REM sleep our brains are devoid of noradrenaline, the chemical associated with the 'fight or flight' response. During REM sleep, the low-noradrenaline environment allows the brain to process the memories clearly without getting tied up in the emotional upset associated with these thoughts when we are awake. When we wake up, we can then call up the memory without the emotional trauma. Without REM sleep, every time we think about the traumatic event, it can also fire up the original physical, emotional response associated with the experience. Not getting enough REM sleep means depriving ourselves of our free internal therapist who helps us process painful experiences every night, putting them in perspective. This may explain why we get angry or upset much more easily when we are sleep-deprived, especially in situations that resemble experiences that caused upset in the past.

3. Sleep deprivation leaves our nervous system in an overactive mode; a constant low-level fight or fight state. This increases our heart rate, prevents our blood vessels from relaxing and results in chronic raised levels of the stress hormone cortisol in the body. This leaves the body in a perennial jumpy state, ready to overreact emotionally and physically. Little wonder, then, that when we are sleep deprived we are less capable of remaining calm in stressful situations and may overreact to minor annoyances or disappointments. One of the virtues you need in abundance when dealing with children is patience, in particular

the ability to remain calm and rational despite being frequently tested to your limits. Even with sufficient sleep, I struggle to handle rapid-fire questions about Fortnite characters while trying to reverse into a tight parking space. And Job himself would struggle to keep it together after pleading with his children for the fifth time to turn the Xbox off and come down for dinner. Without sufficient sleep every night, none of us has a hope in hell.

Weight gain

The less we sleep, the more we eat. And the bad news is: when we are sleep-deprived, we are drawn to eating all the wrong things. This is because sleep deprivation increases endocannabinoids in the brain, which specifically increase our appetite for sweet food (like cookies, chocolate and ice cream), carbohydrates (like pasta and bread) and salty snacks (like crisps). On top of that, our body is less able to handle the calories it is taking in. And with less sleep, we have less energy and therefore feel less like exercising to offset the additional (and unhealthy) food we are eating. Unsurprisingly, the combined result is that we put on weight – insufficient sleep alone could be responsible for weight gain of about 6 kg per year.

This might explain why, as a hungry and sleep-deprived mother of young children, the magic bullet I sometimes grabbed when passing a café was a vanilla milkshake (i.e. sweet food) containing a double shot of espresso! Although many of us turn to caffeine during the day, it turns out this is counterproductive to getting good quality sleep. When we are tired, caffeine helps us feel more alert because it dampens down our body's urge to fall asleep. Our daily sleep cycle is regulated by a chemical in our brain called adenosine, which slowly builds up over the course of the day from the time we wake up. When the amount of adenosine reaches a critical level, this creates the urge to fall asleep. When we drink a cup of tea or coffee, the caffeine is absorbed into our blood and one of the places it goes is the brain. Caffeine competes with adenosine to sit on the adenosine receptors in the brain and by effectively blocking some of the receptors, the brain is fooled into thinking the adenosine level in the brain is lower than it really is. In effect, caffeine buys us time, by deferring the urge to sleep for a while. If we drink caffeine past a certain point in the day, though, at bedtime the caffeine might still sitting on the adenosine receptors in our brain. When this happens, even if we are in bed, the brain is still in an alert state instead of being relaxed and ready for sleep. Therefore, we are deprived of part of the seven to nine hours of quality sleep we need, making us feel even more tired the next day.

Reproductive health

Getting adequate sleep each night is important to both women and men who are trying to conceive. Women who routinely sleep less than six hours a night typically have 20% lower levels of a hormone critical for ovulation called FSH (Follicle Stim-ulating Hormone). Studies in healthy men in their mid-twenties have shown that restricting sleep to four to five hours per night lowers their testosterone to the levels of men ten or fifteen years older. They also suffer a 29% decrease in sperm count compared to men getting a full night of restful sleep. While trying to survive the sleep deprivation that comes with being the parent of a baby or young toddler can be enough to put some people off any plans for a little brother or sister, should you be game for more, sleep deprivation may limit the chances of this happening.

Weakened immune system

Sleep helps keep our defences strong. Not getting sufficient sleep, even for one night, reduces the body's ability to protect itself against infection, meaning we are more likely to become sick. Exactly what you don't need when you are already flat out! Professor Walker describes a study where doctors deliberately squirted the common cold virus up the nostrils of one hundred and fifty volunteers and then monitored them for a week in quarantine. They found that the less sleep an indi-vidual had had the previous week, the more likely they were to become infected and develop symptoms. Among people who were sleeping around five hours a night, the rate of infection was about 50%, while among people who were getting a full night's sleep, it was only 18%.

Long-term consequences of not getting enough sleep

In the short term, not getting enough sleep has serious implications for our ability to remember things, process and retain new information, cope emotionally and think creatively, but the long-term consequences are even more serious. When Prof. Walker uses the phrase 'chronically sleep restricted' to describe individuals in his studies, he is referring to people 'who are getting less than seven hours of sleep a night on a routine basis'. By *routine*, he means for as little as ten days. By that definition, millions of us are chronically sleep restricted ... Practically every mother of a new baby, most parents of babies and toddlers and a large proportion of parents who manage the majority of the Invisible Job. Despite all the valuable insights on the importance of sleep in his book *Why We Sleep*, not once does Matthew Walker mention mothers as a group who personify practically every aspect of chronic sleep deprivation. If he ever wanted to recruit participants for an observational study of sleep quality under optimal conditions, he need only place a discrete advert on Mumsnet saying 'Wanted: participants for a week-long study on sleep. Soft pillows, restful rooms and all meals provided. No phones, partners or children allowed.' He would have 100,000 mothers at his door the following morning.

People who are chronically sleep restricted are also at significantly higher risk of suffering from long-term conditions such as raised blood pressure, heart attacks and stroke, type 2 diabetes, cancer and Alzheimer's disease.

So why are you up so late? Come to bed!

This is a line I used to hear from my husband sometimes when I'd eventually fall into bed, exhausted. As if I had been randomly surfing YouTube for hours! It's all very well to say I should come to bed earlier but it would be more helpful if he offered to do more of the Invisible Job keeping me up so late!

IMPACT ON YOUR RELATIONSHIP

When a woman is left to manage the lion's share of the Invisible Job week after week, particularly on top of a paid job, it can become a source of much resentment in a relationship. Among couples I have spoken to, it tends to be the most common cause of major arguments.

Managing the Invisible Job is very different to managing a professional workload. At work, even when you face gargantuan projects with obstacles and setbacks, you can usually plan effectively and creatively with a clear head, negotiate with stakeholders, reach agreements, cancel or defer less important projects, or pull in additional support as needed to move forward.

Frustratingly, the same logic doesn't seem to apply at home. Instead, it feels like all the plates you are spinning are important and you cannot drop any. You have no issue attending to any one of these responsibilities – that's just part of being a parent. It's only when women find themselves doing (almost) all of them that they become resentful. It's not that husbands aren't busy, too; life is very busy for all parents of young children. But it can feel as if men get to choose what they do, to opt in whenever they feel they have capacity to do so, whereas women have no choice. In a home where both parents work, a wife can feel hard done by if her husband regularly stays late at the office if he has work to finish while she always has to be home at 6.30 p.m. on the dot and immediately shift gears to become cook, cleaner, listener, referee, homework checker, counsellor and general fixer for as long as it takes. She may have had an urgent work deadline, too, but it will be at least 9 p.m. before she can open her laptop and finish whatever she was working on when she left the office.

When she eventually falls into bed, exhausted from a day of work, followed by three hours of the Invisible Job, one thing that is unlikely to be uppermost on her mind is sex. Women are unlikely to be interested in physical intimacy when they are exhausted. When men fail to realise this however, it can lead to feelings of rejection, further compounding the stress in a relationship. Most men feel that their wives don't initiate sex often enough; some even suspect sometimes that women are not interested in sex at all. But that's not true! Women do want and enjoy sex but men and women differ fundamentally when it comes to what makes them want sex and when.

If a man has a bad day, sex may be high on the list of things that would make him feel better. It makes him feel wanted and orgasm releases endorphins in the brain that relax the body and drain away the stress of a bad day.

If a woman has had a bad day, however, sex may not necessarily be top of her list of remedies. She is very likely to be receptive to kind or thoughtful gestures. Should these not be forthcoming, a dopamine hit from watching some feel-good TV, indulging in chocolate or a glass of wine – or even all three – may help. After that, who knows – sex might even feature!

A woman is much more likely to be interested in sex when she feels good. To any man wondering exactly when that elusive window might be, although it is a highly individual question, this is more likely to be when:

- She is not exhausted after a day trying to get through the Invisible Job
- Her mind is not spinning with half-finished jobs and logistical updates
- She is feeling at least vaguely feminine because someone recently looked after the children long enough for her to relax and care for herself
- She has had a break to go for a walk, watch a tiny bit of Netflix or sit in the garden with a book for fifteen minutes without hearing someone shout 'Mommy!'
- Her husband/partner, noting that she looked exhausted, cleaned up the kitchen after dinner and made tomorrow's school lunches. Or simply told her he appreciates her.

The Ladybird book *The Mum — How it Works* understands this perfectly (33):

When she was single, Debbie had nightmares about being left alone and unwanted. For the last three years, someone has called for her every two minutes and watched her every time she has taken a bath or sat on the toilet.

Debbie now dreams of being left alone and unwanted, even for just a few minutes.

IMPACT ON YOUR MENTAL WELLBEING

Most women with caring responsibilities don't have the same freedom as their male colleagues to perform to the best of their ability every day at work. They often must accomplish more in a shorter time and perform at the highest level, frequently on insufficient sleep. They often feel as if they are struggling professionally. At the same time, they may also feel inadequate for falling short of the image of the perfect mother. This can lead to feelings of frustration and inadequacy for women at both a professional and personal level.

Often, they view it as a personal failure, some ineptitude on their part to keep all the plates spinning, believing (incorrectly) that other women can do it all. Individual women are quick to feel that they are personally at fault. In fact, what is at fault is the situation they find themselves in. But even when women know that the playing pitch is not even, the unwritten rules of the handbook for succeeding at work dictate that you must never admit that your Invisible Job even exists. Above all, it must never be seen to compromise your capability at work. Admitting that you got hardly any sleep last night because your two-year-old wet the bed twice (meaning you were up for hours changing sheets and cajoling them back to sleep), is not conducive to promoting your professional image as the best person to lead today's pitch with an important client.

Juggling multiple commitments is even more challenging when we are not getting sufficient sleep because raised cortisol levels mean we are operating at a higher baseline level of anxiety throughout the day. It also makes it harder to unwind at the end of the day. In individuals with mental health issues such as depression or bipolar disorder, even a few nights of insufficient sleep can be enough to trigger a manic or depressive episode.

There are certain behaviours that many women who are chronically sleep-deprived will identify with but which they might not realise are linked to a lack of sleep. For instance, a heightened desire for activities or substances that generate dopamine (the chemical that corresponds to pleasure or reward) in our brains. Such behaviours might include an increased desire for alcohol – almost every mother I know sometimes experiences 'wine o'clock' – i.e. feeling badly in need of a drink by 6 p.m. Alternatively, we may feel the urge to binge-watch a TV series late at night, even though our rational brain is screaming at us to go to bed. It's as if we need a fix of something good, something fun, something that will give our brains its dopamine hit. This increased need for pleasurable experiences may be due to the striatum (the part of the brain that generates our reward/pleasure feeling in response to dopamine) becoming hyperactive in people who are chronically sleep-deprived (32). Unsurprisingly, such behaviour is detrimental to our wellbeing. Both alcohol and staying up watching TV will further reduce the quality and quantity of our sleep, creating a vicious circle.

WHEN IT ALL BECOMES TOO MUCH

The social infrastructure in most countries expects women to work like they don't have children and raise children as if they don't work. Eventually, some women decide that succeeding at work and at home is simply not possible; that they have reached the point of wanting to scream, 'Stop the world, I want to get off!' When this happens, something has got to give. For those who have the financial option to do so, what 'gives' is often their career, meaning they give up work or switch to a less demanding role, i.e. either one with less responsibility or fewer hours. By reducing the number of hours in paid employment, a mother gains more hours to attend to family/household demands. Other members of the household are likely to benefit from her taking care of (even more!) things on their behalf and family life will probably feel calmer and more manageable for everyone. I know a mother of four who quit her high-profile job in international strategy when her youngest child started primary school. She said that when she did, quality of life improved instantly for everyone in the house – including for her. However, it came at a huge personal cost. In her own words, 'I lost my identity'.

Women often carry on for years, not fully realising the impossible burden they are carrying. They just keep going stoically, telling themselves to try harder: 'This should all be doable; it must just be me.'

After a while, running all day starts to feel normal. In fact, you can keep going like that for many years. However, you may not realise how close you are to the edge until some big boulders are thrown into the mix to test what you can cope with.

For me, one of these boulders came from my job. I lost a key member of my team and slow HR processes meant it took more than six months to appoint a replacement, significantly increasing my already heavy workload. The really big boulders, though, are the ones that threaten the health and wellbeing of the people you love. In a short space of time, I lost two close relatives to cancer unexpectedly. My son had two medical emergencies. And both my parents had serious health issues requiring intervention and support.

The straw that broke the camel's back was the au pair announcing she was leaving – tomorrow. So much for the six-week notice period! My husband and I both had work in the morning as usual and the children had school. While we muddled through for a while with no childminder, this was just one boulder too many. It was time for one of us to stay home and dedicate time to looking after our family and restoring some calm. With only one applicant for the post of stay-at-home parent, 'we' decided this someone would be me.

IMPACT OF COVID-19 LOCKDOWNS ON WOMEN

The restrictions imposed in many countries around the world in response to the Covid-19 pandemic revealed very clearly just where the buck stops when it comes to who really carries responsibility for the Invisible Job. With schools and crèches closed and millions of employees asked to work from home, women around the world found themselves in an impossible situation. First, they became home-schooling teachers (which is what remote learning entailed by the time you had deciphered the log-in instructions and spent several hours locating, supervising and correcting whatever activity the teacher had apparently set the class to do).

Second, they became 24-hour restaurants, as their children not only needed breakfast and dinner cooked for them but also lunch and snacks throughout the day. During all this, they were also expected to carry out their own job as normal, despite having to work from perhaps their bedroom or the kitchen table while being interrupted every fifteen minutes by children who were bored, hungry or confused.

While fathers were also working from home, rather than share the burden of managing children in these challenging circumstances equally with their wives, many focused intently on their work in a quiet corner of the house, only coming out to enquire what was for lunch/dinner.

In September 2020, just as the school term was about to start, over 1.1 million workers aged 20 or over dropped out of the labour market in the USA, meaning they were no longer working or looking for work. Of these, 80% were women (34). The joint McKinsey–LeanIn 2020 survey of US workers found that during the first lockdown, women (despite already doing most of the parenting and housework responsibilities) saw their workload in these areas increase disproportionately compared to men. Without access to childcare and other regular support services, mothers were 1.5 times more likely than fathers to be spending an extra three or more hours a day on housework and childcare – the equivalent to 20 hours a week – on top of their existing responsibilities. More than 70% of fathers surveyed believed they were splitting household work equally with their partner during Covid-19 – but only 44% of mothers agreed (35). As one mother explained:

> I have weeks when I feel burned out. Before the pandemic, my parents helped with childcare, but now everything falls on me. I feel overwhelmed at least two or three days a week. It's hard to put toddlers and babies on a schedule and have them entertain themselves. The biggest challenge is meetings. I need to be available for meetings at core business hours, and it's very hard to focus when my kids are in the room.

In some ways, the impact on women was like a magnification of the impossible path many mothers who work outside the home find themselves on eventually. In the words of one survey respondent:

> I feel like I am failing at everything. I'm failing at work. I'm failing at my duties as a mom. I'm failing in every single way, because I think what we're being asked to do is nearly impossible. How can you continue to perform at the same level as in the office when you had no distractions, plus being asked to basically become a teacher for kids and everything else with online learning? I'm doing it all, but at the same time I'm feeling like I'm not doing any of it very well. I also worry that my performance is being judged because I'm caring for my children. If I step away from my virtual desk and I miss a call, are they going to wonder where I am? I feel

that I need to always be on and ready to respond instantly to whatever comes in. And if that's not happening, then that's going to reflect poorly on my performance.

Consequently, many mothers are considering downshifting their careers (switching to lower or part-time hours, taking a less demanding job, taking a leave of absence or leaving the workforce completely). Interestingly, significantly fewer fathers are having similar thoughts. One woman in the survey commented:

There were times when I said to my husband, 'One of us is going to have to quit our job.' And I remember thinking, 'How come I'm the only one thinking about this, and my husband isn't?' I don't think him leaving was ever in question.

The survey found that senior-level women are significantly more likely than men at the same level to feel under pressure to work more and as though they have to be 'always on'. Women at this level are 1.5 times more likely than their male equivalents to think about downshifting their careers or leaving the workforce because of Covid-19. Almost three in four cite burnout as the main reason.

While the Covid-19 lockdown has been challenging for mothers with professional careers, having to juggle their work with increased childcare and domestic responsibilities, in many ways the women who have fared worst are those who work in service jobs, such as cleaners and childminders. As these jobs cannot be done online, many women have simply been unable to work at all, and unlike professional women, they may have no financial safety net to protect them.

22

To Work or Not to Work?

Caring for children and the home is a role that in many societies has long been associated with women. Perhaps we should not be surprised, therefore, that some people presume that this is what all mothers want to spend their whole day doing! While mothers obviously care deeply about their children and the wellbeing of their family, women are also highly capable individuals with outside interests and a lot to contribute professionally.

Conversely, men have traditionally been designated responsibility for earning enough money to support their families. However, many of today's young fathers articulate a desire to be much more involved in their children's lives than fathers were a generation ago. A 2015 survey of millennial fathers in the UK found that their top priority in life since becoming a father was spending time with family (23). A US survey found that almost as many working fathers as working mothers (48% and 52% respectively) said they would prefer to be at home with their children but could not afford to do this because they needed their salary (36).

So, has the world changed? Can gender stereotypes be eliminated when it comes to discussions between you and your partner about how best to balance looking after children and earning a living? Do women want to stay home or continue their careers? Would men like to break free of the chains of tradition and be the primary caregivers in their families? And when is the best time to start a family in terms of balancing it with a career and other personal goals?

Before exploring these questions, it's important to be very clear on one point: there is no right or wrong answer when it comes to whether either a mother or a father should stay at home full-time to engage in caring duties. Ideally, this decision should be based on what a couple feels is right for them/their family, bearing in mind that this perspective is likely to change over their lifetime. It may also be influenced by financial and personal circumstances, what stage they are at in their career and the age of their children. Some mothers or fathers might want to be a full-time carer to their children for a short period, some might want to do it for most of their lives, while for others it might hold little appeal whatsoever.

It can be hard to figure out what is right. Would you like to continue working full-time if you become a parent? Or would you love to stay at home full-time to look after your child? Or would you like the option of doing both (assuming there was adequate support to make this possible) – perhaps by working part-time or taking a break from your career for several months or years? Until you have tried it, it can be hard to know. And whether it works out or not, whether you feel fulfilled, whether you can cope, depends on many external factors.

A global comprehensive survey carried out by the International Labour Organisation and Gallup examined exactly what people's preferences were, when it comes to doing paid work versus doing unpaid caring work for their family (9). It found that, globally, 70% of women, including women with children, would rather be in paid work, given the choice. And that two-thirds of the men interviewed also wanted women to be in paid jobs. In high-income countries, the figures were even higher, with 80% of women stating they would prefer to be in paid employment and 77% of men echoing this view. This is in line with research carried out in the US in 2010, where young adults (aged 18–29) were asked how they would prefer responsibilities in a marriage to be structured. Some 72% said they would favour an arrangement where both the husband and wife have jobs and take care of the household and children. Only 22% favoured a marriage where the husband provides for the family and the wife takes care of the household and children (37).

The ILO report also found that women who engaged in paid work were more likely to describe themselves as 'thriving' compared to those who did not. However, although 70% of women want to work, the reality is that only 45.3% of women globally actually have a (paid) job. This figure has not increased at all between 1991 and 2019; in fact, it has declined slightly. In contrast, 71.4% of men have a paid job.

The main reason for this enormous mismatch between women's desired and actual occupations is the unpaid caring responsibilities they are lumbered with. For generations, societal norms have labelled the care of children, the home and older relatives as 'women's work' and the lack of access to affordable care services to assist them means women have little or no time to pursue paid work, despite being highly capable of it.

Women enter the workforce in equal proportions to men, but many of them exit it again sometime after having children. The ILO report examined how being the mother of young children impacts women's participation in the labour force. It found that in high-income countries, women with young children are much less likely to be in paid employment than those without young children. Conversely, being a father of a child aged under six doesn't diminish your chances of working. In fact, fathers are more likely to have a (paid) job than men without young children.

Thus, becoming a mother reduces your chances of having a paid job. This is referred to by some as the 'motherhood employment penalty'. Between 2005 and 2015, the global motherhood penalty increased further, as the employment rate of both women without young children and (all) fathers increased more than employment among women with young children.

Currently, more than 41.5% of women with a university degree are classified as being 'unemployed' or 'outside the labour force', compared to just 17.2% of men, a gender gap of 24.3%. Things are even worse for women with lower levels of education: among people with only primary school education, the gender gap in paid employment is 41.1% globally.

Our level of education also shapes our views about whether it is acceptable for a woman to have a (paid) job, if she wishes to. While even asking this question will seem prehistoric to feminist men and women, some people remain fundamentally opposed to women having this choice. When an international Gallup world poll carried out in 2016 asked men and women asked whether it is perfectly acceptable for a woman to have a paid job:

- 13.2% of men (and 8% of women) with a university education interviewed do not believe that it is perfectly acceptable for a woman to have a paid job if she wants one
- Among people with second-level education, 18% of men and 11.9% of women shared this view
- And among respondents who only completed primary education, almost a quarter of men and almost a fifth of women felt this way (13)

It therefore appears that a significant proportion of people (both men and women) are fundamentally opposed to true gender equality in the workplace. Why?

Aside from the obvious sexism, perhaps these views signify something else; namely the value that many people place on having a parent at home. However, even if this is the reason, it indicates respondents exclude the possibility of this parent being the father.

Another possible explanation is the outlook of 'traditionalist' men described in *The Second Shift* (38). These men believe that if they earn enough money to obviate the financial need for their wife to engage in paid work, this should entitle them to the privilege of having a wife who stays home to look after her husband, children and home. Hochschild also encountered a small number of 'traditional women' in her research, i.e. women who desired to stay at home and play that traditional role, articulating views such as, 'I don't want to be equal with [my husband]. I want to be feminine ... I want to be taken care of.' Even thirty years ago, Hochschild estimated that women with this outlook accounted for fewer than one in ten of the women she encountered. Regardless of whether a woman feels at any given time in her life that it would be best for her to focus on her career versus being a full-time parent, today's educated women certainly do not view themselves as anything less than equal to their husbands/partners.

TACKLING THE INVISIBLE JOB AS A WORKING MOTHER

When I became pregnant with our first child, I was really enjoying my career. Since I was little, I'd been interested in being things – an air hostess (age four), a pilot (ages six to ten), a computer hacker (age eleven), and later all kinds of other things. I studied hard and things worked out well for me academically, meaning I was fortunate to be able to choose whatever I wanted to do at university. By then I had decided I wanted to work in international pharmaceutical marketing, so I did a degree in Pharmacy followed by graduate studies in Business and French. I then landed my dream job as a marketing manager in a French pharmaceutical company. From there I went on to several other roles in the pharmaceutical industry. It was diverse and interesting work, with plenty of learning opportunities and exciting international travel. My partner (now husband), who worked in a completely different field, also enjoyed his job, which required a lot of international travel too.

Although becoming parents was very much something we had planned, looking back I realise that how we were going to manage being parents was not. We were aware that we did not have a clear picture of how it would transform our lives but at the same time, somehow trusted that things would turn out OK. Maybe I thought the knowledge would kick in with the oxytocin right after birth; downloaded to my brain like Neo acquiring a new skill in The Matrix. Or maybe, like the philosophy of the theatre owner in the film Shakespeare in Love (39), everything just works out, somehow:

[Theatre owner trying to explain to an investor that his upcoming play will still be profitable although the theatres have just been closed due to the plague]: 'Allow me to explain about the theatre business: The natural condition is one of insurmountable obstacles on the road to imminent disaster'.
[Investor]: 'So what do we do?'
[Theatre owner]: 'Nothing. Strangely enough, it all turns out well'.

[Investor]: 'How?'
[Theatre owner]: 'I don't know; it's a mystery'.

We knew people with children. Granted, not our immediate friends (that wave was just beginning to hit), but acquaintances and relatives. And their lives seemed to be continuing. (Admittedly, we had never enquired too closely exactly how their lives were continuing and whether it was different from before). But maybe, like the theatre business, although it may not be obvious how, parenting just works out. If not, surely there would be global carnage – the equivalent of a two-mile pile up on the M25 every morning as thousands of new parents got into a car and tried driving for the very first time.

Just in case the *Matrix* download wasn't going to happen, I was also reading as many books as possible about parenting/babies during my pregnancy. And we both attended (two lots of!) antenatal classes. But while we were gathering a significant amount of baby advice (some very practical, some distinctly wacky), a clear picture of how our life was going to work with a baby in the mix was still worryingly elusive. For me, a critical piece of the jigsaw was missing: the bit that explains how people manage having a baby and having a job.

As my due date approached, HR wanted to know if I would be coming back to work once the baby was born. My brain said 'Duh! Why wouldn't I?!' (Although I really hope whatever I said was more articulate.) At that point, becoming a stay-at-home parent had never crossed my mind. This was not the 1960s, where women automatically opted out of the workforce just because they had children, relegated to a life of changing nappies, making dinners and supporting their husbands in their important jobs. My husband and I considered each other equals. (Or at least that's what we said). We also earned equal salaries and we would need both for a mortgage to (hopefully) move one day from our two-bed London flat to a house.

But even leaving finances aside, it had simply never occurred to me to chuck in a career I enjoyed and had worked hard to achieve. I remember meeting some of the mothers from my antenatal group during maternity leave and the conversation was all about when we were going back to work.

'What about you?' I asked one mum, who hadn't said a word. 'When are you planning on going back?'

She laughed a little nervously and simply said, 'Oh, we're very lucky.'

As nobody really seemed to get what she meant, she expanded ...

'You see, John has got a very good job so I won't need to go back to work.'

The nervous laugh had been because she didn't want to openly flaunt how financially 'lucky' she was to be giving up her job as a teacher in order to stay home looking after a baby. As she saw it, the rest of us didn't have that marvellous option; instead, we *had* to go back to work. However, we cannot presume to know what other women would choose to do, given the choice.

Most women go back to work following maternity leave. For some, this is because their careers are important to them, offering mental stimulation and forming part of their identity. Some go back to work full-time for financial reasons. Others might love to be a full-time mother, either permanently or for several years. And if they have the financial means to do so (perhaps because they have a partner who earns enough money to support them), this is also a valid choice, made in the interest of children's well-being. However not all women have the option to choose, and even for those who do, what feels right can change over time.

I stayed home on maternity leave after our daughter was born. At the time, it seemed like a no-brainer, in so far as my employer would pay my full salary for six months, provided I came back to work afterwards. On the other hand, my husband was only entitled to two days of paid paternity leave. For that reason, I don't think we even considered there were any alternatives; it was simply what all new mothers did, while their husbands went back to work after (at most!) a week at home. We still had no idea what magic solution would enable us to function when my maternity leave ended. Although looking after a baby at home all day felt tougher than being at work, I remember the closer I got to my return date, the more impossible the prospect of leaving my daughter felt. How could I possibly be separated from this little thing, who had never been out of my sight for more than two hours in her life? I didn't know which of us would be more traumatised.

In the end though, just like the theatre owner predicted, it did all work out. My wonderful sister, who at that point didn't have children of her own, volunteered to give up a month of her summer holiday to look after her godchild when I went back to work. As she is the most caring and capable person you could imagine, this meant I was able to walk out the door knowing my daughter could not be in better hands. It also helped my husband and me realise that finding a nanny would be the perfect childcare solution for us.

While this solution would enable us both to continue working, I also came to realise that I couldn't bear the thought of being away from my daughter for five days every week. I therefore contacted my manager, a young Australian called Mark, to ask if I could switch to a four-day week when I came back to work. Although this would mean earning less, it would enable me to spend three full days each week with my baby. But his response to my perfect plan was ... no! Mark was only a year or two older than me and relatively new in his job, with no children of his own yet. I therefore don't know where he got his wisdom from, but to his enormous credit, he said that it would be irresponsible of him. Why? Because he suspected that I would diligently ensure I did my job just as well as before, but in only four days, even if that meant staying late or taking work home. In his view, this would not be fair, as I would only be paid 80% of my previous salary. Instead, he recommended switching to a compressed week (something I had never even heard of), which meant working four longer days each week but getting paid my full salary. He even put me in touch with a colleague who already worked compressed hours to find out more and set it up. What a guy!

The compressed week worked out brilliantly and I will be forever grateful to Mark for introducing me to the concept. In the beginning, the challenge of doing my job just as well as before in just four days was daunting. But I was determined that nobody would be able to say that becoming a mother meant I was any less capable than I had been before. Therefore, like many other mothers, I became the epitome of efficiency, trying to get everything done between 8 a.m. and 6 p.m., so as to be home on time for the nanny.

I had always been disciplined about creating daily, weekly and monthly priority lists at work, but I got better at it. I also became ruthless at sifting out everything that wasn't essential. I learned to say no to meetings I didn't feel were necessary to attend. And I pushed back on meeting invitations without an agenda. Whenever I ran a meeting myself, I ensured it had an agenda with clear timings and kept to them. When reviewing documents, I trained myself to focus, so that whenever possible, I would only need to read it once. I tried not to defer decisions and where I didn't have all the information to make a complex decision, I scheduled time to speak to the relevant people or find the answers I needed elsewhere. I learned to write shorter emails. I ate lunch with other women who were keen to be back at their desks within twenty minutes. And 'coffee breaks' consisted of a dash to the coffee machine and back. At my annual appraisal, my manager said my performance in my role was outstanding but he had one critical observation: that I wasn't spending enough time 'hanging out at the water cooler talking to people.' Damned if you do and damned if you don't!

Less than a year after coming back from maternity leave, I was promoted to a European role that involved frequent travel to Paris. While I needed to be in the Paris office Tuesday to Thursday every second week, I structured my work and travel schedule to minimise time away from my daughter as much as possible. I therefore avoided meetings before 10 a.m. on Tuesdays or after 4 p.m. on Thursdays so that I could catch the 7 a.m. Eurostar from St Pancras to Gare du Nord on Tuesdays and be home again on Thursday by 6.30 p.m., working solidly on my laptop for the two-hour train trip each way. I worked late in the office on Tuesday and Wednesday evenings because in Paris there was nobody to rush home to.

Shortly after my promotion, I discovered I was pregnant again. Because of this, my new boss – a chic, older French woman who didn't have children – openly expressed her scepticism about my commitment to the job. Keen to prove to her that I was indeed dedicated to my job, I took a short maternity leave following the birth of my son, which I now regret. With this one exception, though, I never consciously experienced gender bias during my career or felt as if there was a glass ceiling for women. It helped that there were plenty of strong female role models in the company I worked at; all highly qualified and many of them members of the senior management team.

The only aspect in which I felt the playing field was not level for women who were mothers related to time. I had many female friends at work in senior positions, who all performed at a high level, but we all had to play a game, pretending that there were no external responsibilities that impacted our ability to contribute at work; no secret clock dictating what was humanly possible. I watched these women arrive early to work, fully prepared for every meeting, and saw how they assigned their time throughout the day with surgical precision, ever-conscious of their deadline to get home to attend to children. If a three-day meeting in Spain was announced at short notice, while my male colleagues surfed online for the best restaurants, female colleagues with children sent frantic texts trying to rearrange childcare. Externally, they remained calm; the duck's feet paddling furiously in high heels beneath the water while maintaining perfect feathers and mascara above.

For the first ten years we were parents my husband and I worked full-time in busy jobs requiring frequent overseas travel. This meant constant diary coordination to ensure that one of us was home every night and that children never fell through any gaps in the schedule. For the first four years this was made possible by Tedie, our amazing live-out nanny. She cooked delicious food for the children, played with them, read books and brought them on walks through Kensington Gardens, to the Science Museum and the Natural History Museum. They attended storytime at the children's library, had picnics in the park and tea parties with dolls in the lounge. She was incredibly capable and utterly dedicated. While most of my salary went directly to Tedie, she was worth every penny.

When our son was two-and-a-half, Tedie decided to retrain as a nurse. As our daughter was already in preschool and our son would soon be old enough to join her, from then on they would only need childcare in the afternoons. Therefore, instead of looking for another nanny we decided to see if we could manage with an au pair. This required moving out of our two-bed flat and renting somewhere bigger so the au pair would have a bedroom. Although we didn't realise it at the time, this was the beginning of a hectic phase of our lives that would last about five years, involving four house moves, two job changes and leaving the UK permanently. During this period, our lives functioned (just about) through of a steady stream of au pairs and emergency assistance from grandparents when needed.

People say moving house is the second-most stressful life event (after divorce). Moving house four times in three years is therefore obviously a recipe for disaster. However, it was not intentional. The first move to a small house in north London was to gain a bedroom for an au pair. Six months after that, our daughter was unexpectedly offered a place in an Irish-speaking school in Dublin and my husband was offered an exciting new job, also in Dublin. And while London had been great for thirteen years, I'd always dreamed of moving back to Ireland one day. We decided to go for it.

Much earlier in the year – not envisaging any of this – we had booked a holiday for the last two weeks in August. Two days after the holiday, a big truck containing everything we owned drove from London to Liverpool and took the ferry to Dublin. A day later, the movers were unloading furniture and an endless stream of cardboard boxes into our rental house as we tried to keep pace, directing where everything should go. When the truck drove off, at least there were beds, sofas and wardrobes in the right rooms. Another 24 hours and dozens of cardboard boxes later, we had located the essentials for sleeping, eating and getting dressed, including the all-important school uniform. Just as well, because the following day was the first day of big school for our four-year-old!

In the weeks that followed, we did our best to unpack as many boxes as possible every night after the children were in bed. The days were already full of all the normal stuff (i.e. a full week of work on top of the Invisible Job). In addition, we had to jump all the administrative hurdles that moving to a new country entails – new bank accounts, mobile phones, social security, tax registration, vehicle registration, healthcare and utilities. There wasn't much left in the tank when it came to unpacking boxes, but we plugged away at this most nights until well after midnight. Although we had moved in on 30 August, I think the first time we sat on a couch was 26 December.

We had rented the house for a year, hoping to find a house of our own to buy within that period. We registered with estate agents and property websites and scoured the property supplement every Thursday for anything on sale in the area. We dragged the children along to house viewings and put offers on several but were always unsuccessful. Unable to extend our lease, we had to move to another rental house for a year while we continued searching. Twelve months later, we finally managed to buy a house – and began the whole packing-up-everything-we-own-thing for the fourth and final time.

When we first moved to Dublin, I continued in the same job I had been doing in London, commuting to Paris for three days every other week. My husband also needed to travel abroad frequently for work. Our definition of a great midweek night was simply one where we were both home and neither of us was getting on an early-morning flight. We knew this wasn't good. Something had to change.

I was approached with a job offer from a London university to set up a commercial clinical trials unit. They envisaged the role would only require me being in London once a month (for meetings), and the rest of the time I would be able to do my job remotely from Dublin. This would mean half the amount of travel associated with my current job, which sounded good for our family. I accepted the job.

However, the promise of only needing to travel to London once a month was wildly inaccurate. The reality was that I needed to be there at least every second week and sometimes more often. The job was challenging and involved long hours but I told myself that this was simply par for the course in the early phase of any new job, especially one involving setting up new structures and systems.

For five years our life was very hectic. Much more than I was even conscious of at the time. There was no one component that was the problem. The issue was everything together. I could handle my job fine, despite its many challenges. I could pack an overnight case in ten minutes and knew exactly how many minutes I needed between my alarm going off and climbing into a taxi, make-up in hand to do en route to the airport for an early-morning flight. Running with my wheelie suitcase case through airport terminals and London pavements had become second nature.

Each day, I tried to get through my work as efficiently as possible, ever-conscious of my Cinderella deadline when, ready or not, I needed to have morphed into my other job: mother, schoolteacher, cook, cleaner, listener, organiser, fixer, seamstress, au pair counsellor, children's social secretary, doctor, storyteller. If my husband had deadlines to meet or work to finish, he stayed late at the office. Not having that option, it was only when the demands of the evening were seen to and the children were asleep that I could log back on to my laptop to finish off whatever I had been doing when I had had to cut and run at 6 p.m.

Every year life evolved: our children opted into or out of various interests; school routines were tweaked; friendships with classmates formed and shifted; urgent house projects clamoured for attention; mini-disasters had to be managed. And you just keep juggling all the balls. Additional balls appear so quietly that you barely notice them; you just have a vague suspicion that someone is adding a new one every time you look away.

WORKING FROM HOME – THE WORST OF BOTH WORLDS?

When I took up my new job in London, I naïvely thought that working from home in Dublin might be a wonderful alternative to commuting to an office. After all, isn't that meant to be the Holy Grail for parents? Creating extra hours in your day by eliminating unnecessary commuting as well as allowing you to skip doing your make-up in the morning?

Strangely enough though, for me it was anything but. In fact, in some respects, it was harder. Initially, I worked from the study in our home but soon realised this would not work out with a three-year-old who finished playschool at 1.30 p.m. It was impossible for him to understand that he couldn't run into the study screaming when I was midway through a conference call with colleagues or clients. I would hit the mute button as fast as I could, desperately hoping no one on the call had heard the furore, while the au pair did her best to entice him back out. Naturally, adult logic carries no sway with a stubborn three-year-old intent on recalibrating my interpretation of 'important' and 'urgent' to his worldview.

> [Me, frantically whispering]: 'I'm sorry honey, Mommy's working. You can't come in here right now. But I'll come find you as soon as I can, I promise.'

[Foot-stomping response from three-year-old]: 'But Mommy, this is impor-tant! Iron Man is broken! You have to fix him now!'

For a few months I resorted to renting an office to be sure I could get my work done, but after a while I realised that simply threatening to go to the office was enough to stop my children hammering on the door. So I gave up renting the office ... but obviously didn't tell the children!

If you are a diligent employee by nature, when you work from home there's a risk you will become even more diligent (due to paranoia that someone in the office might think you are slacking off). With nobody to blame for any possible distractions, you feel that any failure to meet your deadlines can only be your fault. Even if those deadlines were self-imposed, optimistic or downright unachievable!

Every morning I was at my desk by 8.30 a.m. and worked solidly for two hours before running downstairs for a ten-minute coffee break, unloading the dishwasher or washing machine at speed while the kettle boiled. (Knowing what an evening with a house full of children will be like you feel compelled to make every minute of the day count). When it was sunny, I stepped into the garden for a moment to drink my coffee, envious of my retired neighbours pottering in their garden and listening to the birds. But I'd no time for that. Coffee downed, I dragged myself back to my desk and continued working until there was a suitable gap for a quick bite of lunch. Without colleagues around to prompt you, when immersed in work, you may only realise it's already 2 p.m. because your stomach is growling. Fifteen minutes later, I'd be back at my desk, cracking on with the afternoon work window, ever-conscious that only part of it was guaranteed to be childproof.

When you step through the door after commuting home from work, you are stepping into the 'childrenworld' – little faces excited to see you and tell you what they did today (or more often, what their big sister/little brother did to them today). It's a wall of noise and a change of gear you are ready for as you put your key in the door, having said goodbye to the 'adultworld' of work. Immediately, there are woes to hear, fights to referee, homework to check, school notes to sign, various requests (for a toy they desperately want or a playdate with a friend you need to arrange urgently).

However, when you are working from home, it's the other way around; that is, the childrenworld steps into your adultworld. And often before you are ready for it. You may have thought you had another thirty minutes before closing your laptop and putting on your Mom hat, but that is not necessarily how it works. Instead, that half an hour is gobbled up as the childrenworld invades prematurely because somebody is hungry or can't find a certain toy or simply wants a hug. Whatever it was you needed to finish in the adultworld must then fall asleep for a hundred years ... or at least wait until your children fall asleep.

While many people might consider working from home a wonderful way of cutting out commuting times and maximising the hours in your day, it doesn't work for everyone and there are certain drawbacks. Some people struggle to maintain focus without the structure of an office and interaction with the people around them. Especially for extroverted people who thrive on being able to bounce off others, it can be hard to stay motivated and the day can feel very long. For others, that's not a problem at all; some people are at their most productive working alone.

However, for people charged with doing the majority of the Invisible Job, working from home can be a double-edged sword. While you no longer have to commute to work, you are losing a window that you usually spent doing something other than your (two!) jobs, such as listening to the news or a podcast, reading a book or at least getting some fresh air and exercise on your walk to the bus stop. Instead, you may be tempted to squeeze a household job into that window, like clearing the breakfast table or loading the dishwasher, before logging on to your computer. And since, technically, you are not running out the door, your partner may feel (even more than before), that it's OK to leave this job to you.

Another problem to contend with if you're working from home is that not every-body believes you are actually working. A mother who works from home told me about a time her in-laws came to stay for a week at short notice. While they completely respected that her husband was not free to entertain them on weekdays as he had to go to work (*real work*), they were less convinced that what *she* was doing (a full-time paid job operating from her home office) was actually *real work*. They seemed disappointed that she would *not* be preparing hot breakfasts or lunches and was *not* free to go sightseeing with them.

TACKLING THE INVISIBLE JOB AS A STAY-AT-HOME MOM

After juggling many balls as a working mother for ten years, I eventually took a career break. Having jealously eyed the stay-at-home mothers dropping off their children at school for years, I must confess that I envisaged this would be an easy gig, with copious amounts of 'me-time'. Naïvely, I immediately drew up a big list of all the projects that my husband and I had put on the long finger for years, thinking I would plough through them in a couple of months. Things like replacing the roof on our house, installing solar panels, planting a vegetable garden, catching up on overdue continuing professional development modules (mandatory study to retain my licence to practise as a pharmacist), writing wills and making photo albums. Who knows, I might even get to play tennis! This was going to be great.

However, that wasn't quite how it worked out.

No longer having any childcare support whatsoever, I discovered what being responsible for children five days a week felt like and, for the first time, began to appreciate just how enormous the Invisible Job is.

My first job every morning was to get the children up, dressed and fed, then make the school lunches. After locating schoolbags and establishing what else they needed to bring with them that day, I began the daily battle of trying to get out the door to school on time. It is difficult to explain why it is impossible to get two small(ish) people into coats, hats, gloves and helmets and onto bikes – without losing the schoolbag, swimming bag, science project or whatever else they were holding in their hands just ten seconds earlier. But somehow, it just is. Eventually, with (hopefully) everything in tow, we would race off down the road to school. After locking the bikes in the yard and kissing them goodbye, I raced straight back home again.

Keen to make progress on my project list, each day I tried to dispatch whatever housework needed to be done in the shortest time possible. However, by the time I'd cleared up the breakfast things, unloaded and loaded the dishwasher, washed up any pots from the night before and maybe swept the kitchen floor, it was easily already 10:30. (Assuming I hadn't received a phone call from the school to say one of my children had forgotten something that morning and could I please bring whatever-it-is to the school as soon as possible.) Next, I might throw a load into the washing machine and/or sort and put away the dry clothes on the rack. One morning each week, a grocery shopping had to happen (which takes up two hours, even if you literally run around the shop, once you factor in driving there and back and unpacking all the groceries). If I was lucky, sometimes I had time for a quick sandwich before getting back on my bike to collect the children from school at 2.30 p.m.

After that, the chances of doing anything on my project list were very slim indeed, as afternoons were a blur of homework, music practice, driving to and from after-school activities and refereeing sibling fights. Dinner was needed each evening too. And since I no longer had a job, I somehow felt that home cooking was now something I was morally obliged to do. On days when I knew the afternoon would be full-on with various after-school activities, I needed to prepare dinner in the morning to avoid arriving in the door at 6 p.m. with 'hangry' children and nothing to eat.

On top of these boring daily staples, there were various other elements of the Invisible Job to do too. During all the years I had worked full-time while trying to juggle all the other balls in my life, it had always felt impossible to stay on top of family and home responsibilities. However, it wasn't until I gave up my job to attend to these on a full-time basis that I started to appreciate the following about the Invisible Job:

It is enormous

No wonder it had always been impossible to stay on top of! If you allowed it to, it could easily take up your whole day. And unlike most kinds of paid work, it doesn't have a defined boundary that marks the start or end of the workday.

It is invisible

Firstly, because so much of what you do needs to be repeated every day, it can feel as productive as raking the beach between waves. And secondly, because the better you do it all, the more invisible it becomes. Nobody sees a clean house! Nobody notices if your children are wearing shoes that fit correctly. Nobody looks twice if the bins have been emptied. Or if we haven't run out of milk.

It is thankless

Firstly, you experience little internal acknowledgement or sense of personal achievement for much of it, because compared to, say, completing a project at work, many elements are repetitive (and will need to be done all over again tomorrow).

Secondly, as far as external acknowledgement (for all the things you do on behalf of your family) is concerned, don't expect this to come from your children because ...well, simply because they are children. (None of us ever understood or appreciated what our parents did for us when we were children.) So that narrows down the number of people (other than you) who could, and should, acknowledge your efforts to ... well, just one person. That is why, regardless of whether you are doing the Invisible Job full-time as a stay-at-home parent or on top of your paid job, it's important that your partner understands and appreciates what you are doing. Assuming that the security, wellbeing, health and happiness of your children is something you both value, it follows automatically that the thousands of hours you spend attending to this (on behalf of both of you) should be valued. The same goes for all the things you do to create a home that feels good to be in. When relationships struggle because the Invisible Job is not being shared equally, what usually causes the most hurt is that all the things that one partner is doing (on behalf of everyone) are not acknowledged or appreciated by the other partner.

It has little or no status

We live in a society where our status is often linked to what we do. While it should not be the case, the job of being a full-time carer carries very low status in society compared to most professions. This is true both for people engaged in paid caring work (for instance, those looking after elderly people in nursing homes) and unpaid caring work (for instance, parents looking after young children or people caring for older relatives).

Earlier I mentioned a woman I spoke to who gave up a senior role in international strategy to stay home and look after her four children. While the quality of life for everyone in the family went up, for the first time in her life, she felt as if she no longer had an identity. Another woman I spoke to, who had given up her job to look after her three children and the home, told me how she felt somewhat intimidated in the school yard by the mothers in pencil skirts and high heels who dropped off their children en route to their law firms. When debating issues at school committee meetings, she felt that her opinion no longer counted as much as theirs.

When someone asks you what you do, it can therefore feel like a loaded question, as you worry the answer may relegate you to some lowly status in that person's mind. Even if you are a highly capable and intelligent person, who has lived an exciting life, achieved many worthy goals and who contributes in important ways to society, when you describe your current occupation as mother or homemaker, people can often appear somewhat underwhelmed.

Perhaps that's why women I know who work even one or two days a week in a paid job usually define themselves as 'a dentist', even though most of their week is spent as 'a mother' doing the Invisible Job. One of the women interviewed by Arlie Hochschild in *The Second Shift* (38) describes how when she told someone at a dinner party that she was at home looking after children, she often felt instantly dismissed as unimportant. Harry Enfield's 'A Very Important Man' sketch (available on YouTube) is essential viewing for further insight on this.

Men who choose to stay at home to look after children and the home have arguably even more prejudices to overcome, especially as men tend to view other men's worth in terms of their career status. Thankfully, less so than in the past, as more men choose to perform this role, either on a part- or full-time basis. However, some men still consider this an exclusively feminine role and may therefore view men who choose to do this as less masculine or as underachievers professionally. Conversely, increasing numbers of women view fathers who opt to take on or share this role as enlightened, feminist and comfortable with their masculinity.

23

Achieving a Balance

While some parents say they would love nothing more than the opportunity to spend every day with their children, others would rather run a mile to the office over hot coals. I believe that, given the choice, most mothers (and fathers) would like a balance. They want the opportunity to participate in the labour force (in a job that stimulates them), while still having time to attend to caring responsibilities as a parent and home maker. The need for balance is indeed something that those concerned with the social and economic wellbeing of European citizens are conscious of, as the European Survey on Quality of Life (ESQL) report confirms: 'Reconciliation between work and life is a long-standing concern of the EU, its Member States and social partners' (15). However, the report recognises that achieving this balance – or even defining what it looks like – is not straightforward: 'The research literature on work–life balance indicates that the terminology of "balance" somewhat masks the difficulties and conflicts that are inherent to reconciliation'. It proposes that balance can be defined as 'satisfaction and good functioning at work and at home with a minimum of role conflict'.

The authors of the report recognise that to achieve balance, in this context two resources are critical:

1. Time
2. The means to address conflicting demands and the related stress

Indeed, it is the absence of these two critical resources that most impacts people who are struggling to balance the conflicting demands of their paid job and the Invisible Job, especially where they are responsible for most of the latter. Both jobs are important and people in this situation want to do them both well. But as a society, if we persist in not recognising the Invisible Job as something real, something important to the welfare of every family and, above all, something that takes up a significant amount of time, we will never be able to cut our cloth to fit our needs. Unless we recognise that the way we work needs to enable men and women to accommodate both paid work and the responsibilities of the Invisible Job, we will continue trying to do the impossible. Or at least women will. And until employers expect the Invisible Job to place equal demands on male and female employees, society will continue expecting responsibility for it to fall exclusively to women.

There is a limit to how much we can do each day before we feel we have lost a semblance of balance. The ESQL tried to explore when this balance is lost by asking respondents to define in the survey when they:

- Were too tired from work to do household jobs
- Experienced difficulties fulfilling family responsibilities because of time spent at work
- Had difficulties concentrating at work because of family responsibilities

There was a clear relationship between number of hours in paid employment and ability to deal with household responsibilities (see Table 23.1).

Table 23.1: Proportion of respondents in employment reporting work–life balance issues at least several times a month (15)

Hours worked per week	Too tired from work to do household jobs	Difficulty fulfilling family responsibilities because of time spent at work	Difficulty concentrating at work because of family responsibilities
1–29	49%	23%	15%
30–39	56%	31%	18%
40–49	60%	40%	19%
50+	73%	59%	26%

Data based on aggregate responses from both men and women

Unsurprisingly, the more hours an individual spends at work each week, the more they struggle to cope with family responsibilities. Among people who worked <30 hours per week, only 23% felt they had difficulty coping with family responsibilities. For people working 31–40 hours per week, this rose to 31% and among people working 40–49 hours per week, 40% reported this was a problem. The proportion experiencing difficulties was highest among those working 50+ hours per week. It is interesting to note that the correlation was much weaker the other way around – i.e. even for those in jobs with the longest hours of paid work, family responsibilities did not prevent them concentrating on their paid work. Since women tend to carry the mental load for all the Invisible Job entails, it is not surprising that the survey found that women experience tiredness more often than men. Tiredness was most marked in women aged 34 (the age group most likely to have at least one child under five), two-thirds of whom reported feeling too tired from work to do household jobs at least several times a month (15). Men also reported feeling too tired to face parenting and housework responsibilities when they come home. The survey found the peak period where men report the most difficulties in terms of work–life balance is age 35–49. Therefore, during the busiest phase of life for parents – which is generally age 30 to 49, would it not make more sense for us all to go about this differently? What if, during this period, men and women both had flexibility to reduce their hours of work to, say ten, twenty or thirty hours per week, depending on what combination would work best for the couple. This would afford both the stimulation of paid work while freeing up time to participate more fully in parenting and household responsibilities. Research from the US found that working fathers were just as likely as working mothers to say they would prefer to stay at home raising their children than working for pay but they couldn't because they needed the income (48% of fathers versus 52% of mothers interviewed) (36). It is important to temper this enthusiastic attitude by highlighting that it is not clear whether any of the people interviewed had ever experienced looking after children full-time! Especially when you have children under five years old, the day-to-day reality can be rather less fun that you would imagine. In fact, without respite, much of the potential joy from spending time with children can be extinguished. It is well documented that having more than one role (provided this is in a balance or proportion of our choosing) is beneficial to our overall wellbeing, compared to spending all our time on caring responsibilities. (15) And it is this mix which might bring greater happiness and balance to both men and women.

Research comparing actual versus preferred work among couples found that in Ireland, as in many other European countries, the male breadwinner arrangement (male employed/female not employed) was much more common than preferred: while 29% of working-age couples had this arrangement, it was preferred by only 9% (2).

Countries with the greatest flexibility in working hours and the most egalitarian approach to sharing parenting and home responsibilities experience the least difficulty when it comes to managing the conflict between (paid) work and home responsibilities. Whereas 66% of respondents in the UK and Ireland reported feeling too tired to face household jobs, in Denmark, Sweden and Finland, this was the case for just 53% of respondents (15). Is this yet another endorsement of the ethic of egalitarian working practices and shared male–female responsibilities for household activities in Nordic countries?

A manageable and equitable balance between professional work and home responsibilities would offer benefits to both men and women. For women, it would offer the variety, mental stimulation and identity that comes from engaging in professional work. Provided their partners increased the number of hours they contributed to the Invisible Job by a corresponding amount, the wellbeing of the family/home need not suffer.

For men, spending more time with their children when they are young also brings important benefits. It gives them the opportunity to bond with their baby and create closer long-term relationships with their children. It also ensures they are not excluded from developing the practical parenting skills that they may otherwise lack if not regularly involved in a hands-on capacity. In addition, participating as a caregiver to their children has a beneficial effect on men's relationships with their partners.

WHEN IS THE BEST TIME TO HAVE CHILDREN?

Deciding when is the best time to become a parent is complicated and involves many social, economic and personal factors. These include the financial cost, availability of affordable childcare, cultural norms, relationship status, perceptions of feeling ready to be a parent – and the suitability/readiness of your partner (40). Until government and employers enable shared working and caring roles to become a viable reality for men and women, trying to figure out the best time to have children remains a difficult decision for women who want to have a career and a family.

While in theory the window of opportunity for a woman to have children stretches from her teens to her forties, in reality it is much narrower. To make the best start in their careers, most women will want to progress their education as far as possible, i.e. not only complete secondary level education but third level, too. If she completes secondary education around 18 years of age and continues straight to third level, a woman may have completed undergraduate studies by the age of 21 or 22, depending on the course. If she takes a year off before going to university or decides to pursue graduate studies, she may be 25 or 26.

Some women might consider having a child in their mid-twenties. At this age, a woman's chance of becoming pregnant are high and arguably she might have the most energy to handle being the parent of a young child. However, having recently graduated, at this point most career-oriented women will be keen to establish themselves and get experience in their field. This is the point when graduate training schemes in companies are available and when competition is hot for essential entry-level positions in many professional fields. Another factor is that at this age, most women/couples won't yet have the financial security to afford support services such as cleaners and childcare that make the experience of being a parent more manageable.

By her early 30s, a woman is more likely to feel sufficiently established in her career to risk stepping out of it for a while. She is also more likely to have the resources for this period to be less stressful financially. However, women's chances of becoming pregnant begin to decline gradually but significantly from the age of 32 and even more rapidly from the age of 37 (41). This means that trying to become pregnant in your late thirties or later is more likely to be a stressful and expensive process involving IVF, a lower chance of becoming pregnant, a higher risk of pregnancy loss and/or complications.

It would therefore appear that the window of opportunity for starting a family is very narrow indeed! It is therefore not surprising that the latest European data indicate that the average age at first birth of European women is 29.3 (42). In the UK, the figure in 2019 was 30.3 years old (43) and in Ireland it was slightly higher, at 31.3 years (44). In the absence of affordable childcare, if most of the responsibility for looking after children falls to women, little wonder that women are so time-starved between the ages of 30 and 45, precisely the period when both men and women are also busiest in their careers. In her much-cited article, 'Why Women Still Can't Have it All' (45), Anne-Marie Slaughter (an international lawyer and political scientist who was Director of Policy Planning in the Obama administration) wonders if there might be a work-around to this problem within the current system. Even if women end up stepping back from (or completely out of) the workforce during this period to raise a family, could they perhaps refocus on their career when their youngest child is finished school and they are less encumbered with caring responsibilities? As she puts it, would it be possible for women 'to rise to the top in their late 50s and early 60s'? While there are examples of senior women in public life whose careers did indeed peak late in life (such as Hillary Clinton) at this stage, many career options are closed off because women seeking to re-enter the workforce will be competing against their younger selves. As Slaughter acknowledges, 'Personally, I have never seen a woman in her 40s enter the academic market successfully, or enter a law firm as a junior associate, Alicia Florrick of The Good Wife notwithstanding'.

PART III

WHY DOES THIS IMBALANCE EXIST AND HOW CAN WE END IT?

24

Why Is Most of the Invisible Job Done by Women?

Why does a curious imbalance exist in countless heterosexual relationships in terms of what should be jointly shared responsibilities? Why does the vast majority of the Invisible Job somehow end up falling to the woman?

When exchanging vows 'to have and to hold', is there some small print that says, 'Regarding almost every aspect of your joint life responsibilities, the wife shall be ultimately responsible and the husband only needs to get involved when he chooses to opt in or is specifically asked to?'

I don't think so.

And if this future (hypothetical) arrangement had been proposed, do you think many egalitarian women would have signed up to it?

Hell no!

So why is it that even in relationships where both partners have paid jobs, the majority of the Invisible Job is all too often done by women? And why don't we notice it happening?

THEORY A: THE X CHROMOSOME

Does the X chromosome mean that women (exclusively) are genetically programmed to ensure a successful long-term relationship with a mate and offspring, where everything on the domestic front is tickety-boo, regardless of the cost to them personally?

Among some species, the responsibility for building a den/nest and bringing up offspring is indeed often borne by the female, with males contributing little to the daily grind of catching food, teaching youngsters and removing ticks from fur. In prides of lions, for instance, females are responsible for hunting all the pack's food, in addition to rearing cubs and teaching them to become independent adults. The leader of the pack is usually the most dominant female. The only responsibility the adult males have is defending the pack against predator attacks. An important role, certainly, but one which leaves males free to lie in the shade snoozing 90% of the time, while females take care of pretty much everything else.

Mind you, prior to securing a female as a mate, the male in almost all species will go to great lengths to impress her. The bowerbird in Papua New Guinea devotes long hours to constructing a magnificent nest to demonstrate to any would-be mate what a wonderful future home he has built for them to share. The female surveys all the nests built by males vying for her affection and carefully evaluates their quality before making her decision. She also takes into consideration the singing ability of the nest builder – after all, who wouldn't want their champion nest builder to also be a great singer?

On the other hand, there are also some exemplary egalitarian animal species that share the burden of raising and providing for a family equally. One of these is the Emperor penguin. Both the male and female spend long and lonely hours in the freezing cold diligently tending a single egg, keeping it warm and preventing it from coming into direct contact with the ice by balancing it carefully on their feet. They share this job equally. While one parent holds the fort (or rather egg) at home in sub-zero temperatures, the other goes out to sea for long periods, fishing. They continue this sharing once the chick is born; parents taking turns to look after the hatchling chick and protect it from gulls until the other arrives home from fishing with a bellyful of sardines ready to regurgitate to the hungry chick.

Or does some transformation occur when women become mothers? Does an instinct to nurture and provide for her child lead a mother to blindly cater to the needs of this tiny human without question? Certainly, most mothers rapidly develop a strong impulse to protect their new baby and do everything they can to ensure its happiness. On the other hand, it would be hard to believe that men don't also develop this deep sense of responsibility as the parent of a helpless infant.

Many fathers describe feeling terrified initially to pick up their new baby; while bursting with eagerness and pride to hold her, they may be reluctant to do so, worried they might drop her at any moment. Many assume that somehow their partners naturally know what to do, when in fact most women are equally clueless – unless they have had occasion to hold a baby in the past. And while few men may have experienced holding a tiny baby before the arrival of their own first child, to be fair, most women probably have. This is not due to any absence of paternal instinct in men; it's simply that women are more likely to have done a stint as an au pair or babysitter at some point, both roles that are (unfairly) more available to girls than boys. Even if they have not had either experience, whenever women find themselves in situations where a friend, relative or colleague has a new baby, it is usually presumed that all other women are just dying to hold it, even if no such signals are forthcoming. When the mother enthusiastically stretches her arms across to you asking, 'Would you like to hold her?' it's practically a rhetorical question. You have a baby in your arms before you've had time to start the getaway car. Having experienced it once (even if the baby cries non-stop when ousted from the familiar arms of the mother into your terrified ones), at least the fear factor is forever diminished. Next time, you will feel less intimidated by the prospect of holding a baby – or if holding babies is not really your thing, you will make sure you have a well-rehearsed excuse at the ready.

When women become mothers – whether by birth or adoption – does this generate in them a sixth sense that enables them to hear their baby cry in the middle of the night, immediately jumping out of bed to resolve whatever is causing the distress? I remember coming across a new baby greeting card once that read, 'Sleep like a baby? Are you kidding me, those little buggers never sleep; you want to sleep like a husband!'

Could it be that women have supersonic hearing? Or is it more likely that mothers choose to get out of bed to attend to baby while fathers turn a blind ear? Is this due to 'maternal instinct' – whether real or one mothers are conditioned to believe they should have?

With practice, a mother gets better at resolving whatever is ailing her baby when he cries at 2 a.m., whether he is cold, hot, wet, hungry, lonely or scared. This is clearly good news for baby. This competence probably also makes mother feel good too. With experience, she even learns to anticipate a baby's needs. The more she looks after the baby, the more competent and comfortable she becomes.

While for some women, being the only one who can calm their baby – i.e. being needed – might make them feel good in the early days, creating an exclusive dependency is not good for either parent.

Knowing how to soothe a crying infant or child is not a skill exclusively available to mothers; with equal amounts of practice at 2 a.m. (or any other time!), there is every chance Daddy would become just as much of an expert, meaning his presence will calm and comfort baby in the way the mother's does.

For that reason, women should never exclude fathers from looking after baby; instead, they should help them become just as capable and confident as they are. For instance, even if she is breastfeeding, when Daddy is nearby Mommy can try to include him in her baby talk and ensure baby can see Daddy. Often breastfeeding mothers will express milk so that Daddy can do occasional feeds. Not only does this enable Daddy to be more involved, but it also allows Mommy to get some essential sleep!

Conversely, if the gap between their capabilities grows, Daddy might even begin to feel that he's not needed at all, since Mommy appears to have the whole situation covered. Developing a reputation for being 'good at' something can lead to being responsible for it forever.

Pigeons and doves have evolved a very efficient system for sharing the load of looking after their young, helped by the unusual fact that both sexes are able to secrete milk. This makes them interchangeable when it comes to feeding but this sharing approach continues after the chicks have dispensed with milk and moved on to solid food. The male and female tag-team to gather seeds and other food for the chicks, with the father flying off to find food in the morning and the mother working in the afternoon. This efficient partnership enables pigeons and doves to complete the rearing of their young very quickly, leaving them free to consider what they want to do next in life, whether this might be having more chicks or focusing on other things, such as the pigeon equivalent of watching Netflix or taking up hillwalking. Perhaps humans have something to learn from this.

A final angle to this possible genetic theory for why women assume most of the burden of parenting and home responsibilities is a numbers one: Female mammals (including humans) have a fixed number of eggs, while males can theoretically generate infinite numbers of sperm. In addition, females are the ones that must grow a new life inside them and give birth. So when it comes to decisions about reproduction, females need to choose carefully who to mate with. Humans live in a society built around an expectation of a two-parent unit, ideally one that stays together forever. Therefore, when a child is born, could it be that women are genetically predisposed to ensuring this happens and that their offspring are brought up safely and successfully? Since they have more 'skin in the game,' might they be willing to do whatever it takes to achieve this (even if this means doing all the work themselves)?

In summary, while the parenting behaviour of humans may be influenced by the presence or absence of an X chromosome, in my view it would be far too simplistic to say it accounts for why most of the Invisible Job is currently done by mothers.

What about housework, though? We're all familiar with the gender stereotype, when it comes to what constitutes clean or tidy, that women's standards are simply much higher than men's. In other words, when a man and a woman look at the same room, although a woman would consider it messy, a man may think it is fine. Well it turns out that this theory does not hold water. Researchers Sarah Thébaud and colleagues asked 646 people to look at a picture of a living room/kitchen area and rate it as clean or messy on a scale of 0–100 and determine whether they felt it needed to be cleaned urgently. There was no difference between how men scored the picture compared to women and whether it needed to be cleaned urgently. In other words, men and women have similar views on mess (46). Where respondents did differ, however, was in terms of whose responsibility it was to clean it! More on this later.

THEORY B: MATERNITY LEAVE

Recognising that newborn babies need to be looked after, most developed countries have a financial mechanism that allows a parent to stay home and perform this function for a limited time. However, except in a handful of enlightened countries this financial support is offered exclusively in the form of maternity leave (rather than parental leave – i.e. accessible to either/both parents), so it is largely predetermined that the person who takes on this role will be the mother. But is this right? If a couple decide to have a baby, surely this means both want to become parents. If so, why should caring for the baby be automatically designated the mother's role? By exclusively offering financial support to mothers, 'maternity leave' ensures that women start out as the main carers of their children. This sends the mother down a path that leads her deeper and deeper into the parenting role, while the father is encouraged to progress his career as the financial provider of the family.

After giving birth, a period of immediate maternity leave is indeed welcome. Jesus, the damage it can do to your undercarriage! Emma Thompson expresses this well in the film *Bridget Jones' Baby*, where she plays Dr Rawlings, Bridget's obstetrician. Bridget is not sure whether the father is Mark Darcy or Jack Qwant. Therefore, both men are in the labour suite when Bridget gives birth. After they initially position themselves at Bridget's feet as she lies with her knees spread, Dr Rawlings casually counsels against this location: 'I'm not sure how much there is to gain from you two being at the coalface if I'm honest. My ex-husband said it was like watching his favourite pub burn down' (47).

Suffice to say that there is a need for rest and recuperation after giving birth. To enable far-flung bits to return to their rightful location, stitches to heal and bruises to subside, every new mother needs a period of rest. And after an extended labour, sleep feels like manna from heaven. However, most public maternity hospitals in the UK and Ireland only afford new mothers one night in hospital after giving birth. And poor Mum may get very little sleep at all because her baby is likely to cry every hour or two for any number of reasons – he may be hungry, too cold/hot or just confused and lonely after leaving his cosy surroundings of the last nine months. And if you are in a public ward with five other new mothers, five out of six times the baby crying isn't even yours!

After a day or two, Mum will head home, probably still exhausted, and very possibly still quite sore. She would love the chance to bond with her baby and get to know everything about this unique little being while nursing her wounds (physical and emotional) with large doses of sleep. She is definitely not interested in cooking (for herself or anyone else), trying to keep a house clean or feeding babygrows and bedsheets to the washing machine all day! If 'maternity leave' meant a chance to recuperate peacefully at home while someone attended to all the rest, it would be an opportunity women would welcome with open arms.

In reality, it's more like trying to recuperate in a war hospital on the front line. The bombs keep coming relentlessly, in the form of baby feeds and nappy changes every couple of hours and pacing around exhausted in the wee hours trying to release wind that may or may not be the reason your baby is not sleeping. As for attending to your wounds (whether stitches following a Caesarean section or tears to sensitive areas) and getting on with those pelvic muscle exercises, well ... most days you're lucky if you manage to shower.

In short, most women would feel that a period of maternity leave is necessary. But once they feel physically and emotionally recovered from the birth, however long this might take, the question of how two parents should manage looking after the baby between them for the next few months should be an open discussion.

Looking after a baby is harder than going to work

When a woman goes on maternity leave, she possibly leaves behind a stimulating workplace, where she interacted daily with colleagues and/or clients, and suddenly finds herself at home with only a baby to talk to. I remember being in this situation when my daughter was about a week old. My husband had stayed home for a few days after the birth, both of us trying to get our heads around our new world. The first few days were a blur of excitement and confusion. We muddled along as best we could, figuring out how to breastfeed (me), change nappies (both of us) and between us, tried to make informed guesses about what might be the problem whenever our daughter cried, while gently trying to dissuade visitors from staying for hours.

After a few days, he went back to work and I was alone. Initially, I did not feel daunted. In fact, on paper, it all looked easy. My husband would be working all day to support us financially while all I had to do was mind a baby – how hard could it be? At least that's how I (deludedly) saw the situation.

Each morning I had a mental to-do list of various household things I needed to do that day – such as clearing up the kitchen, putting on the dishwasher or washing machine and emptying the nappy bin – which I envisaged getting through in about an hour.

There was also a rapidly evolving must-do list being dictated by health professionals, books, well-meaning relatives and friends. Things like:

- Register baby with the GP, book postnatal check-up and arrange her immunisations
- Register her birth officially and obtain birth certificate

- Research crèches and childminders
- Apply for baby's passport so we can fly to Ireland to introduce her to my family
- Open a child savings account with the £250 government voucher that had arrived in the post
- Arrange a postnatal visit with the district nurse to check on my stitches
- Attend postnatal physiotherapy and breastfeeding clinics at the hospital

I also had a list of activities that I was keen to do, my try-to-do list. Things like:

- Contact that nice girl from the antenatal class who suggested meeting up for coffee once the babies were born
- Write thank you notes for all the presents and cards we received
- Start a baby diary to note down all the things baby is doing
- Get some pictures of baby printed to send to parents/siblings and frame one to put on the wall
- Contact local church about the christening
- Find out about the baby yoga my friend recommended – she says it's great for their physical development
- Do my pelvic floor exercises
- Read the baby books I bought (or had been given) about feeding, sleep routines, swaddling and baby development
- Learn how to do baby sign

Day after day, I failed to even get halfway through the to-do list of household jobs – the ones I expected would only take an hour. The rate of progress on the must-do list was like the rate that glaciers retreat in Patagonia. And don't even mention the try-to-do list!

At work, I had been responsible for planning and executing a wide range of projects, working with colleagues and experts from around the world. I was now attempting only a tiny fraction of what I would normally get through in a day but failing miserably. It was frustrating and demoralising. When you are a sleep-deprived new mother, however, you do not realise how incredibly difficult the job of looking after a baby is. In hindsight, I appreciate that daily goals that include anything beyond eating, sleeping and looking after your baby are a stretch. But if nobody has ever told you this, how are you supposed to know? Instead, you think you are failing. And when you are not used to failing, instead of screaming for help, you will just try harder because clearly it must be your fault.

There is a really important point that new mothers on maternity leave need to realise. You and your partner have (presumably) made a joint decision that you will take maternity leave while he goes back to work. Quite possibly, this period will be the maximum period that your employer or the state will subsidise you financially to look after your baby. This makes sense for many couples, given the limited paternity support options available to fathers in most countries. However, if choosing this route, two things should be appreciated by both partners from the outset:

1. Looking after a new baby is much harder than going out to work

In the roller coaster you find yourself on after giving birth, you know the going is tough but you don't appreciate just how tough until you have something concrete to compare it to. I presumed that my husband was having just as tough a time each day at the office as I was having at home with the baby and that the problem must simply be that I simply wasn't very good at this 'mothering' business. My first day at work after maternity leave was therefore an eye-opening moment. I had been a little anxious about it, wondering if I'd be able to jump back in at full pace. However, I distinctly remember my first day back. For the first time in months, I was free to carry out a task from start to finish without being interrupted, I could engage in intelligent conversation with other adults – even go to the toilet on my own! It felt fantastic. To my surprise, I realised that this job was infinitely easier than the one I had been struggling with on maternity leave for the last seven months. All this time, I had been beating myself up trying to manage everything at home, not realising just how easy my husband's life had been by comparison. Therefore, whichever parent is at home looking after baby should cut themselves some slack and deserves as much support as possible from their partner.

2. Being on maternity leave should not mean you are responsible for baby 24 hours a day, seven days a week

Instead, the hours that you have sole responsibility for looking after your baby should mirror the hours that your partner goes out to work. Outside of say, 8 a.m. to 6 p.m. Monday to Friday, responsibility should be shared equally between you. Remember that the person going out to work has the easy gig; they do not have a small person permanently attached to them; they have two hands; they have space to think clearly; their brain enjoys the regular dopamine rewards of completing tasks throughout the day while you juggle ten unfinished tasks at any one time; they do not have strange-smelling milk regurgitated on them several times a day; in short, they get to conduct themselves as a normal adult. Under no circumstances, therefore, should your partner presume that you should have sole responsibility for baby-related activities in the evenings and at weekends! Another common mistake most new mothers make: having developed skills which your partner does not have, when you are stuck for time, it can often feel easier/quicker to just do something yourself instead of taking a moment to show your partner how to do it. Tempting as this may be, try to resist!

Setting a precedent

Eventually, it all gets easier: baby starts to sleep a little more; you get a little more sleep and the haze you had been stumbling through for months starts to lift – possibly just around the time you are preparing to go back to work.

However, two detrimental things tend to happen during maternity leave:

1. Without being conscious of it, many women take on the lion's share of both parenting and household responsibilities. They are usually not aware this is happening, firstly because this evolution is so gradual and secondly because nobody tells them (or even asks them!) to take on these responsibilities. Women tend to simply identify when something needs to be done in the interests of their family – and do it.
2. This sets a precedent for who is responsible for most of the parenting and household responsibilities when maternity leave ends: when women go back to work, rather than splitting these responsibilities with her husband, women tend to carry on doing them on top of their own (paid) job.

This is why maternity leave (i.e. where a mother exclusively takes time off work to look after a baby but the father does not) plays a critical role in establishing the imbalance in 'ownership' for responsibilities that should be shared by both parents.

The financial side

In most countries where paid parental leave is provided (by the state or an employer), it tends to be assigned to the mother. This is a key determinant for why mothers are almost always the ones who stay home to look after a new baby.

The duration of paid maternity leave varies enormously from country to country and depends on who your employer is. In the UK, women are entitled to take up to 52 weeks of maternity leave. They also receive 'statutory maternity pay' during this time but only for 39 weeks. 'Statutory maternity pay' (paid by the state) entitles mothers to 90% of their average weekly earnings for six weeks. For the next 33 weeks it only pays £148.68 (before tax) per week. And if this equates to more than 90% of their average weekly pay (before tax), women only receive the lower of the two amounts (48).

This weekly amount of £148.68 is the equivalent of an annual salary of £7,731.36. It's hard to imagine how any woman could survive on this, once basic outgoings such as paying rent/mortgage, food and transport are factored in. So what hope does a woman who has just had a baby (and may even have other children to support already) have? On top of her existing outgoings, she now has to meet significant additional costs associated with a new baby. For instance, all the baby clobber she needs to buy – nappies, a Moses basket, cot, pushchair, blankets, perhaps formula feed, baby bottles and steriliser, baby clothes (which they grow out of every three months), toys and books. While she is contending with these additional financial outgoings, she is also unable to be as thrifty as she might normally be because she has absolutely no time! In other words:

- No time to cook (and therefore probably has to rely on buying ready-made food)
- No time to clean (and so may need to employ a cleaner)
- No time to plan (e.g. research to find the best prices or travel to larger shops to buy reasonably priced goods; instead, she may have to shop locally even if prices are higher)
- She also may frequently need to make emergency purchases (because it is easy to forget to bring a bottle of water, snack or nappies with you when you are chronically sleep-deprived and focused on the needs of your baby)

Therefore, for most mothers in the UK, it is almost impossible to survive on statutory maternity pay for 39 weeks without some other source of finance, whether this is savings, a partner who is reasonably well paid or help from family. And it certainly does not provide for the luxury of paying for external help with household chores, meaning women have no means of outsourcing these responsibilities during the very period they need this help most.

It is formally acknowledged that there is a big difference between 'paid maternity leave' and 'well-paid maternity leave'. According to the International Network on Leave Policies and Research (49), 'well paid' is defined as receiving 66% or more of your salary. Using this index, Table 1 in the Appendix of this book summarises the maternity leave entitlements across a range of countries. It highlights huge disparities – with some countries (such as the US) having no statutory provision whatsoever for well-paid maternity leave, while others offer up to twelve months. There are also marked differences between countries when it comes to flexibility around transferring part or all this leave to fathers, with few countries facilitating this in a meaningful way.

Facilitating shared parental leave

Why is it that in most societies, the onus of looking after babies/children seems to fall automatically on women? The question is almost always

- If/when a mother plans to go back to work (in other words will she quit her job to become a 'stay-at-home mother' permanently or just temporarily?)
      NOT
- Whether a father plans to quit his job to become a 'stay-at-home father' (even temporarily!)

Scandinavian countries are lightyears ahead of most of the rest of the world in facilitating men and women sharing this responsibility equally. Since 1974, Swedish couples have had access to parental leave (i.e. leave that can be shared between them), while in most countries the only viable option available to couples is maternity leave, as the table in the Appendix outlines. In 1993, Norway was the first Nordic country to introduce leave earmarked exclusively for fathers – initially for four weeks, later increased to twelve. Currently, the total parental leave allocation in Norway is 49 weeks, paid at 100% of salary. (Alternatively, couples can opt to take 59 weeks at 80% salary). Mothers are allocated thirteen weeks exclusively (three weeks before the birth and ten weeks after), while fathers get twelve weeks exclusively, with 26 additional weeks that can be shared between the mother and father.

Sweden and Iceland followed Norway's lead in assigning a share of parental leave exclusively to fathers. In Sweden, it is now generally frowned upon if men don't opt to spend at least several months looking after their baby. As a result, it is completely normal to find young men in parent and toddler groups (most of which are organised for free by the government of this forward-thinking country) out having morning coffee with baby in tow. Outside of the Scandinavian utopia, men may be given a token amount of paternity leave by employers but it is usually unpaid and may be as short as two weeks – hardly a realistic option for a couple who wish to share child-rearing equally.

In Iceland, parents of new babies are entitled to nine months of paid parental leave, three of which must be taken by the mother and three which must be taken by the father, with the remaining three months shared between the couple as they choose. If a mother or father does not take their allocated three months of paid parental leave, it cannot be transferred to their partner; i.e. you either 'use it or lose it'. And use it they do; in Iceland uptake of parental leave by fathers is 91%!

Many groups have been calling for other countries to put in place adequately paid paternity leave to enable fathers to become actively involved in the care of their new babies. In the UK in 2018, there was an active campaign for the introduction of a twelve-week 'use it or lose it' paternity leave to encourage fathers to spend more time with their infants, like the system in Iceland.

There are many potential advantages for both men and women associated with a measure like this. A 2018 EU report on the benefits of fathers taking leave found that it offered benefits for everyone – fathers, mothers, children, employers and families (50):

- *Benefits for fathers:* Fathers involved in their children's lives have longer, healthier lives, better relationships and more personal satisfaction.
- *Benefits for children:* Fathers' participation in children's lives from birth has positive, long-lasting outcomes for child development, such as improved cognitive and emotional outcomes and physical health.

- *Benefits for mothers:* Acknowledgement by employers that both mothers and fathers have caring responsibilities leads to greater gender equality in the labour market.
- *Benefits for employers:* Paid leave has positive impacts on businesses, promoting and reducing employee retention, increasing morale and productivity, and reducing absenteeism and staff turnover.
- *Benefits for families:* More equal share of professional and domestic responsibilities has a positive impact on work–life balance in families.

Having a baby is one of the biggest stress tests of a relationship and the role fathers play in looking after the baby is critical. When men elect to take time off work to participate in taking care of their baby, it significantly strengthens their relationship with their partner. A recent Norwegian study showed that playing a more active role in childcare makes men better appreciate the childcare work their partners do (51). When men understand what looking after a child entails, they are likely to show more empathy for, and support towards, their partner when she is doing much of the parenting work.

Another positive for the mother is the free time this affords her to engage in something she wishes to do, increasing her sense of wellbeing and fulfilment, as well as her satisfaction with her overall work–life balance. It also gives her the opportunity to engage (at least part-time) in paid work, which may make the relationship feel more egalitarian, especially for women who are not fans of the traditional male breadwinner model. The proportion of total childcare that the man did correlated positively with how the woman viewed the relationship.

A study carried out at University of Manchester based on a large UK cohort of UK couples found a direct correlation between involved fatherhood and the long-term stability of the relationship (10). Fathers who took sole charge of their baby for an extended period during the baby's first year of life were up to 40% less likely to break up with the baby's mother within seven years of the child's birth. Paternal involvement in four childcare and three housework tasks were found to be sufficient to account for the significance of this outcome. When interviewed on the study findings by *The Guardian* (52), its lead author Professor Helen Norman said, 'Our results show that relationships are less likely to break down over the long term if the dad looks after the baby on his own, without the mother being there, at least a few times a week during the first year. This correlation holds regardless of all other variables such as ethnicity, gender-role attitudes and household income'. A key factor in this study was that fathers were looking after the baby without the mother being there. This enables fathers to learn for themselves what taking care of a small baby is really like. It is easy for men to believe they are contributing significantly simply by virtue of being present – i.e. 'potentially available' to help their partner. However, whether they are helping with a particular task or even doing the task themselves, there is still an enormous difference between doing one task and having sole responsibility for a baby's needs for a period. Any individual task is manageable; it is only when they have responsibility for all of them, with nobody to call on for help, that fathers experience this reality. For instance:

- When the doorbell rings midway through changing a particularly messy nappy on the bed: while your mind frets about whoever-it-is walking off before you get to the door, your child wriggles off the change mat, smearing poo across the duvet.
- Attempting the apparently simple task of getting out to the park for a few hours with a six-month-old: all too often, women shield men from experiencing this solo. Instead of letting fathers figure things out for themselves, mothers make it an artificially easy experience by handing them a fed, dry and suitably attired baby, already installed in the pushchair complete with baby bag (containing nappies, wipes, Vaseline, plastic bags, spare babygrow, emergency pot of purée and bottle of milk for baby, water and a snack for Daddy), along with detailed advice about baby's feed/sleep times. Even still, given the opportunity, some men will walk the pushchair straight to their mother or mother-in-law's house so she can dote on the baby while he pulls up a chair at the kitchen table. He will return from the walk proudly announcing that it was a breeze (In other words 'I don't know why you make such a fuss about this being so hard').

Instead, mothers should gift fathers the learning opportunity of surviving solo with baby for 48 hours early and often, by walking out the door on a Friday and saying, 'See you Sunday night, darling!' It is only when they have to cope by themselves that men realise that what their wife/partner has been doing for the last few weeks is much harder than it looks. Remember, the better you do a job, the more invisible it is to people who never do it. Without the invisible support, Daddy will have to figure out for himself what's involved and rely on his wits, skill and creativity to make it work. From then on, even if he is not the one doing it most of the time, he will better understand what it entails and is therefore more likely to demonstrate his appreciation to his partner. He may do this verbally or by taking on a different task to help – perhaps preparing lunch or tidying the kitchen while his wife is busy looking after the baby. The experience will not only enhance his capability as a parent and build confidence in his own ability as a father, but, importantly, it starts him on a path to playing a lifelong, more hands-on role in his child's life.

The second reason that relationships in which a man regularly takes sole responsibility for a baby fare better is that mothers really need little breaks. Looking after a baby can be all-consuming and frequently frustrating. Being able to switch off, even for a short time, allows a mother to recharge her batteries and gain perspective. It also gives her a chance to do something for herself, which reduces feelings of resentment towards her partner and makes the relationship feel more like an equal partnership. When fathers truly share the load of parenting and household responsibilities during this very challenging period, it is hardly surprising that it results in more stable relationships in the long term. So why is facilitating paid paternity leave for all fathers not a no-brainer? And if all men were offered the opportunity to spend a month (or more) at home with their baby during the first few months after birth, without suffering any financial penalty, would they jump at the chance or pass? Here are two interesting case studies on this question: one from Portugal and one from Spain.

The impact of making paternity leave available in Portugal

In 2009, the Portuguese introduced new legislation (Labour Law 2009) that replaced maternity leave with the more gender-neutral 'initial parental leave' and with it, three major changes came into effect:

1. Paid paternity leave was increased to four weeks.
2. A 'sharing bonus' was introduced, which affords couples an extra month of fully compensated leave, provided the father takes four weeks or more of initial parental leave on his own, after the first six weeks reserved for the mother. Couples could choose between five months of leave at 100% of previous earnings or six months at 83% of earnings.
3. 'Complementary parental leave' was introduced (payable at 25% of previous earnings), if taken immediately after initial parental leave.

Fathers in Portugal therefore became eligible to take paid initial parental leave and complementary parental leave. So, did they use it?

A report on this (53) found that with the new policy, fathers' leave periods indeed became longer, and their use of initial parental leave increased substantially. Before the 2009 reform, only 0.6% of fathers took leave. In 2010 (just one year after its introduction), 20% of parents divided the initial parental leave between them, either in the form of the longer six-month option (58%) or the shorter five-month option (42%).

According to the authors of the report, four factors encouraged the use of the scheme by fathers:

1. It offers full earnings compensation.
2. It allows parents to prolong childcare when the child is still very young (5–6 months).
3. It was facilitated by paternity leave (taken at the same time as maternity leave during the first month after childbirth), which increased from 17% in 2000 to 82% in 2014.

4. Lastly, compared to men who began to take up leave in the mid-1990s, this generation of fathers grew up in a society where the meaning of fatherhood was starting to shift dramatically.

A paper looking at the changes in attitudes and practices with regard to unpaid labour in Portugal over the period 2002–2014 found this policy had led to marked progress towards gender equality (54). The authors found that:

- Regardless of age, men take a larger part in household work.
- The division of unpaid work between men and women is more equal.
- There is an increasing perception, among men and women, of fairness in the division of household work.
- A concept of caring masculinity is being disseminated – reflected, for example, in more men taking leave.
- Popular attitudes about men's early involvement in paternal care are changing in line with the egalitarian leave policies.
- Evidence of changing gender roles, including a perception that men have as much responsibility as women in family life.

This endorses the long-term impact that putting in place adequate measures to encourage men to take at least 30 days of paternity leave shortly after birth has on changing behaviours and gender roles.

The impact of making paternity leave available in Spain

In 2007, Spain introduced several changes to its family benefits system as part of a wider system to foster gender equality in areas such as law and electoral rights. One of the new initiatives was the creation of additional paid paternity leave. In addition to promoting gender equality, one of the aims of the new family benefits system was to encourage couples to have more children because fertility rates in Spain were lower than desired. Before we look at the outcome of this scheme, it's worth explaining the situation.

Prior to 1989, Spanish women were entitled to fourteen weeks of paid maternity leave, while fathers were only entitled to two days. In 1989, a sixteen-week parental leave system was introduced; of this, six weeks were compulsory and exclusively reserved for the mother but the remaining ten weeks could be taken by either the mother or the father. Fathers could take leave either at the same time as the mother or on their own, any time after the first six weeks. However, although entitled to take parental leave, only a negligible number of fathers opted to use any part of their entitlement. Under the 2007 reforms scheme, the sixteen weeks of parental leave was extended to eighteen weeks, with the additional two weeks being available exclusively to fathers and non-transferable to mothers.

This measure led to an immediate and dramatic increase in the number of fathers making use of parental leave. Within one year of implementing the 2007 'use it or lose it' two-week paid parental leave, 279,756 fathers had taken it, which represented 54% of all new fathers, a more than 400% increase! At the same time, it was observed that this resulted in women taking shorter maternity leave, as can also be seen from Figure 24.1.

Figure 24.1: Number of mothers and fathers taking maternity/paternity leave in Spain (55)

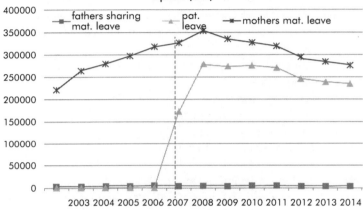

Two Spanish university researchers examined whether the new 2007 legislation resulted in any longer-term changes to Spanish society. The researchers were interested in finding out what impact (if any) men taking two weeks of parental leave after a baby's birth had on:

• Men taking on a greater share of household work
• Women's participation in the labour market
• Men's longer-term involvement in childrearing
• Future fertility decisions of couples (as mentioned, the Spanish government hoped the new parental leave would encourage couples to have more children)

Impact on father's participation in childrearing and household chores

While there was huge uptake by men of the two-week 'use it or lose it' paid paternity leave within the first few months of their baby's birth, fathers' involvement in childcare was short-lived: beyond the age of three months, men were no more likely to stay home from work to look after a sick child than before (55).

This contrasts with the long-term benefits observed in Portugal. The authors comment that perhaps two weeks is insufficient to lead to any significant change in behaviour and that more intensive reform, such as equalising the duration of parental leave for both genders, may have a stronger effect on the division of child-care chores. This view is in line with the 'International Review of Leave Policies and Related Research', which found that where fathers take parental leave, this can lead to greater sharing of care for children by gender (49).

Impact on mother's employment

Following the introduction of the 'use it or lose it' paternal leave, women in Spain were 11% more likely to be back at work four months after the birth of their child. This suggests that women took up the option to return to work a couple of weeks earlier following childbirth, while their husbands stayed home to look after the child instead. This has the advantage of deferring the need for paid childcare by a few weeks. However, beyond a period of one year after childbirth, no change was observed in the numbers of women in paid employment compared to before the introduction of this policy. This suggests they were no more liberated than before from looking after children and managing a household.

Impact on fertility among couples

Given that one of the reasons for introducing the new measures was to encourage couples to have more babies, the outcome of this question was keenly awaited. Some speculated that women may be more inclined to have more children if they know their partner is going to be more involved in their care and if the direct cost to them (in terms of paying for childcare and being absent from employment) is lower. On the other hand, there was a chance men might be less inclined to have more children if the policy meant they would be expected to play a more hands-on role in their care by taking parental leave. Before the new paternity leave measures were introduced, men were more likely than their partners to want a large family. They also spent less time with their children than their partners did.

Overall, the study found that where the father had participated in the two-week parental leave, couples now took longer to have their second or subsequent child, with men stating their ideal number of children was now lower than the number they originally wanted. Before the parental leave reforms were introduced, 13% of women were likely to have another child, while afterwards this had dropped to 7.7% (i.e. the fertility rate was lower!) When the researchers dug into the data further, they found this outcome was mainly driven by families who were not college graduates – i.e. those less likely to be able to afford paid childcare. This may suggest that where fathers actually had to do the hands-on childcare them-selves, it led them to reconsider how soon they wanted to have another child. (Note that this applied principally to women who were older having their first child, with limited impact on younger mothers.)

An OECD report on Sweden concluded that fathers who take parental leave continue to be more involved in childcare in the long-term (56). It recommended that government and employer policies should encourage more equal sharing of parental leave by increasing the amount of time ringfenced for each parent, as is the case in Iceland. Where the allocation of parental leave is left up to a couple, evidence suggests that the split is influenced by cultural attitudes. Especially for men, long absences from work to attend to childcare responsibilities may be frowned upon in terms of perceived career commitment.

A 2018 article in *The Guardian* (57) argued that the reason men don't embrace parental leave in the UK is that it is simply not financially viable. 'Allowing' men (or women) to stay home to help look after their new baby without pay is meaningless when many people simply cannot afford to do so.

It is true that not many countries provide real financial encouragement to fathers to take leave to look after their child after birth (see the Appendix, Table 2 for a summary of the 'International Review of Leave Policies and Related Research' (49)). In many countries, men have no statutory entitlement to leave whatsoever, some countries only allow a few days, and several have provision for up to two weeks. The authors of the review highlight that even where fathers have a statutory entitlement to take parental leave, unless this leave is well paid, men tend not to use it. ('Well paid', as outlined earlier, is defined as receiving 66% or more of your previous salary.) However, there are only a few countries where 'well-paid leave' for a period of thirty days or more is available to fathers, namely Brazil, China (in some cases), Croatia, Finland, Iceland, Norway and Slovenia.

Another effective incentive is to offer a bonus where both fathers and mothers take some parental leave. Ten countries offer such a bonus: Sweden has a 'gender equality bonus' that provides a financial incentive for families to divide parental leave more equally; Germany extends paid leave by two months if fathers take at least two months of leave; Japan also offers an extra two months of leave if both parents use some of their leave entitlement; and as described earlier, Portugal offers a bonus to families where the father shares part of the initial parental leave. Other countries with incentives for fathers to take leave are Austria, Croatia, France, Italy, Korea, Norway and Romania.

In addition to financial barriers, another significant factor behind the very low number of men currently opting to take extended periods of paternal leave following the birth of their children is the attitudes of their colleagues or employers. One woman I know is expecting her first baby in a couple of weeks. Following the birth, her husband plans to take two months paternal leave so they can look after the baby together. She grew up in a family with traditionalist gender roles – i.e. her mother did all the housework and looked after the children while her father had a paid job. Her husband is aware of this dynamic and is himself a strong feminist. Both want to break free of the dynamic of the previous generation and ensure they share the responsibility of parenting and family management equally. However, when he announced to his colleagues his intention to take two months of parental leave, the response was one of incredulity. This doesn't mean his colleagues don't believe a baby would benefit from the love and attention of a father; rather, their response simply reflects their internalised sexism when it comes to perceptions of men's and women's parenting roles. Most men in his age group (30–35) have been conditioned to view looking after children predominantly as a woman's job. At the same time, they were led to view a man's identity in the family as being tied tightly to his role as a financial provider.

Breasts

Men who believe that women are obviously designed for staying home to look after babies may claim they are better physically suited to do so. Certainly, breast-feeding has many benefits for both babies and mothers, and while it can be intense and difficult in the early weeks, while learning the ropes (especially without guidance from a midwife or breastfeeding expert), once established it can fit into a woman's life more easily than often imagined. Mothers can continue to breastfeed after returning to work, either expressing milk while away from the baby, visiting baby during lunch or breastfeeding breaks to feed (if working nearby), introducing some formula feeding during the day, or, once baby is established on solids, simply feeding baby before and after work, with baby eating food and drinking water while away from mom. Of course, not all women do choose to breastfeed. It takes a lot of energy and therefore a physical toll on the body that does not appeal to all. In France, where beauty and femininity are of high cultural importance, breastfeeding ranks low. In fact, France has the lowest breastfeeding rate in the Western world. French women are quite open about their concerns that breast-feeding (especially for a protracted period) may result in saggy breasts, replacing what they perceive as their formerly powerful feminine weapons of seduction. As a Frenchwoman once told *Guardian* correspondent Fiachra Gibbons (58), 'Your breasts are for your husband, not your baby.' However, this is a myth. It is, in fact, pregnancy, not breastfeeding, that affects the shape of women's breasts. In any event, mothers who wish to continue breastfeeding but are returning to work may be able to adapt their baby's routine to include some formula feeding during the day or, alternatively, find a quiet space to express milk at work. Depending on their job/employer, some women may be able to work from home to accommodate breastfeeding. And once baby is established on solids, mothers can simply feed baby before and after work, with baby eating food and drinking water while away from mom. In short, breasts are not a dealbreaker when it comes to which partner should be a primary caregiver to a baby.

THEORY C: SEXISM AND THE OPPRESSION OF WOMEN

Restricting well-paid parental leave exclusively to mothers is one way of determining that the role of parenting falls mainly to women. However, there are even more overt ways in which state measures can ensure that 'a woman's place is in the home'.

Constitutional barriers

Article 41.2 of the Irish Constitution refers to the contribution of women to the state as being 'through her life in the home', and obliges the state to

'ensure that mothers shall not be obliged by economic necessity to engage in labour to the neglect of their duties in the home' (59).

There is currently work afoot to reform this strongly gendered provision in the Irish constitution. Its intention was presumably well-meaning, aimed at ensuring that families with young children are neither economically destitute nor bereft of parental care. And it was introduced in an era when women had no access to birth control, meaning they were unable to plan for children in accordance with their means to support them. However, it formally establishes expectations in Irish society that parenting and managing a home are the responsibility of women (exclusively).

My mother is a very smart woman who had a senior role in the Irish civil service before getting married. However, she was obliged to give up this job when she got married due to a law enacted by the Irish government in 1932 called the Marriage Bar. It required single women to resign from their job in banks, the police service or any part of the civil service upon getting married and disqualified married women from applying for vacancies. The rationale was that allowing a married woman to work was 'unfairly depriving a man of this job'. The rule applied in Ireland up until 1973 but was lifted in the case of primary school teachers in 1957 (probably because the government was unable to recruit enough male primary school teachers).

Sexism

The most likely reason for the ongoing inequality between men and women in terms of the Invisible Job as well as paid work is sexism.

Sexism can be confusing because we are led to believe that (as Father Ted might say), 'that sort of thing' doesn't go on anymore. Instead, it's just a fossil from the era of *Mad Men* or the film *Nine to Five*. Today's employers, broadcasters and politicians go to great lengths to demonstrate their feminist credentials. Apparently, women can achieve anything in today's equal society; they can even 'have it all' – i.e. a top career, great relationship, happy family and wonderful home!

Mothers are led to believe (by lifestyle magazines, advertising and the media) that they should have immaculate homes, serve home-cooked family meals and have plenty of time to play with children, all of whom are well-adjusted and doing great at school. In addition, they are expected to look fabulous. However, the whole notion of 'having it all' is a falsehood cleverly designed to preserve the status quo. Women never asked to 'have it all'. What they want is simply to be able have a family *and* a career, if they so wish. Just like men. As for the additional strings attached to 'having it all' (looking fabulous, maintaining a perfect home and catering to the emotional needs of everyone around them), it seems unlikely this is something any woman ever asked for. At the heart of the message that 'women can have it all' lies a dangerous Trojan horse: Women can *have* it all, provided that they *do* it all. Women can have a career and a family provided they single-handedly manage all that this responsibility entails. Instead of images of perfect homes, why do so few glossy lifestyle magazines show tired women opening their laptops at 10 p.m. to start wading through school emails (having just got their children to bed, cleaned the kitchen and hung up the washing)? Is it because it would shine an uncomfortable light on the gender imbalance surrounding the Invisible Job today and highlight how unrealistic the glossy images are?

If this messaging about their expected role in society is fed to women throughout their lives, it is little wonder that they eventually internalise (accept) it. When a working mother then finds herself struggling to achieve this promised outcome, she assumes it must be her fault. Women blame themselves, when in fact they have been set up to struggle by the oppressive system they find themselves in. We are all so used to this system that most of us barely realise it exists. It is only when we become aware of it that we can consciously reject it.

I realise that 'oppression' is a weighty word; a huge concrete block menacingly hanging in the air. For most people, it conjures up scenes of cruelty and immense injustice, such as the treatment of Black slaves in the US a century ago or a time when women were not permitted to vote or own land. While most view this kind of oppression as manifestly wrong, it's easy to think that oppression itself has been safely relegated to history. However, slavery still continues in some countries today, Swiss women only got the vote in 1971 and women in Lesotho have only been permitted to own land since 1979. And most of us are unaware of the more subtle ways that oppression occurs in everyday life for all of us, especially in situations where we are the ones doing the oppressing. Although I found it hard to accept myself at first, the imbalance between men and women when it comes to sharing the responsibility for the Invisible Job is in fact due to the ongoing oppression of women by men in society. Deep breath. In his book *Personal Struggles*, the psychologist Dr Seán Ruth describes oppression as 'the systematic, one-way mistreatment of the members of one group by those of another group that has become institutionalised and is defended' (60).

He explains that we all belong to several groups based on sex, sexual orientation, class, ethnicity, etc. Often the members of one group enjoy certain advantages and privileges that other groups do not, and cause others to be disadvantaged. The elite/dominant groups are described as oppressing other groups.

Being a member of each of these groups strongly influences our experiences in positive and negative ways. If you are a member of an oppressed group, you will have noticed some of the associated disadvantages in your own life. However, if you happen to belong to an oppressor group, you may be almost unaware of any advantages you enjoy because of it. If you are a man, you may never have been asked during an interview whether you plan to have children soon. While it is now unlawful in many countries to ask interview candidates this question, it is terrain many women have frequently had to navigate.

You can be a member of several oppressor groups and/or oppressed groups at the same time. For instance, if you are a white, gay, working class male you belong to two oppressed and two oppressor groups. It's easy to acknowledge the oppressed groups you belong to (e.g. black or gay) and point to some of the disadvantages that people in your group experience because of it. But it can be very hard for us to identify as members of an oppressor group (e.g. straight or male) because we may fundamentally believe we have never personally done anything to oppress anyone from the other group. Note that being a member of an oppressor group doesn't necessarily mean that you personally have oppressed members of an oppressed group. But it does mean that the group as a whole has done so, and continues to do so.

While I now understand that being a woman means I have had to contend with elements of oppression that apply to women universally (even if I didn't realise it at the time), I am also aware that growing up I benefitted from oppression. For instance, the privileges that come from being White, straight, non-disabled and middle class (although we were certainly not rich, I had the privilege of a secure home and access to a good education).

The fact that responsibility for the Invisible Job is implicitly understood to rest with women is an example of the oppression women face. People who believe that parenting and housework are essentially a woman's responsibility may not realise that this view is oppressive. They are not inherently 'bad' people; instead, their viewpoint is simply a result of their experiences, background and cultural context.

What is remarkable is that this view (held by many people) has gone unquestioned for so long. The fact that many women all over the world accept it is a form of internalised oppression. This means that, as a group, women have lived with this unfair situation for so long that many of them no longer question it. Even though it is unfair in principle, it may never have occurred to some to question it. Although a woman knows she has significantly less leisure time than her husband because she bears responsibility for the majority of the Invisible Job, provided she can cope, she may just accept this inequity. Before becoming a parent, I had no idea the Invisible

Job existed. In fact, for my first ten years as a parent, it remained invisible. It wasn't until I took a step back from my job that I first began to be aware of it, and that the Invisible Job (and its impact) started to become visible for the first time.

In the study I mentioned earlier (where respondents were asked to look at a photo of a living area and consider whether they thought it needed to be cleaned), the researchers discovered some powerful conditioning at play in the minds of the respondents. When they were told that the occupier of the flat was a woman called Jennifer who worked full-time, 95% of respondents felt she should assume responsibility for cleaning it herself (as opposed to hiring a cleaner to do it). However, when they believed the occupier was a man called John who worked full-time, only 84% felt this job should fall to him, with 16% feeling a cleaner should do it, a statistically significant difference. When they were told that John or Jennifer was a full-time stay-at-home parent, in both cases respondents felt that responsibility for cleaning lay with them, regardless of gender (in other words, that is simply part of the job of a stay-at-home parent). However, when respondents were told that the occupants were a married couple, both of whom worked full-time, significantly more people felt that cleaning was the woman's responsibility, rather than the man's (46)! This study is one of the first experiments specifically designed to test whether individual or societal gender assumptions result in women doing more housework than men and if so, how. The authors consider their findings 'evidence that men and women are differentially held accountable for housework'. They conclude that 'Men and women both incur dramatic [social] penalties for having a messy (vs. a clean) room. But our finding that respondents generally expect women, not men, to be responsible for housework indicates that, in practice, these penalties are disproportionately borne by women'.

Once oppression has been internalised, the oppressor group (in this case men) doesn't need to continue actively oppressing women because the unfair status quo has been accepted by women. A husband may not even realise all the ways that his wife makes his life easier or appreciate the sacrifice it entails; instead, he may presume it is just one of the perks of being a man.

But just because an oppressive system has become internalised does not mean that it is right or that it should remain. Once women become aware of the oppressive system and how it impacts their lives, they can challenge and change it.

According to Dr Ruth, an effective system of oppression is one in which the oppressed side does not even realise it is oppressed. While individuals know they are struggling, the system is very good at making them believe it is because there is something wrong with *them*, specifically, not that it is due to a system that is inherently rigged against them. At the same time, people in the oppressor group will not attribute their lack of struggle to the fact that they belong to an entitled group. Instead they just see their position in society as normal and any achievements as being due to their own merit.

Women who find themselves struggling may turn to self-help books, many of which, unhelpfully, reinforce the myth that they can indeed 'have it all'. Most women know they are capable of being or having these things, but somehow achieving everything at the same time seems so much harder than they were led to believe. However, the oppressive system aims to ensure they never recognise why this is the case. Instead, it is happy to facilitate endless self-help discussion on approaches individual women could follow in their efforts to conquer what is portrayed as their personal failure to be the perfect mother, wife and professional. Suggested solutions may advocate getting up earlier, being more assertive, being mindful, leaning in – which women obediently try to emulate. Others may suggest opting for a more submissive approach – i.e. to stop beating yourself up and just accept your 'failings'.

However, both strategies obscure the large elephant in the room, by feeding the narrative that a woman's struggle is her own fault, i.e. something she is (or isn't) doing. Instead, the real problem is that she is running a race with lead weights around her ankles, which nobody will acknowledge exist. Therefore, none of the self-help approaches we try can ever solve the problem because the problem isn't us, it is the system we were operating in.

Once a woman eventually realises what is going on, she is not likely to continue to put up with it. While she may not be able to bring down the entire oppressive system on her own, right now she can at least address it in her own relationship.

25

Preventing This Imbalance in Your Own Relationship

In most cases, the inequality that most women in long-term relationships fall blindly into is avoidable. It simply requires both people to understand the enormous portfolio of responsibilities that lie ahead of them before deciding to have children (or better still, before committing to a lifelong relationship).

FIND OUT IF WHAT YOU EACH WANT FROM LIFE IS COMPATIBLE

There is much to be said for the adage that prevention is better than cure. To avoid finding yourself in a relationship where most of the burden of the Invisible Job falls to you (unless this is an arrangement you feel you want), choose wisely when deciding on a life partner. In other words, before making a lifelong commitment to someone, find out whether what you each want from life is compatible.

You would probably encourage twenty-five-year-old-you to have frank and honest conversations with any potentially serious partner about gender roles. If you both feel you would like to have children one day, get a sense now of what you each envisage your future roles would look like.

When you are 25, initiating a casual discussion on the topic of having children at all can be daunting because it may feel like a very heavy topic to bring up early in a relationship – especially if you don't even know yet if this might be a long-term thing. But since the perspective of your life partner on gender roles is ultimately critical, why waste any time on someone whose expectations are very different to yours?

Even men who consider themselves feminists may not have considered the implications for them personally of life on an equally weighted seesaw: i.e. that you can't both be up at the same time. Right now, you may feel like equals, chasing your individual dreams and careers. However, when difficult choices need to be made in the future, will he still see you as an equal partner? When you are both on the career ladder in your early 30s, aiming to make partner in a firm, reach consultant grade or get on the senior management team, will your partner presume that his career automatically comes first? And that the Invisible Job will therefore become your responsibility?

It's useful to establish which of the following categories described by Prof. Arlie Hochschild (38) you feel you fall into:

1. *Traditionalist:* 'Even though she probably works, a traditionalist woman wants to identify with her activities at home (as a wife, a mother, a neighbourhood mom), wants her husband to base his identity on work and wants less power than he has. The traditional man wants the same.'
2. *Egalitarian:* 'Wants to identify with the same spheres her husband does, and to have an equal amount of power in the marriage. Some want the couple to be jointly oriented to the home, others to their careers, or both to jointly hold some balance between the two.'
3. *Transitional:* 'A transitional woman wants to identify with her role at work as well as at home, but she believes her husband should base his identity more on work than she does. A typical transitional wants to identify both with the care of the home and with helping her husband earn money, but wants her husband to focus on earning a living. A typical transitional man is all for his wife working but wants her to do the lion's share at home too'. Hochschild highlights the character Evan in her book *The Second Shift* as an example of a transitional man, who 'felt it was fine for Nancy to have a career, if she could handle the family too'.

While most educated women today would describe themselves as egalitarian, if your partner's outlook is transitional or traditional, there will always be conflict in your relationship when it comes to the Invisible Job, which will be very difficult (if not impossible) to resolve. Which is why it is better to find this out now.

DISCUSS RESPONSIBILITIES EARLY AND OPENLY

When you and your partner move in together, certain patterns will begin to be established, so it is important that you both start as you mean to go on! Unless you want to permanently assume responsibility for the majority of the Invisible Job, it's a good idea to discuss the main household responsibilities and who'd like to do what. Maybe you detest hoovering but don't mind walking the dog, while he doesn't like putting the bins out but enjoys cooking. If you have little time but lots of disposable income, outsource what you can. And as new jobs come up, decide between you how you want to handle them.

HAVE 'THE TALK' (I.E. DISCUSS THE INVISIBLE JOB) BEFORE YOU HAVE CHILDREN

It is important for couples to understand what being a parent will entail and to honestly and openly discuss (in principle) how these responsibilities will be shared. Some elements listed in the Invisible Job Description will already apply to couples before they have children but many never even crossed my twenty-some-thing-year-old mind. The increase in workload created by the arrival of your first child is exponential, even without the handicap of chronic sleep deprivation. Both partners should understand from the outset what the Invisible Job will entail. That way, you can at least try to come up with a plan for how you will manage it between you in a way you both feel is equitable.

Even if you and your partner both have (paid) jobs, unless you make a clear plan, responsibility for most of the Invisible Job tends to fall to mothers. The satirical Ladybird 'How it Works' series for adults explains the role of mothers in a little book called *The Mum* (33), mentioned earlier. The first page shows a picture of a woman with a dishtowel in her hand watching her children. As you'd expect from a Ladybird book, it explains things very clearly in large letters:

> *This is a Mum.*
> *A Mum has two very important jobs to do.*
> *One is to look after the children.*
> *The other is to do everything else as well.*

While the tongue-in-cheek illustrations on each page suggest the book was written in the 1970s, it observes with wisdom and razor-sharp wit precisely what it means to be a mother today.

> *(Illustration of mother breastfeeding)*
> *Being a new mum is full of wonder.*
> *Sally wonders if her left shoulder will every stop smelling of sick.*

(Illustration of mother at the school gate).

Alice is a successful biochemist. She publishes at least one highly regarded academic paper and year and has won the Colworth medal.

At the school gate, nobody knows this. Alice does not even have a name. Everyone calls her Olivia's Mum.

All laughing aside, if a woman's role really is to be a mother and do everything else as well, of course she will begin to will feel as if she is failing, either at work or at home. Or, as happens to most women, both. Women must therefore reframe their expectations – and more importantly, the conscious or unconscious expectations of their partners – right from the start.

Different approaches

One woman I spoke to described how her relationship with her husband had been very equal before they had children. They both had high-flying careers but contributed equally at home, gravitating naturally towards jobs they didn't mind doing, and sharing others. However, once children came along, the rules changed. Her husband prioritised *his* time and *his* career over hers. If she had an unexpected evening meeting at work and asked her husband to pick up the children from school, he would refuse if he had a conflicting work need or even a tennis match. She would therefore be forced to forego her meeting. Like the mother in the Bible story of King Solomon or a high-stakes game of chicken, the husband knew that his wife would always cave.

Another woman told me how she and her partner had tackled the career conflict. Both had been high achievers in the financial services industry, working long hours, chasing up the career ladder. When children came along, they consciously decided to 'crash one career' – by one of them continuing to focus on work while the other attended to everything else. Unsurprisingly, it turned out to be her career, not his, that was 'crashed'. But at least this was a conscious decision made together in the knowledge of what this implied for her future.

I remember asking a friend of mine, a consultant anaesthetist with two children, how she managed. I wondered whether, like Sheryl Sandberg, she had a husband who was happy to take a back seat and keep the home fires burning whenever she had to work nights or do weekends on call at the hospital.

'No', she said. 'I had a wife!'

Seeing my confusion at this revelation, she elaborated: since her children were very little, my friend explained, they had had a woman from the Philippines living in their home who looked after the children and did most of the housework. She took the children to and from school and was a warm and stable presence in the home for the children while they were doing homework each afternoon. She prepared meals for the whole family, did the grocery shopping, made the beds and kept the house clean. They paid her a generous salary, along with private health insurance. Once the children were no longer in school, the woman continued to live and work with them, and took on part-time work with another family, given their much-reduced needs.

Reflecting on this conversation, I had a light-bulb moment: a 'wife' is exactly what most women would love! Not necessarily the arrangement described above, but just a clone of ourselves. Why should men be the only ones to have the privilege of an unpaid, highly devoted, capable person attending to the interests of the whole family 24 hours a day, who requires zero direction or training? Men are free to 'opt in' whenever they want – to do whatever elements of the Invisible Job they choose, when it suits them, but are not compelled to do so. In other words, à la carte parenting. What woman wouldn't want the same?

Equally, what man or women does not love the feelings that a warm and loving home evokes in all of us? An electricity advert that featured on Irish television about twenty years ago still brings a tear to the eye of most men and women when they see it now (Google 'ESB ad I think I'm going back'). It features a man in his early twenties being picked up from a provincial train station by his father, after a long absence. While we listen to the nostalgic words of Dusty Springfield singing 'Going Back', the advert evokes powerful emotions of yearning – for home, and being cared for by loving parents somewhere warm and secure and welcoming. For those lucky enough to have grown up in a nurturing environment like this, it is only natural that we instinctively want to give the same experience to our children. At the same time, I know a wonderful woman who never experienced such a home environment growing up. Yet it is precisely for this reason that she has subconsciously prioritised ensuring that her own children *do*.

ENCOURAGE AND ENABLE YOUR PARTNER TO PARTICIPATE FULLY AS A FATHER RIGHT FROM THE START

When you become a mother, you will automatically find yourself on a very steep learning curve encompassing every aspect of looking after a baby. There is no glory in doing this alone. Instead, aim to ensure you both acquire these skills. Developing competency in looking after a new baby will not only be good for your partner's confidence as a father, but it will prevent the situation where there are many parenting tasks that only one of you can do. Therefore, ensure that your partner gets frequent opportunities to look after baby solo by being absent early and often! Go for a walk, have a nap, read a book in the park ... and remember to turn your phone off.

SHARE PARENTAL LEAVE

If paid parental leave is available to your partner, encourage him to take up this opportunity for at least a month, ideally within the first few months of the birth. Even if his only option is unpaid (or poorly paid) parental leave, if you can afford it financially, it is worth doing. Fathers taking parental leave benefits both parents, whether you take parental leave at the same time or sequentially. In the early days, given that babies need to feed every few hours, your sleep is likely to be hugely impacted every night, making it very challenging to function normally the following day. Having your partner at home with you gives each of you an opportunity to catch up on vital sleep during the day, while the other keeps the show on the road. It also enables you to accomplish the essentials every day, such as eating properly. And if you suffered complications during the birth, or had a Caesarean section, a second pair of hands in the first few weeks is invaluable in giving your wounds a chance to heal. Even the companionship of experiencing parental leave together can transform it into a very special time.

Alternatively, your partner taking parental leave when you go back to work can also work well. When women go back to work, even if they are now working 30+ hours a week (or even full time) in a paid job, they often retain ownership for most of the baby and household jobs out of habit. If your partner takes a period of parental leave when you go back to work, this enables responsibility for the primary parenting and household responsibilities you have assumed during maternity leave to be temporarily transferred to your partner. This will help him appreciate what doing the Invisible Job entails and enable him to better understand how he can actively play his part in sharing this load with you when you are both back at work.

CREATE SPACE FOR EACH OTHER – APART AND TOGETHER

Right from the time your baby is born, it is a good idea to ensure that you and your partner have designated times where you are each free to do what you want, as well as designated time to spend time together as a family. For instance, you might divide weekends into segments: Saturday morning could be a designated time for you to spend as you please, while your partner assumes full responsibility for baby and everything else. Sunday mornings might be the opposite, with you taking the reins. Saturday and Sunday afternoons might be family time, where you do things together with your child(ren) (and perhaps extended family).

Having designated free time each week is beneficial to both of you, as we all need to clear our heads, relax, exercise, maintain our friendships and do something fun. Without designated free time, the boundaries of what one partner considers free time can easily be misunderstood by the other partner. When my husband would go out cycling on Saturday mornings, this often meant I had sole responsibility for two toddlers from 8 a.m. until about 2 p.m. As far as my husband was concerned, though, these six hours only equated to two hours of 'free time' for him because that was how long the actual bike ride was. He didn't realise that it made little difference to me whether he was cycling, doing bike-related things in the garage or having lunch. The point was that throughout this six-hour period, he was free to do whatever he chose because I was looking after the children. Simply being in the vicinity was irrelevant to me; unless he was available to actively participate in parenting/household jobs, he may as well have been on the moon. It's therefore much more straightforward to set fixed times when you give each other complete freedom to do whatever you want, wherever you choose. Time to be officially 'up' on the seesaw (i.e. free), while your partner is officially 'down' (i.e. in charge of children or housework). How you each use your freedom is entirely up to you.

Having equal designated free time also avoids falling into another common trap, where one person's personal goals result in them monopolising the other person's free time. For instance, if your partner decides they are going to enter a marathon, this will clearly require them to engage in many hours of training each week. Not wanting them to fail in this challenge, you may obligingly spend midweek evenings and Saturday mornings looking after the children while your partner goes running. Although this may be at the expense of whatever activities you had hoped to do during this time, you may feel that your singing group or Pilates class are no match for the gravitas of training for a marathon and therefore not question this sacrifice. If this temporary imbalance is reciprocated later – for instance, the following year you might decide to commit to intensive swimming training for three months or get in shape to walk the Camino (while your partner spends additional time looking after the children) – that's fine. However, setting personal commitments at the direct expense of your partner's free time is not OK. As Tom Jones sang in the theme song to the Bond movie *Thunderball*, this leads to a dynamic where 'His needs are more so he gives less'.

One woman I spoke to told me about her husband's response when she joined a cycling club. She needed to attend a six-week induction course on Saturday mornings before being allowed to participate in regular club rides. However, her husband was furious about this because he liked going cycling on Saturday mornings with his pals. Although she had looked after the children on Saturday mornings for years to facilitate this, he was not prepared to stay home for six Saturdays to enable his wife to have the same opportunity.

26

Addressing Imbalance in Your Relationship: Having the Talk

But what if it's too late for all these chats in the early days of your relationship about sharing responsibility for the Invisible Job and having equal dedicated free time each week? What if you are already at the point that many women reach in their thirties or forties, i.e. ready to crack from the constant struggle caused by a huge imbalance between you and your partner when it comes to the Invisible Job? Obviously, this will create huge resentment if you feel your partner should really be doing more to help.

There is a great Australian sketch called 'A mystery all men and women can relate to', available on YouTube. (If you can't find it, here is a transcript of the conversation, which takes place between a woman and her boyfriend):

Boyfriend: 'Babe, did you say you were gonna make dinner? I couldn't remember.'

Girlfriend: 'What? I just wish you'd take some initiative and cook your own dinner for once. I've been at work too, you know, and now I get to come home and pack the dishwasher ... and unpack the dishwasher ... and cook dinner and put the washing on ... and you know what? I can't continue to live like this because it's not for me.'

Boyfriend: 'Hey, hey, relax! It's gonna be alright.'

Girlfriend (with incredulous look on her face): 'How?'

Boyfriend: 'Here, I'll show you.' (He leads her to the kitchen where he points to a basket on top of the washing machine).' OK, I've been doing this since you moved in. See this basket thing? I don't know how it happens, if it's the house or what ... but any dirty clothes you put in this basket, somehow, the next day, they're just clean, folded and in a perfect pile on your bed.'

Girlfriend: 'You're not serious!'

Boyfriend: 'I couldn't believe it at first either. That's why I didn't tell you; I didn't wanna jinx it.'

Girlfriend: 'You are insane!'

Boyfriend: 'Try it, you'll see! Unless ... it's only chosen me. See, I dunno.'

Girlfriend: (turning to leave) 'I can't do this!'

Boyfriend: 'No wait! There's other things, too!' (He leads her to a table in the lounge). 'See this table? Plates, cutlery, pizza boxes, dirty tissues, just about anything you leave on this coffee table ... just disappears overnight. I mean sometimes I'll just see how far I can push this thing and I'll just leave shit everywhere and sure enough, the next day, it's all gone!'

The next scene features the boyfriend reporting the overnight disappearance of his girlfriend to a male and female police officer who have arrived at the house:

Boyfriend: 'No, she wouldn't have left me. Here's what I think happened: She must have got up in the middle of the night, to get a drink or something. She must have fallen onto the magic coffee table and just vanished.'

Female police officer: 'Are you insane?'

Male police officer: 'No, he's not insane ... I've got the same coffee table at home.'

If you have never had a discussion with your husband/partner about more equitable sharing of parenting and household responsibilities, believing instead that surely he'll take the initiative and just do it without being asked, this is going to be like *Waiting for Godot*. It's time to have the Talk.

It's never too late to calmly discuss with your partner what the Invisible Job involves and the impact that shouldering too much of it is having on you.

Explain you are keen to figure out together how to manage it between you for a happier and fairer relationship – with minimum stress and maximum free time for both of you.

If approached correctly, not only is this outcome achievable, but you will have taken the first step towards a more fulfilling relationship of mutual appreciation, equality and interdependence. For the Talk to go well, however, a little careful planning is essential!

There is absolutely no point in launching into an angry tirade about how fed up you are doing 90% of what should be joint responsibilities, with little appreciation or support from your partner (even if this is exactly how you feel). Instead, you need to choose a calm moment to plant the seed. Mention that you'd like to find some space in the diary to have a chat about an idea you've got about organising stuff you both need to do that should make things easier and less stressful for both of you. Agree a time when you and your partner will be free to talk, uninterrupted, in a relaxed setting – e.g. an evening in with a nice bottle of wine or escaping out for an hour or two while a babysitter holds the fort.

In advance of your get-together, as described in Part I, you'll need to draft a version of the Invisible Job Description that you feel reflects all the responsibilities you are currently managing between you. (Remember, you can download a version you can edit at www.theinvisiblejob.com). Print two copies.

When you meet up, set the scene by explaining the following:

- On a day-to-day basis you are both busy – so busy that it can be hard to even keep track of all the things going on in your family life.
- You feel it would be a good idea for you both to have an overall understanding of what these things are to figure out a better way of handling them between you.
- You'd like to figure out a way of making life less stressful for both of you that would allow time for more fun. It's unlikely you will encounter any pushback in the conversation at this point.
- To help explain what you mean, tell him that you have made a list of all the things that you are currently trying to manage between you and you'd like to go through it together. Some of the things on the list are ones that your partner manages but there are also quite a lot that you manage – and you feel that it's getting too hard to stay on top of everything.
- You'd like to talk about a better way to share the load in a way that is fair for both of you, that will hopefully leave you both with more time to do fun stuff and that puts less stress on your relationship.

Give your partner a copy of your Invisible Job Description. As you go through each element and your partner starts to realise the impact that shouldering most of this burden has had on you, he may say one of the following:

1. 'I had no idea (you were doing all this).'
2. 'Why didn't you ask me?'

'I HAD NO IDEA'

I genuinely don't believe there are many partners today who would deliberately absolve themselves from sharing household and family responsibilities and feel that this is OK. Certainly, these men existed in the past and even today, some men seem unaware of many aspects of the Invisible Job. They can be surprisingly blind when it comes to noticing the myriad things their partner does for their joint benefit. As a wise friend of mine astutely observed, 'The better you are at doing something, the more invisible that thing becomes.'

Even if men genuinely had no idea about all the parenting and household tasks their wife/partner manages in a typical day (often on top of a paid job that may be just as demanding as his), it is curious they tend not to be too eager to inform themselves about it. Or even to be informed by their partner.

Sometimes, when I got to the end of a hectic workday, successfully managing unanticipated domestic and mechanical emergencies and last-minute rescheduling of children's activities, I felt like Jason Bourne. A day of non-stop thinking, packing the near impossible into the hours between 7 a.m. and midnight. Although exhausted from (literally) running much of the day, as my head hit the pillow, my mind going back over the day's events, I felt pretty proud of all I had somehow managed to achieve. I might excitedly start to recount bits of my day to my husband, thinking he would also be interested in all the minor successes I achieved on behalf of both of us. The funny thing was, though, he didn't want to hear about my day at all.

'Babe, it's OK. I don't need to know'.

He tells me he's tired. He says he's had a busy day too but he doesn't regurgitate his workday to me, so why do I feel the need to do it to him? He switches off the bedside light on his side and I no longer feel like Jason Bourne.

The thing is, sometimes men don't want to know what the Invisible Job entails because it's easier not to know. It's best for the shoemaker not to make any detailed enquiries about the elves who come night after night and turn the leather and felt into beautiful shoes, asking for nothing in return. Just in case the elves should ever turn around and say, 'Actually, about that ...'.

Just as my friend observed, so much of what women do for their partners/families is invisible. And when something is invisible, there is little chance that their partner will (even silently) appreciate the effort involved, never mind express this appreciation.

But it's essential that husbands and partners understand what the Invisible Job entails – i.e. the enormous number of seemingly invisible things you do on behalf of both of you every day – and have possibly been doing for a long time. Simply listing them on a page and explaining what is involved should enable him to form a mental picture of what it entails and understand the diverse skills needed to do it. Hopefully, it will inspire him to volunteer his services as a full-time member of the team. Or at least up his game a bit.

When one woman I know had the Talk with her husband, she calmly showed him a page on which she had written down all the things in her Invisible Job, asking him to choose which of these he would like to take responsibility for from now on. Her husband read though the list in silence. His response was: 'I had no idea you did all these jobs. To be honest, I had no idea some of them even existed!'

WHY DIDN'T YOU ASK ME?

Some men seem to assume that unless their partner asks them to do a specific job, she either doesn't need or want any help. This is a surprisingly widespread misunderstanding.

Before clarifying this for my husband, he would often continue watching the Tour de France highlights or fixing his bike in the kitchen while I ran around trying to take care of several child-related jobs simultaneously. It's not that he was being lazy or incompetent (as he is neither). Instead, like many men, he just didn't have the antennae that women automatically sprout as part of their evolutionary struggle to survive as a parent. For most mothers, it is practically impossible not to be constantly aware of their immediate environment and what needs to be done – and most importantly, be proactive in doing it.

When I exclaim, 'Do I have to do everything myself?' he looks genuinely surprised (and even a bit offended) and replies calmly, 'Look, there's no need to get upset. If you needed help, why didn't you just ask me?'

To any men reading this, please note that if your partner is under pressure trying to manage several things simultaneously and expresses her frustration at your lack of contribution, be wary of responding, 'Why didn't you ask me?'

As the French journalist Emma concludes in her comic book *The Mental Load* (61),

What our partners are really saying, when they ask us to tell us what needs to be done, is that they refuse to take on their share of the mental load.

While they are willing to do a specific task if their partner asks them – i.e. meaning they would opt in – up until then, the responsibility for everything rests with her. She is the default full-time project manager and they are just a zero-hours contractor, available to help, but only if specifically asked to.

Some men might feel this position is perfectly reasonable. However, to women who believe they are in an equal relationship, it's actually not. Even if they were to individually delegate 50% of all the jobs that need to be done each day to their husband/partner, this still means that on top of doing the other 50% of jobs, women are carrying out a second, much bigger job, that of project manager.

Firstly, women have no wish to be the eternal project manager of what should be their joint responsibilities. Just because she might be a highly capable project manager doesn't mean she wants to be the project manager of the home and family. Instead, it's more likely that she would prefer her partner to be a joint project manager; a partner equally capable of identifying for himself what needs to be done and when – and simply getting on with it!

Secondly, women don't feel they should have to *ask* their partner to do things that they are jointly responsible for.

BARRIERS TO HAVING THE TALK

Some women will be reluctant to have the Talk with their partner, even though they know this is an issue that needs to be addressed. There are many reasons they may feel hesitant, including:

- Fear about their partner's anticipated response to being asked to do their fair share of the Invisible Job.
- Fear of discovering that, deep down, their partner does not see them as an equal – or fundamentally believe that men and women are equal.
- Fear of jeopardising the relationship.
- Belief that their partner is not actually capable of independently managing much of what the Invisible Job entails (we'll come back to this one later).*
- Reluctance to articulate how they feel because this would be akin to admitting to failure – as a partner, a mother, or a capable professional (or all the above).

However, if you don't confront the issue, things are not going to improve. You will simply become more resentful and your relationship will deteriorate further. You will waste time and energy asking your partner to do specific tasks time and time again – leading him to accuse you of 'nagging' (that terrible word), while you continue to resent having to constantly point out to him when something you should be jointly responsible for needs to be done. The dynamic can feel like managing a child, rather than living with a capable equal. And all the while, your life continues to be impacted negatively in all the ways described in Part II of this book.

While there is no guarantee the conversation will be easy – or that your partner will immediately recognise the imbalance in your relative contributions up to now – you need to take this proactive step towards establishing balance in your life and equality in your relationship. And don't forget, while you may be shining a light on a touchy problem, you also have the solution!

WHAT HAPPENS WHEN YOU HAVE THE TALK?

Once your husband/partner understands what the Invisible Job entails, he will hopefully appreciate its huge value to you as a couple and family. After all, if you have discussed it in detail together, these constitute the responsibilities you have jointly agreed are essential to your family's welfare, based on what you both feel is most important in your life right now. When he realises the impact that bearing most of the burden for this job has had on you up to now, if he shares your egalitarian ethos, he will recognise that this is something you should be jointly responsible for. If so, you just need to agree (and write down) which elements he will be responsible for from now on and ensure that for each one, he understands what needs to be done and how.

This is where the ASMART criteria described earlier come in: you must both agree on (and then write down) the expected outcome for each element – i.e. exactly what needs to be done and by when. It is also really important to ensure he has all the information he needs to carry this out, so that he has full autonomy to do it properly, by the required time, without your help or needing to be reminded.

There are many advantages to both of you for assigning full responsibility for a given element to a specific person:

- It avoids any misunderstandings about who is responsible for what, ensuring that nothing falls between the cracks.
- It avoids wasteful duplication of effort – where you both spend time and effort trying to achieve the same thing without realising it.
- It avoids one person misguidedly thinking they are contributing equally to a job. For example, where one person believes 'Oh we share cooking; sometimes my partner will cook, sometimes it's me. It depends who gets home from work first', when the reality is that the other person actually cooks 90% of the time. Remember that there is a huge difference between 'opting in' to cook when it suits you and being the person specifically responsible for preparing meals on specific days, whether it suits you or not at the time.
- It allows each person to plan and manage their individual responsibilities as efficiently as possible with maximum advance notice, rather than the annoy-ance of having to do something at the last minute when you have other things to attend to.
- It eliminates 'nagging'. If the responsibility for an element lies with one person, you must trust that they will attend to it, without the need for any reminders. If they fail to, the consequences may teach them to be accountable in future.
- It allows you to completely remove an element from your mental load – i.e. the mental list of responsibilities we carry around with us every day and which most women feel is the most onerous aspect of the Invisible Job. This is possibly the

most liberating aspect of handing over complete responsibility for an element to your partner.

- When something one of you is responsible for planning and executing goes well, they (deservedly) feel a sense of internal accomplishment – and may even get some external acknowledgement from their partner.

By one person having full autonomy and responsibility for a specific element, this avoids the other person having to remind them to do it, as well as arguments about whether it has been done as agreed.

*Note that providing clear and adequate guidance at the start is also the solution to allaying concerns you may have about your partner not being able to do something properly. Provided you each take on elements that align best with your strengths, with adequate initial guidance, you will figure it out. Have a little faith!

CHECK IN REGULARLY WITH EACH OTHER

Just like when any new process is implemented in an organisation, it is essential that you check in with each other about how things are going. Things will never run perfectly from the start so don't expect them to! Instead, recognise that this new partnership for managing the Invisible Job will require regular tweaking – and also that the Invisible Job will evolve as time goes on and your circumstances and priorities change. It is therefore a good idea to schedule another chat, to see how you both feel things are going. So set another date in the diary, about two to three weeks from now, where you can get together again in a low-stress environment. The perfect excuse to order a takeaway and open a bottle of wine!

Be mindful that since signing up to this new way of managing the Invisible Job between you, your partner has probably got more on his plate than before, and more than likely is getting to grips with some new responsibilities.

- Highlight where you have observed he has taken on new responsibility and give praise for all the effort being made.
- Give each other the opportunity to say how you feel about how this new plan for sharing the Invisible Job is going. Listen carefully without interrupting.
- Discuss how you each feel about the current balance. You may decide to reassign responsibility for some elements if one or other of you is struggling with your overall load. You may even wish to swap some responsibilities; e.g. if one of you has been responsible for cooking midweek meals for a whole month, it might be a welcome break to hand this responsibility over to your partner and take on a different responsibility in return.
- Just like when anyone starts a new job, don't expect your partner to be able to do all (or perhaps any) of the new elements perfectly from the outset. Even if you

feel you would be able to do a particular element much better or faster yourself, remember that you acquired that capability over time. Don't be tempted to simply take back ownership; instead, offer constructive feedback and guidance to help your partner manage it better and improve his capabilities.

Treat your joint management of the Invisible Job as an ongoing partnership. One where you each trust the other to be accountable for elements but also where you still value each other's opinions. You should still consult with one another, especially on key decisions. For instance, even if you have taken on responsibility for finding a suitable school for your child(ren), while you may carry out all the research to establish what the available options are, this is surely something you would discuss together before enrolling your child in a specific school. Similarly, if your partner has taken on responsibility for getting a new bathroom, while you would be delighted if he independently researched possible contractors, bathroom layouts and colour schemes, more than likely you would like to be consulted on the proposed plan (and cost) before he signed the contract with the plumber and ordered the tiles!

Communication and mutual consideration are key. There will always be things that you will need each other's help with – for instance, a diary clash where you need to drive two children to separate destinations at the same time and can't arrange a lift for either of them. Of course it is OK to ask your partner for help or swap some responsibilities to get around the problem in good time. What's not OK is to dump a problem on them at the last minute because you simply haven't made an effort, like saying at 7 p.m., when the children are starving, 'I've no idea what to make for dinner, can you just do it?'

Also remember that, over time, the content and your priorities of the Invisible Job will change. Some elements become less important; some may disappear completely, while others start to feature for the first time. Sometimes a huge project or life event may come up unexpectedly. If you decide that one of you should focus on attending to this, the other person should temporarily take on some of their responsibilities to ensure life remains manageable for both of you during this period. You should continue to review your Invisible Job regularly (at least once a month) and adapt it in line with what you both feel are your joint priorities, in accordance with the time available to attend to them.

CHANGING AN OPPRESSIVE DYNAMIC

Even if your partner genuinely believes he is an egalitarian, he may not be immediately enthusiastic about changing the status quo. He may have no objection whatsoever to helping with children or housework in theory but when it comes to it, he may really mean helping on an opt-in basis only. In other words, he may agree to 'do more' but may not wish to sign up to specific responsibilities, especially ones that need to be done urgently or at specified times. Opting in (more than before) still allows him to retain his status as a zero-hours contractor, while doing a few more hours of whatever he chooses, when it suits him. But as we know, it is not the total time spent on the Invisible Job that makes women feel there is a large imbalance; it relates to time spent on tasks

a. That need to be done very frequently (e.g. cleaning the kitchen and cooking midweek meals)
b. That have low flexibility around when they must be done (i.e. even if you have an urgent work deadline, the children's dinner needs to be cooked now)

If you could choose which elements of the Invisible Job you wanted to do and when (i.e. à la carte parenting), it would be much less arduous. But that would mean leaving someone else to pick up all the pieces that we don't ever feel like doing and the ones we are too tired or busy to do *right now*.

Sometimes even men who perceive their partner to be their absolute equal may prevent them from being equals in practice. While egalitarian in theory, deep down they don't want to accept joint responsibility for the Invisible Job because it impacts their freedom and their time. Without being conscious of it, they may hold assumptions around gender roles, i.e. that men should not be encumbered by day-to-day domestic inconveniences when they have other important things to do.

When confronted with the dilemma of being aware that they are not contributing equally to joint responsibilities but at the same time, not really being willing to do more, often men will look for a third option: by either rationalising that the job doesn't need to be done at all or looking for a solution that doesn't impact them. For instance, if a woman tells her husband she is tired of cooking every evening, rather than offering to cook dinner tomorrow, he might suggest they order takeaway instead.

I know a man whose wife spent her whole married life diligently looking after their children and the home. Although she didn't have a paid job during this time (she had willingly given up her job to be a full-time mother), she also spent a lot of time helping to develop her husband's business. Recognising the imbalance and lack of social interaction in her life, the husband proactively encouraged her to get out more and do something for herself, like joining a club. She replied that she would be delighted to, but he would therefore need to take on some of the work she did in the home, for instance, supervise children's homework or cook dinner. Although he had far more leisure time than his wife (he read extensively and regularly played computer games), he wasn't willing to sacrifice some of this time for his wife to have some leisure time. So, despite his understanding of how this affected his wife's leisure/socialising opportunities, nothing changed.

Having had the Talk, if it turns out that your husband/partner is fundamentally not willing to do this share of the Invisible Job, what then?

Well, that depends. You may decide that even though you know it's unfair that you are managing the lion's share of the household responsibilities, it's not that big a deal. Although it eats up your personal time, you might decide that you have sufficient capacity to manage.

On the other hand, you might just decide that this imbalance or lack of effort from your partner is not something you are prepared to put up with and may even be an indicator of worse things to come. To use the analogy of wading into the sea, if you have only got your feet wet – i.e. if you have no children and are not yet married, you might decide to get out of the relationship – after all, there are plenty more fish in the sea. (And some of them might even know how to use a vacuum cleaner!) If you're already wet up to your waist – i.e. married or pregnant, retreating to dry ground can be much more complicated. And by the time you are barely keeping your head above water with small children, you might feel that even if you tried to swim back to shore, you might not make it.

Changing an oppressive dynamic in your own relationship

The dynamic in the relationship with your partner is the one that impacts your life the most. It is also where you have the most power to effect change. However, to move away from a status quo of inequality requires both people in the relationship to change; to progress through a series of steps until both of you are free of roles that may have seemed inescapable so far. The steps involved in moving from an oppressive dynamic to where both of you are liberated differ for each partner. The following are the stages that a woman (the oppressed person in this dynamic) may experience, adapted from 'Stages of Liberation' in *Personal Struggles* (60):

Stage 1: Oppressed

At this stage, the status quo is in place; it is understood that responsibilities associated with parenting and the household fall primarily to the woman in the relationship. This is also largely unquestioned in society, even though a few individuals may be trying to challenge this. Women are mistreated:

- Economically – e.g. through the factors causing the gender pay gap and longer-term financial insecurity
- Socially – e.g. through messaging in media and advertising that portrays child-care, laundry and hoovering as things mothers exclusively need to worry about (when did you last see a man in a TV advert marvel at the suction strength of a hoover or fret about getting stains out of t-shirts?)

- Psychologically – e.g. through continually being fed the myth that there is nothing preventing women thriving at work or at home, apart from their own inadequacy

At this stage, women have internalised this oppressive system, meaning they accept the imbalance and inequality as unchangeable and part of the natural order of things. Regardless of the hurt and personal struggle it causes them, they feel powerless to change it and are encouraged to continue being subservient and undemanding. Rather than shining a light on the inequality associated with the Invisible Job, men would prefer women just continued doing it as invisibly as possible. In return, men will opt in to help their partners with certain things, if/when it suits them.

Men's behaviours and lifestyle are viewed as something to be admired, especially when it comes to careers. Women can compete in the career game if they wish but it is largely designed for men, by men. The timing of business meetings doesn't need to consider inconvenient truths such as school runs and children's dinner times because those things have never been an issue for men. While women nod and joke knowingly among themselves at the impossibility of managing work and being a mother, there is no widespread revolt at this stage.

Stage 2: Angry

A woman may remain in Stage 1 for a very long time, often because she is not fully aware of the imbalance in her life or the reasons for it. For years she will constantly try to up her game, attempting to keep up with the ever-changing demands of being a mother and maintaining her career. It usually takes a trigger for her to finally challenge the way things are, such as some unforeseen boulder in her personal or professional life that makes it impossible (emotionally or physically) to continue spinning all the plates. Or it may be sparked by an external event like the #MeToo movement or the Covid-19 lockdowns – when many women found themselves at the end of their tethers trying to work from home while home-schooling disinterested children and running a 24-hour restaurant. Acute frustrations during periods like this can lead women to see how out of balance life is.

As this awareness hits home, the relationship with her partner is likely to become charged and resentful. No longer bothered with trying to 'keep calm and carry on', she will instead directly challenge his lack of contribution to their joint responsibilities and his apparent lack of concern for how this impacts her. At this point, a woman may also start to feel differently about her identity. Previously, she may have defined herself more through her career, perhaps even burying her second identity as a mother who also manages the Invisible Job. Instead, she may now begin to take visible pride in her role as a mother, choosing to dedicate time to the

234 | Part III

parts of motherhood or managing a home that feel important to her personally, but which she might not have focused on up to now.

Because she feels angry at her partner about the imbalance in their respective responsibilities and freedoms, she may try to punish her partner, perhaps by announcing that she is heading off on a holiday by herself, leaving her husband to experience what a week of juggling the Invisible Job solo feels like. This kind of reaction is more likely to happen if he defends his behaviour when she explains how she is feeling or if he tries to turn the blame back onto her. (A famous example of this occurred on 24 October 1975, when, fed up of being taken for granted, 90% of women in Iceland decided to demonstrate their importance by going on strike and announced to the bemused men that they were not going to do work of any kind for a day – whether going to the office, looking after children or doing housework. It is known in Iceland as the Women's Day Off and was a watershed moment that set the country on a trajectory towards equality. Five years later, Iceland became the first country in Europe to elect a female president, Vigdis Finnbogadottir, a divorced single mother.)

However, if a man simply listens openly and acknowledges his partner's feelings of frustration – and his possible contribution to causing them – the anger she feels can instead quickly dissipate.

Stage 3: Independent

Over time, she will get through her feelings of anger. She will begin to view herself and men differently. She will notice and celebrate other aspects of herself, and mothers in general, such as their kindness, intelligence, creativity, their desire for fairness and their ability to love and nurture. She may begin to feel very proud of the enormous contribution she has made as a mother to her children's emotional, physical and educational well-being. If her sense of identity and self-worth were previously dependant on her relationship with her partner (or with men in general), she has now moved on to redefining this.

The anger she felt has gone but she is indignant about past, current and future inequalities affecting women and especially mothers. She understands better how this situation can come about for individual mothers, along with mothers collectively, and believes the systems that facilitate this must be changed. She becomes mindful of possible areas within her own sphere where she might be able to influence such change.

At the 'Angry' stage, she would have viewed her partner and men in general as the enemy. Once she has reached the 'Independent' stage, this is no longer the case; instead, she now believes that it is the system that is at fault. While she can see that the system is unfair and damaging to women, she also knows that many men also feel strongly that this inequality should not exist and are personally committed to changing it, both in their personal relationships and in the world of work. Although these men may still behave unfairly towards women at times, they are increasingly aware of the conditioning driving their behaviour and are actively trying to free themselves from it.

Many individual women, as well as women's groups, are at this third stage. While they no longer feel confused about what is going on and feel they have more control over their lives and decisions, it doesn't mean that at a societal level the oppressive system affecting women has gone away.

Stage 4: Liberation

If the system oppressing women was completely dismantled, we would say that Stage 4 (Liberation) had been achieved. At a societal level, we are still quite far from that. However, within individual relationships, I believe that liberation can happen, provided that both the woman and her partner liberate themselves from their old behaviours, feelings and patterns.

(Note that in Dr Ruth's view, liberation at the level of an individual relationship cannot be achieved unless it also happens at a societal level because the relationship is always subject to this ongoing external influence).

Achieving liberation requires women to reclaim and recognise their value and human qualities as women and mothers. They also must become allies to each other in calling out oppression when they witness it so that together, women can challenge the system causing their (collective) struggles. This includes highlighting the existence of the #invisiblejob, so that it ceases to be invisible. As we become liberated, we realise that although we have put up with a lot, we are (and always were) OK. In fact, we are more than OK! If other people could just see how capable, talented, hard-working and resourceful we are, how fair and compassionate, they could only be filled with admiration for all we have achieved, given the circumstances.

A critical part of the process in mothers recognising their struggles for what they are is being listened to and having the opportunity to listen to others who have experienced similar struggles. When we hear other people's stories, we recognise parallels with our own and can relate to how it made them feel. We also feel relief and vindication when we realise that the struggles we felt were also experienced by people we consider to be very smart and capable and that therefore it wasn't just us. We were all set up. The more we listen to other women, the more clearly we see the system that holds women back and causes them all to struggle. Women become empowered to agitate to change the system in order to prevent other women experiencing this same unnecessary struggle and self-doubt.

There is huge benefit in sharing our stories with other women in a safe way. And in women being completely honest with other women about their experiences. Sometimes, instead of being allies, women can feel they are competing against each other – against those who seem to be managing it all better than we are.

236 | Part III

We are reluctant to admit our struggles to others; afraid it will make us appear even bigger failures. However, this simply perpetuates the myth that 'other women' are managing fine (and that the problem must therefore be me). Instead, we should empathise with other women about the daily challenges of the #invisiblejob.

Another reason women can be reluctant to talk openly with friends about the struggles they are experiencing in their lives is fear of betraying their partner (i.e. making them look 'bad' or 'lazy'). They don't believe either to be the case, but are worried that discussing it might portray them as such.

However, it's important that we do talk about our struggles with others, not only because we get to discharge hurtful feelings by being listened to but in sharing our experiences we also help other women progress from oppression to liberation. This is best done among friends or in small groups – i.e. a safe spaces where people trust one another. However, if they wish, women can also support each other on a global scale by sharing their experiences with a wider community online (for details, go to www.theinvisiblejob.com). What you choose to share about your own struggles can be read by other women without judgement and will help them know they are not alone. And as you read the experiences shared by other women, you will appreciate ever more deeply how an oppressive system has caused such struggle, not just to you, but to millions of women.

Collectively, women can work together to call out this oppressive system for what it is and dismantle it. In the process, we will help men discover what it is like to take pride in themselves as fathers and husbands and create a society in which both men and women enjoy more equal and fulfilling relationships and lives.

The steps a man might experience as he frees himself from internalised oppression are as follows, adapted from *Personal Struggles* (60):

Stage 1: Oppressing

At this stage, the status quo is firmly in place. A man may take for granted that his partner attends to all the parenting/household responsibilities. He may feel a sense of entitlement to the home services she provides for him and the family and sees no reason to change things. Chances are, he may even have no idea of the enormous imbalance that exists or what providing these services entails for his partner. He may sometimes make well-meaning (yet paternalistic) gestures that demonstrate his benign power, such as suggesting his wife should 'buy herself something nice'. He does not realise the many subtle ways that he communicates his entitlement to abstain from what he views as women's work, such as referring to looking after his own children as 'babysitting'. Or, where both parents work hard all week (whether paid or unpaid), feeling it is OK to dedicate all day Saturday to his hobbies, without consulting with his partner about childcare.

Stage 2: Denial

This stage represents a man's response to his partner pointing out what she sees as a marked imbalance in their respective contributions to parenting/household responsibilities and their individual free time. He may express shock/surprise that she would question the way things are (and always have been). He may appear hurt at being accused of behaving unfairly. He may strongly disagree that his behaviour could be considered 'oppressive' by highlighting, for instance, that he has never been violent or aggressive, failing to understand how his behaviour has been oppressive in more subtle ways. Don't forget that since this oppressive dynamic has been invisible to women for so long, that it has become so normalised/internalised, that is likely to be even more invisible to men. Therefore it may feel like a deep blow at first. Some men may react angrily to criticism from their partner and the demands she is making. He may point to paid work as his contribution to the family, absolving him of any further input. He might see his wife's efforts to gain equal power in the relationship as an attack on his identity and position in the household (as well as an attack on men in general). He may feel threatened by her independence and her lack of reliance on his capabilities or goodwill. He may try to reframe any struggle she is experiencing as a failure on her part.

Stage 3: Guilt

While some men may get stuck at Stage 2, others will move on to Stage 3. At this stage, there is some recognition and acceptance that mothers are indeed often mistreated/taken for granted. A man accepts that his partner has been unfairly treated, and while he feels somewhat guilty about this, he still has difficulty seeing how his own behaviour and attitude are part of the problem. He supports equality in theory but is not really willing to change his own behaviour in order to achieve this. While he may make token efforts to change the situation, he still operates from a basis of entitlement. Some men may even go overboard, acting submissively towards their partner.

Stage 4: Acceptance

Over time, some men will move on to this stage, where there is an acceptance of their own oppressor conditioning and the need for both personal change and wider systematic change. Where a man may previously have identified with symbols of male privilege, instead he now takes a relaxed pride in his own goodness as a person and a father. His sense of identity is not linked to any feelings of superiority to women. He actively works to change any lingering traces of internalised oppression impacting his own relationship and, at the same time, tries to make other men aware of this imbalance in society and its impact on women.

He actively listens to women to help him identify ways that he can effect change within his spheres of influence. For instance, a man working at a senior level in an organisation may ask women in the organisation how policies can be improved to promote gender equality or encourage greater participation of male employees in parenting responsibilities. He is open to being guided by women on how barriers limiting women reaching senior management level can be removed. His new appreciation of women's ability and resourcefulness may make him an advocate of recruiting external women to senior positions, recognising the huge talent pool of capable and experienced women outside the labour market who might be enticed to join their organisation, given suitable working arrangements.

Stage 5: Liberation

Liberation is achieved when 'patterns of internalised domination are eliminated and replaced with thoughtful, fulfilling and interdependent relationships' (60). The process of moving through these stages of liberation can be uncomfortable for both parties. Yet it is hugely worthwhile. Both partners learn to appreciate their own and their partner's qualities and capabilities. Both take greater pride in their roles as parents and find it more fulfilling. At the same time, they share an understanding of the challenges it generates. Both operate with greater respect for how crucial good parenting is and value the synergy created by trying to achieve this together. Both recognise the essential contribution that paid work makes to the family, along with both the personal benefits and challenges associated with it. At the same time, they also understand how it needs to be balanced against other important roles and responsibilities that underpin the well-being of both partners. Ultimately, it becomes something you can both laugh about. A friend of mine told me a story recently about how her husband (who has been working from home due to the Covid-19 lockdown) had started feeding the cat most mornings. While she welcomed his growing awareness of this element of the Invisible Job (having had the Talk), she gently enquired if, when he emptied a pouch of food into the clean cat bowl, he ever thought of washing out the dirty one next to it. 'Oh there's no need!' he said. 'There's always a clean one right next to it every morning ...'. Even before reaching the end of his sentence, my friend had a big grin on her face and she could almost see her husband's brain whirring as he started to laugh too and said, 'Oh wait....it's the Invisible Job, right?' My brother and my husband (both wonderful men) often jokingly remark to their wives — with genuine masculine pride! — whenever they do something that they now realise is just a normal part of their responsibilities as a kind partner or father, saying 'See? Invisible Man did this!'

27

How to End This Imbalance in Society

The same stages of liberation apply to eliminating the oppression of women in society in general and moving towards a point where women and men are completely free of the oppression both are currently entangled in. Reaching that point will not be easy. But that doesn't mean it can't happen.

Many men are already fully committed to true equality and dismantling the oppressive system that gives rise to gender imbalance, both in their professional and personal lives. Many men are visible contributors to gender equality campaigns such as #pushforprogress and #MeToo and their efforts should be applauded.

Fathers and mothers also have a responsibility to shape the next generation of men and women by raising children to see parenting and household responsibilities as something both parents are responsible for. To change the current imbalance in unpaid caring responsibilities for the next generation, we need to teach our sons to do more and our daughters to expect more.

In *Personal Struggles*, Dr Ruth also highlights a critical point in relation to ending oppression between specific groups: that all systems of oppression are part of a larger injustice. Therefore, if we wish to end one of these (e.g. the oppression of women by men), we also need to work towards ending all other oppressive systems and inequalities. This is especially important to understand where we as individuals belong to an oppressor group. For instance, as a woman, while you are a member of one oppressed group, if you are white, straight or middle-class, you also belong to at least one oppressor group. Or as consumers, most of us are guilty of inflicting damage on the earth through the lifestyle choices we make every day, ignoring the impact our decisions have on the lives of others.

It isn't enough to say we personally are not the perpetrators of injustice. As Edmund Burke said, 'The only thing necessary for the triumph of evil is for good men to do nothing.' (If he was alive today, he would obviously update this quote to share the responsibility with good women as well.) Therefore:

- If we don't speak up when we observe oppression, such as ethnic minorities or gay people being verbally abused in public, we silently condone the behaviour and continue to reinforce an oppressive system.
- If we support policies that fail to create equal opportunities for education in schools for children of all backgrounds, we perpetuate class systems of privilege indefinitely and we also fail to fight xenophobia.
- If we stand in the way of creating public infrastructure that benefits society, such as investing in affordable childcare and healthcare for all, or efficient and environmentally friendly public transport, just because we have the personal wealth to live well without them, we are doing an injustice to others and to generations to come.

In each of these areas, there are possible winners and losers. Huge short-term gains for some at the expense of long-term losses for humanity and the planet. It is incumbent upon us all to aim to achieve the best and fairest outcomes for all in each of these areas, instead of enabling the privileges of the few.

Therefore, if we wish to address injustice to women, we must also examine whether our actions (or lack of action) are contributing to injustice in other aspects of our lives. It is only by aiming to create a world of fairness and shared resources for all that we have any hope of dismantling the unjust but inter-connected systems that wrongly oppress people all over the world.

PRACTICAL ACTIONS FOR GOVERNMENT AND EMPLOYERS

To change the unequal systems that have existed in our society ever since women started joining the workforce several practical policies also need to be implemented by governments and employers:

Provide well-paid parental leave to both mothers and fathers

Unless state and employer supports encourage men to participate actively in the care of their baby during its first year (by taking a significant amount of time off work for this purpose), the job of childcare will continue to fall automatically to women. While men have much to benefit personally by being actively and equally involved in the care of their children, they will continue to be excluded from this opportunity. The state and employers should switch from providing maternity leave to offering shared parental leave. This would ensure that both parents become hands-on participants in looking after their children and understand fully the work it involves. This would be the greatest step towards ending the imbalance in the Invisible Job.

Another advantage of expecting both parents to take parental leave is that it would remove the gender bias of employers who are reluctant to employ or promote women of childbearing age. It would mean a forty-year-old man would be just as likely to take parental leave as a thirty-year old woman.

The cost of providing parental leave should be shared by the state and the employer. While there would be a visible short-term cost to the exchequer, this is only because current economic systems (including measures for estimating GDP) fail to quantify the actual cost of childcare, which is currently met by mothers dropping out of the labour force.

Even designating the financial resources that are allocated to maternity leave as parental leave, to be shared by both parents, would be a vital first step towards gender equality. To be truly effective, though, this leave must be properly paid, both for men and for women, i.e. at 80% of their salary. Intelligent governments already know this is a smart investment in society that increases long-term participation in the workforce in addition to offering many societal benefits. However, if governments or employers perceive offering well-paid parental leave as unaffordable (or erroneously suspect it would encourage couples to have larger families), it could be capped at two children per couple. Current global surveys of childbearing preferences show that women consistently express a desire for two children, on average (62). So fear not, employers!

At 7.7 billion people in 2019, the planet is already struggling to sustain its huge population. According to a 2019 UN report, this is projected to reach 9.7 billion by 2050, with most of the growth occurring in Africa and Asia (62). While fertility rates remain highest in less developed parts of the world, particularly sub-Saharan Africa, history shows us that when women and girls are given access to education and family planning, they choose to have fewer children. An average lifetime fertility (i.e. the number of live births per woman) of 2.1 is roughly the level required for populations with low mortality to have a growth rate of zero in the long run, which would enable greater sustainability of resources and improve quality of life for all the earth's inhabitants. In 2019, the global number of live births per woman was 2.5. In developed countries, however, this figure has been below 2 since 1990. In Europe and North America the average number of births in 2019 was 1.7 and in Australia and New Zealand it was 1.8. In fact, in these low-fertility parts of the world, even managing to have a second child is unachievable for many women, according to the UN, due to 'incompatibility between childrearing and the demands of education and career building, a lack of affordable high-quality childcare, the decline of reproductive capacity at advanced maternal ages and imbalanced gender roles for housework and childcare'.

Provide access to affordable, high-quality childcare for all

Lack of access to good quality, affordable childcare is the primary factor holding women back from participating fully in the labour force and reaching their professional potential. It also prevents many women with children from being financially independent. Parents need access to centrally organised childcare, subsidised for parents, where both the mother and father are in paid employment, as well as for single parents. The childcare on offer must be of high standard in every regard, including the calibre of staff, facilities and diversity of learning opportunities, so that uptake is universal. Otherwise parents with better financial resources will seek out better childcare from private suppliers, resulting in a two-tier system of early education, initiating disadvantage and inequality from an early age. The cost to the state of providing this childcare service would be mitigated through the tax contributions of the additional women (and men) who would be working, instead of being outside the labour force.

Give both men and women flexibility to reduce/modify their working hours if they need to attend to caring responsibilities

We need to acknowledge that for significant parts of their working lives, couples will have caring responsibilities for dependents, either their children or their own parents. Therefore, rather than thinking of employees as either pure workers or pure carers, we should all think of ourselves as 'worker-carers'. The ratio of time we need to devote to these two aspects of our identities will change over the course of our lives. Therefore, workplaces need to be structured in a way that gives employees flexibility to reduce their hours, while still enabling the business to carry on with as little negative impact as possible. This diversity of role and flexibility would be welcomed not only by women but the current generation of men, too.

To enable this flexibility in the workplace, we need to restructure job roles in a modular way, so that employees can be more interchangeable and/or share jobs, for example:

- Working two, three or four days per week (applicable to most sectors of work)
- Maintaining the same total number of hours but with some flexibility regarding when to do them, e.g. by having core working hours of 10 a.m. to 2 p.m. (applicable to most office workers)

- Working early and late shifts (applicable to many sectors, in particular transport, retail and healthcare)
- Working alternate weeks, paired with a designated co-worker (applicable to many sectors, including teaching)

There also needs to be financial recognition at the state level of the value of providing care to older dependent family members. If it were not provided by a family member, in any caring society, it would default to being the responsibility of the state. Many countries prefer to ignore state responsibility for providing and funding such care, leaving it instead to the private market. However, this approach can lead to the commodification of care, which undermines the basis of a caring society, with family at its core (63). There are many benefits to such care being provided by family members where they have capacity to do so. However, they should be financially rewarded for this work. As this responsibility most often falls to women, unless it is paid for by the state, it undermines the financial independence of women, in particular. A system that balances care provided by family members (paid by the state) alongside state care provided by professional care workers would be optimal. The Nordic countries represent the best examples of societies with policies to equitably support the care of both older people and children.

Create an employment culture where neither men nor women are penalised in terms of income/career prospects for taking time off work

Men and women need to be (financially and legally) able to take time off work to look after children or older people when the need arises. In addition, they need a guarantee that it will not negatively impact their careers. We saw earlier how taking time off work to look after children has long-lasting negative impacts for women in terms of income and career prospects. And that younger women face prejudice from employers who presume they will leave to look after children. At the heart of this prejudice is the fact that time dedicated to caring for others is not recognised by the state or employers as having economic value. Conversely, spending long hours at work is viewed by many employers as dedication to your job, when in reality what matters is a person's productivity.

As outlined by Dr Mary Murphy, lecturer in Irish Politics and Society at Maynooth University and member of the Irish Human Rights and Equality Commission, the true value of unpaid work needs to be actively measured and included in national accounts of total economic activity (63). Only then will time taken off work by parents to attend to necessary caring work be viewed as having a value to the state, which should actively encourage employers to facilitate it without penalty. To change gender imbalance, employers will also need to proactively support men in the uptake of their care responsibilities at home. Firms should be accountable for achieving gender balance in the number of male versus female employees who take up care leave. The efforts of proactive employers in this regard should be recognised publicly, which will in turn reap recruitment/retention rewards.

Provide secure employment to those in the care sector, particularly immigrants, to look after children in childcare centres and older people in their homes

Everyone deserves to have access to care and kindness throughout their lives, from childhood to old age. Indeed, it is when we are children and when we are old that we need this care the most. Providing this care in a loving way is something that those closest to us are best placed to do.

However, it may not be economically possible for parents to provide all the daily care their children need. And even if they could afford it financially, not all parents might want to spend their entire day caring for their children. We thrive on diversity and the ability to combine caring duties with other pursuits, such as work that interests us. For this reason, in attending to the needs of their children, most families rely on a mix of external care (from nurseries, schools, grandparents and after-school helpers) and the care that parents provide directly.

Similarly, many of us will need to be cared for in some way in our old age. While most people are keen to maintain their independence, at some point many will need the help of others. This may be due to illness or accidents, or simply due to ageing and being unable to do everything they once did. We may no longer be able to drive or walk long distances. We may even have difficulty using public transport. We may not be able to do our own grocery shopping. Perhaps we may no longer be able to wash and dress ourselves. Or perhaps we might just be lonely.

While voluntary, private and state organisations exist to assist older people with such needs to live independently, in a caring society family and people close to us would ideally be part of this network.

In order to facilitate men and women being carer-workers – i.e. able to engage in paid work as well as attend to caring responsibilities – external support will also be needed. In order for countries such as Ireland and the UK to be able to offer affordable care for older people, along with affordable childcare, they will need to attract a much larger supply of immigrant workers to create a workforce that can fill this caring gap (63). To find suitable applicants to work in childcare or care for older people, the state must be willing to provide high-quality training, along with security of contract, good pay and decent working conditions.

Afterword

Home can feel like a wonderful place. Being a parent can be a wonderful experience. And for children, there can be no better start in life than growing up in a secure home with hands-on parents. While these are all things that most couples would agree are desirable, creating this takes time and effort. The Invisible Job presents many challenges, not least the conflict it creates in terms of demands on our time.

Responsibility for parenting and running a home should be shared equally by both partners, not only because you are equally important but because failure to share this responsibility fairly tends to put a significant burden on women. Embracing it as partners will lead to more fulfilling lives for both men and women and better, more interdependent relationships. Creating a society where men and women are facilitated to balance caring and earning roles is key to eliminating gender inequality and enabling everyone to thrive.

Fathers and mothers both want to do their best for their children. But we all have other things we want – and must – give our energies to also. Acknowledging this is important. While we will never feel we have enough time to do everything in life, doing our best to share and value each other's efforts in carrying out the Invisible Job leads to happier lives for both men and women. Things will never run to plan but that's OK. Generosity of spirit, honest communication and flexibility on the part of both partners is all you can ask for.

In a society where the Invisible Job is shared equally by men and women, women will be free to pursue their other goals in life on an equal footing. But gender equality cannot be achieved in isolation. Instead, we also need to work towards equality in every other aspect of our lives.

While we are many years away from achieving gender equality in society, by appreciating how an imbalance in the Invisible Job prevents equality among couples, men and women can ensure this doesn't happen in their own relationships. Instead of falling into the pothole of gender roles, by being forewarned, young men and women can create relationships based on equal partnership. What 'equal' looks like is entirely up to you to decide. Instead of allowing today's twenty-something-year-old women to follow the well-worn path of women aged thirty- and forty-something (and every other woman before them!), shine a light on the Invisible Job now. This will give them an insight into what lies ahead and the ability to negotiate with their partner on how to navigate it together.

Good men will play a pivotal role in shaking off old gender roles and showing other men how living interdependently with their partners leads to more fulfilling lives, both as men and as fathers. Appreciating and sharing responsibility for the Invisible Job will pave the way for gender equality in work and in society overall. A more productive, balanced and happier life for all is up for grabs. It's win–win, not win–lose.

Employers and governments need to recognise the enormous economic and societal contribution made by the Invisible Job and stop pretending that this unpaid work does not exist. We need financial and legal measures that enable men and women to fulfil their caring responsibilities as decent human beings, in addition to providing financially for their dependents. In economic terms, this will not cost anything. Instead, it will be a worthwhile investment towards building a better world for everyone.

Appendix

THE INVISIBLE JOB DESCRIPTION TEMPLATE

A modifiable Word version of this template is available to download at www.theinvisiblejob.com.

Category	Job Element	Frequency					Flexibility around timing: Low, Medium or High	Heavy lifter? (High freq+ low flex)	Should we outsource?	Person responsible	
		Daily (or more!)	Weekly (or more)	Monthly (or more)	Once or twice a year	Less often				(Name)	(Name)
I'm hungry!	Prepare breakfast for children	X					L	*			
	Prepare weekend lunches for everyone		X				L				
	Prepare school lunches for children	X					L	*			
	Prepare midweek dinners for everyone	X					L	*			
	Prepare weekend dinners for everyone		X				M				
	Assist young children at mealtimes	X					L	*			
	Prepare or source baby food	X					M				
	Set table for meals	X					L	*			

Category	Job Element	Frequency					Flexibility around timing: Low, Medium or High	Heavy lifter? (High freq + low flex)	Should we outsource?	Person responsible	
		Daily (or more!)	Weekly (or more)	Monthly (or more)	Once or twice a year	Less often				(Name)	(Name)
	Clean pots, counters and utensils after food preparation	X					L	*			
	Load dishwasher or wash dishes	X					M				
	Unload dishwasher/put away clean dishes	X					M				
	Identify and fulfil all grocery shopping needs		X				M				
	Put away grocery shopping, throw out anything out of date and rearrange items in cupboards/fridge as needed		X				L				
Laundry	Put all dirty clothes, towels and sheets into laundry baskets		X				M	*			
	Load laundry items into washing machine in suitable batches		X				M	*			

Category	Job Element	Frequency					Flexibility around timing: Low, Medium or High	Heavy lifter? (High freq+ low flex)	Should we outsource?	Person responsible	
		Daily (or more!)	Weekly (or more)	Monthly (or more)	Once or twice a year	Less often				(Name)	(Name)
	Hang wet washing up to dry or put through tumble dryer		X				L	*			
	Sort, fold and put away clean clothes, identifying any that need ironing		X				M	*			
	Iron all items that need ironing		X				M				
	Drop off and collect items that need dry cleaning			X			H				
General housework	Bathrooms:										
	Clean toilets, sink, shower, bath and mirrors		X				M				
	Replenish toilet rolls		X				M				
	Mop floor		X				M				

Category	Job Element	Frequency					Flexibility around timing: Low, Medium or High	Heavy lifter? (High freq+ low flex)	Should we outsource?	Person responsible	
		Daily (or more!)	Weekly (or more)	Monthly (or more)	Once or twice a year	Less often				(Name)	(Name)
	Kitchen:										
	Clear kitchen table	X					L	*			
	Wipe worktops and sink area	X					L	*			
	Sweep floor	X					M				
	Mop floor		X				H				
	Clean stove area		X				M				
	Clean fridge			X			M				
	Clean microwave			X			M				
	Wipe inside/outside of cupboards				X		H				
	Defrost freezer				X		M				
	Bedrooms:										
	Tidy room		X								
	Make beds (adults and children)	X									
	Change (adult) bed sheets and covers		X				M				

Category	Job Element	Frequency					Flexibility around timing: Low, Medium or High	Heavy lifter? (High freq+ low flex)	Should we outsource?	Person responsible	
		Daily (or more!)	Weekly (or more)	Monthly (or more)	Once or twice a year	Less often				(Name)	(Name)
	Change (child) bed sheets and covers			X			M				
	Rest of house:										
	Tidy communal rooms		X				M				
	Vacuum or sweep hard floors		X				M				
	Mop hard floors		X				H				
	Vacuum rugs and carpets		X				M				
	Clean windows inside			X			H				
	Clean windows outside				X		H				
	Waste management:										
	Empty all inside bins to wheelie bin, clean bins and replace liners		X				M				
	Bring out and retrieve wheelie bins		X				L				

Category	Job Element	Frequency					Flexibility around timing: Low, Medium or High	Heavy lifter? (High freq+ low flex)	Should we outsource?	Person responsible	
		Daily (or more!)	Weekly (or more)	Monthly (or more)	Once or twice a year	Less often				(Name)	(Name)
	If not collected, bring recyclable materials to designated centre			X			H				
	Dispose of compostable kitchen waste	X					M				
	Bring unwanted items to charity stores				X		H				
Preventive health	Child immunisations: schedule and attend appointments, manage child health records				X		L				
	Arrange and manage routine dental visits for children				X		M				
	Responsibility for birth control (Frequency variable)	X					L	*			

Category	Job Element	Frequency					Flexibility around timing: Low, Medium or High	Heavy lifter? (High freq+ low flex)	Should we outsource?	Person responsible	
		Daily (or more!)	Weekly (or more)	Monthly (or more)	Once or twice a year	Less often				(Name)	(Name)
Hygiene	Children's bath/shower		X				M				
	Manage children's haircuts: schedule and attend appointments at the hairdresser or cut hair yourself			X			H				
	Ensure children brush their teeth regularly and correctly	X					M				
	Wash and dry children's hair		X				H				
	Ensure everyone has suitable toothbrushes/toothpaste/floss			X			H				
	Clip children's finger-nails and toenails			X			M				
Emergency health (Frequency variable)	Look after children when sick						L				

Category	Job Element	Frequency					Flexibility around timing: Low, Medium or High	Heavy lifter? (High freq+ low flex)	Should we outsource?	Person responsible	
		Daily (or more!)	Weekly (or more)	Monthly (or more)	Once or twice a year	Less often				(Name)	(Name)
	Doctor/hospital visits						L				
	Manage headlice, threadworms and other medical delights						L	*			
	Keep family first aid supplies stocked				X		H				
Long-term childcare	Research possible long-term childcare options and choose one that meets your family's needs			X							
	Manage relationship, contract and payments associated with child-care provision		X								
	Manage transport to and from childcare	X					L	*			

Category	Job Element	Frequency					Flexibility around timing: Low, Medium or High	Heavy lifter? (High freq+ low flex)	Should we outsource?	Person responsible	
		Daily (or more!)	Weekly (or more)	Monthly (or more)	Once or twice a year	Less often				(Name)	(Name)
Short-term and impromptu childcare	Identify suitable short-term childcare options and manage set up, communication and payment arrangements as needed			X			M				
	In advance of school holidays, identify and arrange suitable camps for children, manage enrolment, payment and all communication prior to camp			X			H				
	During holiday camps, manage transport, safety and all communications, ensuring your child brings everything they need	X					L	*			
Baby clothes	Identify and buy baby clothes as needed			X			M				

Category	Job Element	Frequency					Flexibility around timing: Low, Medium or High	Heavy lifter? (High freq+ low flex)	Should we outsource?	Person responsible	
		Daily (or more!)	Weekly (or more)	Monthly (or more)	Once or twice a year	Less often				(Name)	(Name)
	Organise baby clothes in current use			X			M				
	Identify and store/pass on baby clothes that are currently too small/big			X			H				
Children's clothes and shoes	Arrange/sort clothes in current use. Identify when new clothes needed and store/pass on clothes that are too small/big			X			H				
	Buy new clothes when needed			X			H				
	Mend or throw out torn/damaged clothes			X			M				
	Identify when children need new shoes, trainers, boots or sandals; select and buy				X		H				
	Identify and buy school uniform items as needed				X		L				

Category	Job Element	Frequency					Flexibility around timing: Low, Medium or High	Heavy lifter? (High freq+ low flex)	Should we outsource?	Person responsible	
		Daily (or more!)	Weekly (or more)	Monthly (or more)	Once or twice a year	Less often				(Name)	(Name)
	Identify and source Christmas jumpers and other festive or dressing up items as needed				X		L				
	Identify and source sports clothes as needed			X			M				
Children's toys, games books, and art	Identify and buy suitable children's toys, games books, and drawing/colouring materials			X			H				
	Organise and manage toys, games, books and art materials		X				M				
	Admire/encourage children's art...then figure out where to put it!		X				H				

Category	Job Element	Frequency					Flexibility around timing: Low, Medium or High	Heavy lifter? (High freq+ low flex)	Should we outsource?	Person responsible	
		Daily (or more!)	Weekly (or more)	Monthly (or more)	Once or twice a year	Less often				(Name)	(Name)
Children's activities	Research and identify suitable activities for your children to participate in. Manage enrolment, scheduling, attendance, practice, required equipment, communications and any associated parental activities including supervision, transport and volunteering		X				M				
Family scheduling	Create a schedule for family activities and adapt on an ongoing basis as needed Oversee to ensure family life runs smoothly, adapting plans as needed.	X					L	*			

Category	Job Element	Frequency					Flexibility around timing: Low, Medium or High	Heavy lifter? (High freq+ low flex)	Should we outsource?	Person responsible	
		Daily (or more!)	Weekly (or more)	Monthly (or more)	Once or twice a year	Less often				(Name)	(Name)
All that school entails	Research, identify and enrol your children in suitable schools at kindergarten, primary and secondary level					X	M				
	Get children to and from school safely	X					L	*			
	Help with or supervise homework as needed	X					M				
	Be contact person for your child's teachers and the school administrator, managing all school communications and attending meetings as needed	X					M	*			
	Act as parent volunteer for school activities as needed			X			H				

Category	Job Element	Frequency					Flexibility around timing: Low, Medium or High	Heavy lifter? (High freq+ low flex)	Should we outsource?	Person responsible	
		Daily (or more!)	Weekly (or more)	Monthly (or more)	Once or twice a year	Less often				(Name)	(Name)
	Identify, source and label all school materials needed by your children including textbooks, stationery, paper, pencil cases, art materials, folders, maths equipment, electronic devices, key fobs, lunchboxes and water bottles				X		M				
Birthdays, special occasions and acknowledging others	Research, plan and manage all activities associated with hosting your own children's birthday parties				X		H				

Category	Job Element	Frequency					Flexibility around timing: Low, Medium or High	Heavy lifter? (High freq+ low flex)	Should we outsource?	Person responsible	
		Daily (or more!)	Weekly (or more)	Monthly (or more)	Once or twice a year	Less often				(Name)	(Name)
	Manage all activities associated with attending other children's birthday parties, including communications with the party host, getting your child to and from the venue, providing any permissions needed and arranging a card and present			X			M				
	Arrange and send birthday cards and presents to family			X			M				
	Organise, write and send Christmas cards to friends and family				X		M				
	Arrange presents for teachers and/or coaches				X		H				

Category	Job Element	Frequency					Flexibility around timing: Low, Medium or High	Heavy lifter? (High freq+ low flex)	Should we outsource?	Person responsible	
		Daily (or more!)	Weekly (or more)	Monthly (or more)	Once or twice a year	Less often				(Name)	(Name)
	Help Santa arrange presents				X		H				
	Put up and take down decorations at Christmas and other special occasions				X		M				
	Write and send thank you cards				X		M				
	Maintain supplies of suitable cards, stationery, gift paper and stamps				X		H				
Be there whenever children need you	Listen to the day's woes	X					L	*			
	Read to/with your children	X					M				
	Playtime	X					M				
	Bedtime	X					L	*			

Category	Job Element	Frequency					Flexibility around timing: Low, Medium or High	Heavy lifter? (High freq+ low flex)	Should we outsource?	Person responsible	
		Daily (or more!)	Weekly (or more)	Monthly (or more)	Once or twice a year	Less often				(Name)	(Name)
	Create structure and limits	X					M				
	Keep the bowling ball from falling down the gulley		X				M				
Family holidays	Research and make all holiday arrangements				X		H				
	Pack (for children and adults) and unpack				X		M				
Managing a home											
Renting	Finding a place to live					X	M				
	Managing contracts, payment and communication with the landlord				X		L				

Category	Job Element	Frequency					Flexibility around timing: Low, Medium or High	Heavy lifter? (High freq + low flex)	Should we outsource?	Person responsible	
		Daily (or more!)	Weekly (or more)	Monthly (or more)	Once or twice a year	Less often				(Name)	(Name)
Manage utilities	Research, procure, manage contracts, meter readings and billing, arrange servicing and testing as required and act as liaison with providers of:										
	Gas/Electricity				X		H				
	Internet				X		H				
	TV and streaming				X		H				
	House alarm				X		H				
Manage family IT needs	Set up and manage the family's broad-band, computer, tablet, phone and music device needs, as well as internet security and data back up		X				M				

Category	Job Element	Frequency					Flexibility around timing: Low, Medium or High	Heavy lifter? (High freq+ low flex)	Should we outsource?	Person responsible	
		Daily (or more!)	Weekly (or more)	Monthly (or more)	Once or twice a year	Less often				(Name)	(Name)
Manage home storage	Set up and manage a system for storing items not currently in use (e.g. Christmas decorations or beach buckets and spades)			X			H				
	Set up and manage a system for organising children's toys and art materials		X				M				
	Set up and manage a system to file important identity documents and certificates			X			H				
	Create and manage a system for locating essential household records including financial documents, utilities, warranties, receipts and instructions as needed			X			M				

Category	Job Element	Frequency					Flexibility around timing: Low, Medium or High	Heavy lifter? (High freq+ low flex)	Should we outsource?	Person responsible	
		Daily (or more!)	Weekly (or more)	Monthly (or more)	Once or twice a year	Less often				(Name)	(Name)
Minor house maintenance	Fix broken things (such as doors, windows, doorbells, furniture, leaking taps) – either by fixing them yourself or hiring a professional to do it			X			L				
	Preventive maintenance: replace water filters, test smoke, CO and other alarms, clean chimneys, charge/replace batteries			X			H				
	Manage home furnishings: identify and source (as needed) curtains, blinds, furniture, carpets, rugs, kitchenware, beds, sheets, duvets, pillows, lights, lamps and other home furnishing				X		M				

Category	Job Element	Frequency					Flexibility around timing: Low, Medium or High	Heavy lifter? (High freq+ low flex)	Should we outsource?	Person responsible	
		Daily (or more!)	Weekly (or more)	Monthly (or more)	Once or twice a year	Less often				(Name)	(Name)
Major house maintenance	Manage plumbing, drainage or electric issues as needed				X		L				
	Manage home improvement projects (e.g. painting/decorating, extensions, renovation, or energy efficiency projects)				X		H				
Gardening	Mow lawn		X				H				
	Manage essential maintenance e.g. removing hazards			X			H				
	Water and feed indoor plants	X					M				
	Other gardening activities such as weeding, pruning and planting			X			H				
Financial planning	Manage day-to-day family finances	X					M				

Category	Job Element	Frequency					Flexibility around timing: Low, Medium or High	Heavy lifter? (High freq + low flex)	Should we outsource?	Person responsible	
		Daily (or more!)	Weekly (or more)	Monthly (or more)	Once or twice a year	Less often				(Name)	(Name)
	Manage long-term financial planning			X			H				
	Manage wills and life assurance					X	H				
	Set up and manage mortgage repayments and administration			X			M				
Looking after pets	Exercising	X					M				
	Feeding and managing litter	X					L	*			
	Cleaning		X				M				
	Managing preventive and emergency health issues			X			M				
	Arrange care of pets when you are away				X		M				

Category	Job Element	Frequency					Flexibility around timing: Low, Medium or High	Heavy lifter? (High freq+ low flex)	Should we outsource?	Person responsible	
		Daily (or more!)	Weekly (or more)	Monthly (or more)	Once or twice a year	Less often				(Name)	(Name)
Connecting (with family, friends and each other)	Making space for the two of you		X				H				
	Arranging social life of children	X					M				
	Family experiences		X				M				
	Fostering connections with relatives			X			H				
	Taking care of older dependants		X				M				
	Preserving memories and moments			X			H				

Note that the daily work involved in attending to a baby has not been included in the Invisible Job Description (i.e. feeding, dressing, changing, washing, stimulating, comforting, engaging, supporting and general loving). In short, that's because babies require your attention every moment that they are awake. The only thing to remember is that it makes doing any other element of the Invisible Job at the same time very challenging.

NOTE ABOUT HOW TIME-USE DATA REFERRED TO IN THIS BOOK IS COLLATED

There are two main methods of estimating the time spent on caring and household activities.

- The first is *self-reported estimates* based on a person's recall in response to survey questions. This is the methodology used in the EQLS.
- The second method is *time-use surveys*, such as the American Time Use Survey that the US data above is based on, where people fill in a log throughout the day to try to log how much time they are spending on a given activity.

As the authors of the ESRI 2019 report note, measuring the extent of care or unpaid work accurately is challenging for two reasons (2):

1. Difficulties can arise in defining what should be included and excluded in measures of care. For instance, in working out how much time per week you spend on cooking, should you include the time you spent meal planning (assessing what is in the fridge that needs to be used up, then figuring out what to cook based on this and the other ingredients you have available). Presumably, you count time spent preparing and cooking the food, but what about laying the table, serving the food or clearing up afterwards?
2. In the case of self-reported data, it can be challenging for respondents to recall exactly how much time they spent on unpaid caring and housework activities. Why is this?
   a. Well, as any parent who currently doing the Invisible Job will know, the activities don't always happen according to a fixed schedule. Instead, one job frequently leads to another and because you are simultaneously spinning many plates, you often integrate activities to be as efficient as possible. You will frequently end up doing several activities simultaneously – for instance cooking dinner while supervising homework and searching through schoolbags for notes from the teacher. It would be much more straightforward to

accurately measure how much time you spent on each client during your day job! As Russell et al. highlight, 'Unpaid activities of this sort lack the clear time schedule boundaries or contractual obligations that apply to paid employment, making it more difficult for individuals to estimate' (2).

b. Second, how couples perceive the amount of time spent on unpaid work and its division may also be influenced by how couple view each other and the situation. In other words, if you generally feel positively about the contribution your partner is making to the overall relationship, you may generously assign them more credit than is due – and vice versa (38).

c. There is also evidence that unpaid hours are overestimated in self-reports. Nevertheless, time-estimate approaches that are carried out with a consistent methodology are still valuable for making important comparisons between groups, over time, and across countries.

Table 1: Summary of maternity leave entitlements

Adapted from Blum et al., 2018 (49)

Country	Maximum length of postnatal leave (months)			Flexibility#	Part or all leave transferable to father?
	Total	Paid*	Well paid**		
Australia	There is only a 'parental leave' provision in place				Yes
Austria	1.9	1.9	1.9	A	
Belgium	3.3	3.3	3.3[2]	A	
Brazil[1]	4 or 6	4 or 6	4 or 6	None	
Bulgaria	12	12	12[2]	C	Yes
Canada (Quebec)	3.5 – 4.2 / 4.2	3.5 / 4.2	0[3] / 4.2[2]	None / B	
China	2.7	2.7	2.7	A	
Croatia	6	6	6	A, C, D	
Czech Republic	5.1	5.1	5.1[2]	A, C	
Denmark	3.3	3.3	3.3[2]	None	
Estonia	3.7	3.7	3.7	None	
Finland	2.9	2.9	2.9[4]	None	
France	3.3	3.3	3.3[2]	A	
Germany	1.9	1.9	1.9	A	
Greece: Private sector / public sector	8.1 / 3	8.1 / 3	2.1[2] / 3	None / A	
Hungary	5.6	5.6	5.6	None	

Country	Maximum length of postnatal leave (months)			Flexibility#	Part or all leave trans-ferable to father?
	Total	Paid*	Well paid**		
Iceland[5]	There is only a 'Parental leave' provision in place				Yes
Ireland	9.3	6.0	No statutory entitlement	None	
Israel	6.0	3.5	3.5^2	A, C	Yes
Italy	3.7	3.7	3.7	A	
Japan	1.9	1.9	1.9	A	
Korea	3.0	3.0	$3.0^{2,6}$	A	
Latvia	1.9	1.9	1.9	A	
Lithuania	1.9	1.9	1.9	A	
Luxembourg	2.7	2.7	2.7^2	A	
Malta	4.2	4.2	3.3	None	
Mexico	2.3	2.3	2.3	A	
Netherlands	2.8	2.8	2.8^2	A	
New Zealand[7]	There is only a 'Parental leave' provision in place				Yes
Norway[8]	There is only a 'Parental leave' provision in place				Yes
Poland	4.6	4.6	4.6	A, C	
Portugal[9]	There is only a 'Parental leave' provision in place				Yes
Romania	4.2	4.2	4.2	None	
Russian Fed.	2.3	2.3	2.3^2	A	
Slovakia	6 to 6.5	6 to 6.5	6 to 6.5^2	A	
Slovenia	2.6	2.6	2.6^2	None	
South Africa	4	X	X	None	
Spain	3.7	3.7	3.7^2	A, C, D	Yes
Sweden[10]	There is only a 'Parental leave' provision in place				Yes
Switzerland	3.3	3.3	3.3^2	None	
UK	12	9	1.4	C	Yes
USA[11]					
Uruguay Public sector Private sector	3.3 3	3.3 3	3.3 3	A A	Yes Yes

* Paid at a flat rate or (if income-related) at less than 66% of earnings for all or most of period

** 66% or all or most of period at 66% or more of usual salary

[1] Brazil: six months for some public and private sector employees; four months for others.

[2] There is a ceiling on earnings-related pay.

[3] Canada: low-income families can qualify for a higher benefit rate, up to 80% of average insured earnings.

[4] Finland: The proportion of earnings paid is reduced beyond a specific level.

[5] Iceland: The law does not distinguish separate maternity, paternity and parental leaves, referring only to 'birth leave', three months of which is for mothers, three months for fathers and a further three months for parents to divide as they choose. Three months of 'birth leave' is reserved for women to take after birth, of which two weeks are obligatory.

[6] Korea: Maternity pay at the higher rate is capped for earnings-related pay after 30 days.

[7] New Zealand: The law does not refer to maternity leave, only 'paid parental leave' (primary carer leave), which mothers can transfer to their partners. This leave is included under parental leave, along with 'extended leave', which can be taken after 'paid parental leave'.

[8] Norway: The law does not distinguish separate maternity and paternity leaves, referring only to 'birth leave', part of which is for mothers, part for fathers, and part for parents to divide as they choose. Six weeks of parental leave is reserved for women to take after birth, and this is obligatory and included under parental leave.

[9] Portugal: The law does not refer to maternity leave, only to 'initial parental leave', part of which is reserved for mothers (6 weeks for women to take after birth) with the remainder for parents to divide as they choose. This leave is included under arental leave.

[10] Sweden: It is obligatory for women to take two weeks' leave either before or after birth; to receive benefits they must draw on parental leave entitlements.

[11] USA: There is no separate maternity leave but parents may take up to twelve weeks unpaid leave for childbirth or for the care of a child for up to twelve months as part of the federal Family and Medical Leave Act; however, employers with fewer than 50 employees are exempt.

#Flexibility:

A: Additional time allowed for multiple births, higher order births or medical complications.

B: Leave can be taken for a shorter period with a higher benefit paid or for a longer period with a lower benefit.

C: In all cases, maternity leave may be transferred to the father (not including cases where transfer is only permitted in the case of maternal death or incapacity).

D: Part of the maternity leave period can be taken part-time and the length of leave extended. Does not include flexibility in using part of maternity leave before or after birth.

Table 2: Summary of paternity leave entitlements

Adapted from Blum et al., 2018 (49)

Country	Summary of leave	Maximum length of postnatal leave (weeks)			Flexi-bility#
		Total	Paid*	Well paid**	
Australia[1]	X				
Austria Private sec Public sec	X ☐	4	None	None	None
Belgium	☐☐☐	2	2	2*	B, C
Brazil[2]	☐☐☐	1 or 4	1 or 4	1 or 4	None
Bulgaria	☐☐☐	15 days	15 days	15 days*	None
Canada (Quebec)	X ☐☐☐	5	5	5*	A
China[3]	☐☐☐	7–30 days	7–30 days	7–30 days	None
Croatia					
Czech Republic	☐☐☐	7 days	7 days	7 days	C
Denmark	☐☐☐	2	2	2	C
Estonia	☐☐☐	2	2	2*	B, C
Finland	☐☐☐	9	9	9[4]	B, C
France	☐☐☐	2.2	2.2	2.2*	C
Germany	X				
Greece	☐☐☐	2 days	2 days	2 days	None
Hungary	☐☐☐	1	1	1	C, D
Iceland[5]	X				
Ireland	☐☐	2	2	X	C
Israel	☐☐	6 days	5 days	3 days	None
Italy	☐☐☐ OB	4 days[6]	4 days	4 days	B, C, E
Japan	X				
Korea	☐☐☐	3–5 days	3 days	3 days	C
Latvia	☐☐☐	10 days	10 days	10 days	C
Lithuania	☐☐☐	4	4	4*	C
Luxembourg	X				

Malta Private sector Public sector	☐☐☐ ☐☐☐	1 day 5 days	1 day 5 days	1 day 5 days	D C
Mexico	☐☐☐	5 days	5 days	5 days	E
Netherlands	☐☐☐	2 days	2 days	2 days	C
New Zealand	☐[9]	10 days	X	X	C
Norway	☐[10]	2	X	X	B,[11] C
Poland	☐☐☐	2	2	2	B, C
Portugal	X				
Romania	☐☐☐	5–15 days	5–15 days	5–15 days	C, D[13]
Russian Fed.	X				
Slovakia	X				
Slovenia	☐☐☐	30 days	30 days	30 days*	B
South Africa	X				
Spain	☐☐☐	4	4	4*	C, D
Sweden	☐☐☐	10 days	10 days	10 days*	C, D
Switzerland	X				
UK	☐☐	1 or 2	1 or 2	X	C
USA	X				
Uruguay	☐☐☐	10 days	10 days	10 days	None

X: no statutory entitlement to paternity pay.

☐: statutory entitlement but unpaid

☐☐: statutory entitlement, some period paid, but either at a flat rate or (if income-related) at less than 66% of earnings for all or most of period

☐☐☐: statutory entitlement, paid for all or most of period at 66% of earnings or more

*: ceiling on earnings-related payment

[1] Australia: Two weeks' payment for fathers taking parental leave ('Dad and Partner Pay'), on unpaid leave or not working.

[2] Brazil: Longer in public sector; less in private sector.

[3] China: There is no statutory entitlement nationally; the given numbers are for regional provisions that have existed in all provinces since 2018.

[4] Finland: Paid at 70% of earnings, but proportion is reduced beyond a specified level.

[5] Iceland: The law does not distinguish separate maternity, paternity and parental leaves, referring only to 'birth leave', part of which is for mothers, part for fathers, and part for parents to divide as they choose.

[6] Italy: a further one-day paternity leave can be taken if the mother agrees to transfer these days from her maternity leave. In addition, fathers may take three months' paid leave in exceptional circumstances, e.g. the death or severe illness of the mother.

[7] Luxembourg: there is no statutory paternity leave, although fathers can use ten days' well-paid leave 'due to extraordinary circumstances'.

[8] Netherlands: Three days of parental leave can be taken during the first four weeks after birth. This leave is included under parental leave.

[9] New Zealand: the mother (or other primary carer) may transfer part of her leave payment to her partner on paternity leave (known as partner's leave).

[10] Norway: While unpaid by the government, most employed fathers are covered by their individual employer or collective agreements. NOTE: In Norway, total parental leave entitlement is 49 weeks at 100% of pay or 59 weeks at 80% of salary. Three weeks before the birth are reserved for the mother. Of the postnatal period, ten weeks are for mothers (mødrekvoten or 'mothers' quota') and ten weeks are for fathers (fedrekvoten or 'fathers' quota'). The remaining 26 or 36 weeks is a family entitlement and may be taken by either the mother or father (64).

[11] Norway: Leave can be transferred to someone else if the father does not live with the mother, since the purpose of the leave is to assist the mother.

[12] Portugal: The law does not refer to paternity leave, referring only 'fathers-only parental leave'. This leave is included under parental leave.

[13] Romania: The statutory leave is granted for five days only but ten extra days can be granted if the father has completed an infant-care course, for the first child only.

[14] Slovenia: paid at 90% of average monthly earnings; not all income on which parental leave contributions were paid is counted towards the basic earnings (e.g. in-work benefits and other income received in addition to basic earnings).

[15] South Africa: there is no statutory paternity leave, although fathers who wish to take leave at the time of the birth of their child can use their family responsibility leave. However, a private bill was launched in 2018 to amend this gap in the provision.

Flexibility
A: leave can be taken for a shorter period with a higher benefit paid or for a longer period with a lower benefit; B: leave can be taken in one block of time or several blocks; C: can be taken at any time during a defined period after birth; D: additional time for multiple births and large families; E: can be extended in case of maternal incapacity or death.

OECD SOCIETY AT A GLANCE 2011. UNPAID WORK

Minutes of unpaid work per day by main categories (OECD, 2011)

	Routine house-work	Shopping	Care for house-hold members	Care for non-household members	Volun-teering	Travel related to unpaid work
Korea (2)	79	13	29	0	1	14
China	103	20	23	2	1	15
Japan (2)	100	26	18	-	4	15

	Routine house- work	Shopping	Care for house- hold members	Care for non- household members	Volun- teering	Travel related to unpaid work
South Africa	139	9	20	1	1	11
Norway	114	23	26	6	2	17
India	148	12	21	1	0	8
France	133	32	19	8	1	4
Canada	109	30	27	9	2	21
Spain	127	25	22	8	1	15
Belgium	134	26	16	0	5	19
Hungary (2)	128	22	20	-	0	30
Finland	120	28	22	10	4	17
Austria	125	21	34	3	4	17
United States	102	28	31	10	8	28
OECD	**128**	**23**	**26**	**7**	**4**	**20**
United Kingdom	123	29	24	8	2	25
Germany	124	31	19	8	7	23
Ireland (2)	92	28	62	-	8	23
Sweden	128	25	25	7	4	24
Italy	138	27	21	8	2	19
Denmark	128	26	28	10	3	22
Netherlands	118	28	28	8	5	33
Portugal	161	15	17	7	2	20
New Zealand	121	23	30	18	13	22
Poland	145	23	28	13	1	20
Slovenia	166	18	21	7	1	18
Estonia	150	24	25	13	1	19
Australia (2)	132	29	45	-	6	32
Turkey	141	14	32	-	19	40
Mexico (3)	185	17	36	6	1	7

Works Cited

[1] *Notting Hill.* Michell, Roger. [writ.] **Richard Curtis.** [perf.] Hugh Grant. 1999.

[2] *Caring and Unpaid Work in Ireland.* **ESRI.** Russell, H; Grotti, R; McGinnity, F; Privalko, I. s.l. : Economic and Social Research Institute, 2019. Report.

[3] 'Clinical observations related to head lice infestation'. **Mumcuoglu, KY et al.,** 1991, *Journal of the American Academy of Dermatology*, Vol. 25, pp. 248–251.

[4] 'Single-blind, randomised, comparative study of the Bug Buster Kit and Over the Counter Pediculicide treatments against head lice in the United Kingdom'. **Hill, N.**, *British Medical Journal*, Aug 2005 pp. 331–384.

[5] 'Hormonal contraceptives and cerebral venous thrombosis risk: a systemic review and analysis'. **Amoozegar, Farnaz.** Article 7, Feb 2015, *Frontiers in Neurology*, Vol. 6.

[6] *School Holidays by Country.* **Marian, Jakub.** Jakub Marian's language learning, science and art. [Online] 2015. https://jakubmarian.com/school-holidays-by-country-in-europe-map/.

[7] 'Take turns being the fun parent'. **Modern Parent.** *Medium.* [Online] 4 December 2020. https://medium.com/modern-parent/take-turns-being-the-fun-parent-2283a0813016.

[8] *The Unmumsy Mum.* **Turner, Sarah.** London: Penguin Random House, 2016.

[9] *Towards a better future for women and work: Voices of women and men* **International Labour Organisation & Gallup**. International Labour Organisation & Gallup, 2017. Report. 978-92-2-128962-3.

10 'Does Father's involvement in Childcare and Housework affect Couple's Relationship stability?' **Norman, Helen et al.** *Social Science Quarterly*, November 2018, Vol. 99. Wiley Periodicals.

11 'Skip the dishes? Not so fast! Sex and housework revisited'. **Johnson, M. D., Galambos, N. L., & Anderson, J. R.** *Journal of Family Psychology*, 2016, Vol. 30. American Psychological Association.

12 Perceived fairness and satisfaction with the division of housework among dual-earner couples in Italy. **Carriero, R.** *Marriage & Family Review*, 2011. Vol. 47, pp. 436–458. Taylor & Francis.

13 *A Quantum Leap for Gender Equality: A Better Future of Work for All.* **International Labour Organisation.** Geneva: International Labour Office, 2019.

14 *Society at a Glance 2011:OECD Social Indicators.* **OECD.** Paris : OECD Publishing, 2011. https://doi.org/10.1787/soc_glance-2011-graph4-en.

15 *European Quality of Life Survey 2016.* **Eurofound.** Luxembourg 2017.

16 *Women shoulder the responsibility of unpaid work.* **Office of National Statistics.** [Online] 10 November 2016. https://www.ons.gov.uk/employmentandlabourmarket/peopleinwork/earningsandworkinghours/articles/.

17 *Household satellite account, UK: 2015 and 2016.* **Office for National Statistics.** [Online] 2 October 2018. https://www.ons.gov.uk/economy/nationalaccounts/satelliteaccounts/articles/householdsatelliteaccounts/2015and2016estimates#toc.

18 *The Life of Women and Men in Europe.* **Eurostat.** Accessed online 20/04/2020. Eurostat, 2019.

19 *Measuring time spent in unpaid household work: results from the American Time Use Survey.* **Krantz-Kent, Rachel.** *Monthly Labor Review.* July 2009, pp. 46–59.

20 *American Time-Use Survey, Bureau of Labor Statistics 2018 2020.* **US Bureau of Labor Statistics.** [Online]. https://www.bls.gov/tus/tables/a6-1519.pdf.

21 *A Tale of Two Fathers.* **PewResearch**, 15 June 2011. Pew Research Center

22 *Tuning In: Parents of Young Children Tell Us What They Think, Know and Need.* **Zero to Three.** [Online] 2015. https://www.zerotothree.org/resources/series/tuning-in-parents-of-young-children-tell-us-what-they-think-know-and-need#parent-voices.

23 *UK Dads Study.* **Babycentre UK.** 2015.

24 *Parenting in America.* **PewResearch,** 15 Dec 2017. Pew Research Center

25 *GDP.* **Coyle, Diane.** Princeton University Press, 2016.

26 'Should've been you'. **May, Imelda.** 2017.

27 *Women in Management in Ireland.* **IBEC.** Irish Business and Employers
    Confederation, 2019. https://www.ibec.ie/connect-and-learn/
    media/2019/11/03/ibec-published-women-in-management-survey.

28 *They're waiting longer but US women today more likely to have children than
    a decade ago.* **PewResearch**, 18 Jan 2018. Pew Research Center.

29 *The Career Dynamics of High-Skilled Women and Men: Evidence from
    Sweden.* **Albrecht, Jim, et al.** Institute for Evaluation of Labour Market and
    Education Policy, 2018. pp. 1–39, Working Paper. ISSN 1651-1166.

30 'Assessing Unequal Treatment: Gender and Pay'. **Gregory, M.** [book auth.]
    in Bond, Russell, McGinnity. *Making Equality Count: Irish and International
    Research Measuring Equality and Discrimination.* Dublin, Liffey Press, 2010.

31 'Prevalence, Incidence and Obstetric Factors' Impact on Female Urinary
    Incontinence in Europe: A Systematic Review'. **Cerruto**, *Urologica Interna-
    tionalis* 2013, Vol. 90. Karger.

32 *Why we sleep.* **Walker, M.** Allen Lane, 2017.

33 *The Mum: How it Works* **Hazeley, J.A. and Morris, J. P.** Penguin
    Random House, 2016.

34 *Four Times More Women Than Men Dropped Out of the Labor Force in
    September.* **Ewing-Nelson, Claire.** National Women's Law Centre, 2020.
    pp. 1–3. Washington

35 *Women in the Workplace 2020.* **McKinsey & LeanIn.org.** McKinsey &
    Company & LeanIn.org, 2020. pp. 1–63, Joint report. https://wiw-report.
    s3.amazonaws.com/Women_in_the_Workplace_2020.pdf.

36 *Modern Parenthood.* **PewResearch**, 14 March 2013. Pew Research Center.

37 *The Decline of Marriage and Rise of New Families.* **PewResearch.** 18
    November 2010, Pew Research Center.

38 *The Second Shift.* **Hochschild, Arlie.** Penguin Books, 1989.

39 *Shakespeare in Love.* Madden, John. [writ.] **Stoppard, Tom & Norman,
    Mark.** [perf.] Geoffrey Rush. 1998.

40 'Fertility awareness online: the efficacy of a fertility education website in
    increasing knowledge and changing fertility beliefs'. **Daniluk, J.C. &
    Koert, E.**, *Human Reproduction* 2015, Vol. 30, pp. 353–363. Oxford
    University Press.

41 'Female age-related fertility decline'. **American College of Obstetrics
    and Gynaecologists Committe on Gynecological Practice.** *Obstet-
    rics and Gynecology*, March 2014, Vol. 123, pp. 719–21. Wolters Kluwer.

42 *Women are having their first child at an older age.* **Eurostat.** [Online] 15
    May 2020. https://ec.europa.eu/eurostat/web/products-eurostat-news/-/
    DDN-20190318-1

43 *Birth characteristics in England and Wales: 2019.* **Office of National
    Statistics.** [Online] 16 Nov 2020. https://www.ons.gov.uk/

peoplepopulationandcommunity/birthsdeathsandmarriages/livebirths/
bulletins/birthcharacteristicsinenglandandwales/2019.

44 *Press releases 2020.* **Central Statistics Office.** [Online] 29 May 2020.
https://www.cso.ie/en/csolatestnews/pressreleases/2020pressreleases/
pressstatementvitalstatisticsyearlysummary2019/.

45 'Why Women Still Can't Have it All'. **Slaughter, A.M.** *The Atlantic.* 2012.

46 'Good Housekeeping, Great Expectations: Gender and Housework Norms'.
Thébaud, Sarah, Kornrich, Sabino and Ruppanner, Leah, *Socio-
logical Methods and Research,* 2019, pp. 1–29. SAGE Publications. DOI:
10.1177/0049124119852395

47 *Bridget Jones' Diary.* Maguire, Sharon. [writ.] **Helen Fielding, Dan Mazer
and Emma Thomspon.** [perf.] Emma Thompson. 2016.

48 'Maternity leave and pay'. **Gov.UK.** [Online] May 2019. https://www.gov.
uk/maternity-pay-leave/pay.

49 *International Review of Leave Policies and Related Research 2018.* **Blum, S.,
Koslowski, A., Macht, A. and Moss, P.** Research Gate, 2018. Technical
Report. DOI: 10.13140/RG.2.2.18149.45284.

50 *Paternity and parental leave policies across the European Union: Assessment
of Current Provision.* **European Commission.** Govt. Report. Publications
Office of the European Union, Luxembourg 2018.

51 'Fathers on leave alone in Norway: Changes and Continuities'. **Kvande, E
and Brandth, B.** in *Comparative Perspectives on Work–Life Balance and
Gender Equality. Life Course Research and Social Policies.* Springer, Cham,
2017, Vol. 6.

52 'Hands-on fathers less likely to break up with partners'. **Rice-Oxley, Mark.**
The Guardian. 30 Sep 2018.

53 'Fathers on Leave Alone in Portugal: Lived Experiences and Impact of
Forerunner Fathers'. **Wall, K. and Leitão, M.** [book auth.] in Wall, K.
and O'Brien, M. *Comparative Perspectives on Work–Life Balance
and Gender Equality. Life Course Research and Social Policies,*
s.l.: Springer, 2017, Vol. 6, pp. vol 6. Springer, Cham. https://doi.
org/10.1007/978-3-319-42970-0_4.

54 *White Paper: Men and Gender Equality in Portugal.* **Wall, Karin.** Commission for Equality in Labour and Employment. 2017. pp. 1–147. ISBN
978-972-8399-86-3.

55 'Does paternity leave reduce fertility?' **Farré, Lidia and Gonzáles,
Libertad.** DOI: 10.1016/J.JPUBECO.2018.12.002. *Journal of Public
Economics,* April 2019, Vol. 172, pp. 52–66. Elsevier.

56 *OECD Economic Surveys: Sweden 2017.* **OECD.** OECD Publishing,
Paris 2017. https://doi.org/10.1787/eco_surveys-swe-2017-en.

57 'Want men to share parental leave? Just give them equality'. **Fisher,
Duncan.** *The Guardian.* 15 February 2018.

⁵⁸ 'In France, breast is definitely not best'. **Gibbons, Fiachra.** *The Guardian.* 1 April 2011.

⁵⁹ *Bunreacht na hÉireann (The Irish Constitution).* **Government of Ireland,** 1937.

⁶⁰ *Personal Struggles.* **Ruth, Seán.** Cork: Atrium, 2019.

⁶¹ *The Mental Load: A Feminist Comic.* **Emma.** New York. Seven Stories Press, 2017.

⁶² *World Population Prospects 2019: Highlights.* **United Nations.** *United Nations Department of Economic and Social Affairs.* [Online] 2019. https://population.un.org/wpp/Publications/Files/WPP2019_Highlights.pdf.

⁶³ 'Making Ireland a Caring and Equal Society'. **Murphy, Mary.** *Studies,* Jan 2011, Vol. 100 No. 397, pp. 43–53.

⁶⁴ 'Norway country note', **Brandth, Berit and Knavde, Elin.** in Blum, S., Koslowski, A., Macht, A. and Moss, P. (eds.). 2018, *International Review of Leave Policies and Research,* pp. 313–322.